D1556423

The Dutch Naval Air Force Against Japan

The Dutch Naval Air Force Against Japan

The Defense of the Netherlands East Indies, 1941–1942

TOM WOMACK

McFarland & Company, Inc., Publishers

Jefferson, North Carolina, and London

LIBRARY OF CONGRESS CATALOGUING-IN-PUBLICATION DATA

Womack, Tom, 1967–
The Dutch Naval Air Force against Japan : the defense
of the Netherlands East Indies, 1941–1942 / Tom Womack.
p.   cm.
Includes bibliographical references and index.

ISBN 0-7864-2365-X (softcover : 50# alkaline paper) ∞

1. Netherlands. Marine-Luchtvaartdienst — History — World War,
1939–1945.   2. World War, 1939–1945 — Aerial operations, Dutch.
3. World War, 1939–1945 — Regimental histories— Netherlands.
4. World War, 1939–1945 — Campaigns— Indonesia.   I. Title.
D792.N38W66   2006   940.54'5949209598 — dc22   2006000206

British Library cataloguing data are available

Cover photograph: ©2004 Brand X Pictures

Manufactured in the United States of America

*McFarland & Company, Inc., Publishers
Box 611, Jefferson, North Carolina 28640
www.mcfarlandpub.com*

Acknowledgments

In its final form, this book marks the culmination of 11 years of original research, translation, writing and rewriting. The original text was researched, translated and written in just six weeks over the summer of 1991 following my graduation from the University of Texas at Austin. At no point, however, did I plan on spending more than a decade fleshing out the details and expanding and rechecking my facts in order to make this text into what I consider to be the most complete history of the naval air war in the Netherlands East Indies in any language to date.

It would have been impossible to reach this point alone. I have received generous encouragement, support and assistance from not only my family, but also dozens of colleagues across the globe. Thanks to the World Wide Web, I have been able to cross international boundaries to exchange information, seek guidance and debate international perspectives that more often than not differ from our idealized American-schoolroom viewpoint.

Of my fellow historians, amateurs and professionals alike, I have met very few in person. Yet all have proven extraordinarily helpful by providing not only factual information, but also their own unique insight as to the events of the Netherlands East Indies campaign. To each, no matter how large or small their contribution over the past decade, I gratefully give my thanks. While there are far too many names to list individually, there are a few that I remain particularly indebted to.

These individuals include Jan Visser and Bert Kossen of the Netherlands and my fellow Americans Mark Jones and Allan Alsleden. Despite my having met only one of these individuals in person, each graciously and without hesitation volunteered their time and expertise to edit and proofread this 100,000-word book no fewer than three times each. Simply put, all went well beyond what was asked of them by checking everything, from spelling to factual content, to help ensure its accuracy.

In particular, Jan Visser and Bert Kossen provided access to numerous out-of-print Dutch-language sources that would have otherwise remained outside my reach. At the same time, Allan Alsleden's Japanese translations and assistance (particularly with seaplane operations) were nothing short of phenomenal. And Mark Jones— whom I have had the pleasure of meeting in person — provided invaluable guidance with his postgraduate studies and teaching experience in helping me prepare and structure this text for publication.

My search for photographs to illustrate this book led to yet another group of individuals, all of whom showed extraordinary kindness. Most were complete strangers prior to being contacted via email by an unknown American who had just completed a manuscript on the MLD and needed photos to illustrate it. Some work with museums and national archives, while others shared photos from their personal collections, yet all generously provided a wealth of images that I could otherwise never have hoped to obtain.

André de Zwart—founder of the www.dornier24.com Web site—put me in contact with Nol Baarschers, whose uncle of the same name served as a crewman aboard the flying boat *X-15*. An avid amateur photographer, the elder Baarschers took a plethora of photos of his fellow crewmen and their aircraft. Although crewman Baarschers was killed when his Dornier seaplane disappeared in December 1941, his photos survived and were passed down to his nephew, who graciously provided a large number of images that have not previously been published. In addition, André made available his own personal photo collection and donated a number of equally unique images from his Web site that complemented those of Mr. Baarschers.

Alan Renga, assistant archivist with the San Diego Aerospace Museum in San Diego, California, and his staff of volunteers provided stellar assistance in providing a large number of the photos found in this book. I owe thanks, again, to Jan Visser, for putting me in contact with Jan Klootwijk, who provided photos of MLD seaplane tenders from his personal collection. Joshua Stoff, curator of the Cradle of Aviation Museum in Garden City, New York, and the staffs of both the National Archives of Australia and Institute for Maritime History in The Hague, Netherlands, also proved of tremendous assistance in obtaining photos.

My co-worker, George Campbell, was kind enough to draw the maps for this book. Not only did he endure countless revisions, but he did so without a single complaint. Whether or not he had as much fun in the process as he claimed remains unknown! Mark Hancock, a graphic artist whom I have known and worked with for a decade, also helped immensely by cleaning up numerous photos to make them presentable for publication. Without their help, and that of dozens of others who are too numerous to name here, this book would not have been possible.

In closing, while I have attempted to present the most factually accurate account possible, the confusion surrounding the final days of the East Indies campaign lend uncertainty to an era in which it might never be possible to fully learn the entire truth. It was a time when one's primary attention was often devoted to basic survival to the extent that record keeping was often of secondary importance. Likewise, many primary Dutch-language records were destroyed prior to the final surrender of the East Indies, making certain elements of the campaign murky at best.

Nonetheless, as the author I alone bear the burden of accurately portraying these elements and freely acknowledge and accept that any errors or omissions found in this manuscript are solely my own. And to anyone—either living or deceased—whom I might have unintentionally overlooked, misrepresented or otherwise erroneously omitted, I offer my sincerest apologies.

Tom Womack
Dallas, Texas
February 2006

Contents

Militairie Willemsorde (The Military Order of William, 4th Class)
"In the fight against Japan from the declaration of war on December 7, 1941, [the MLD] without exception, provided excellent service and performed outstanding deeds, including reconnaissance, air attack, anti-submarine duties, minelaying and convoy escort, against an overwhelming enemy, giving their utmost effort and lives in uninterrupted air battles to inflict great losses on the enemy."

Her Royal Highness,
Queen Wilhelmina of The Netherlands
April 9, 1942

Abbreviations

ABDA	American-British-Dutch-Australian Command established January 1942 to coordinate Allied defenses in the Far East
ABDA-AIR	American-British-Dutch-Australian Air Command
ABDA-FLOAT	American-British-Dutch-Australian Naval Command
ABDA-GROUND	American-British-Dutch-Australian Ground Command
ABDA-HQ	American-British-Dutch-Australian Headquarters
A/S	Anti-Submarine
BPM	Britse Petroleum Maatschappij or British Petroleum Company
CAP	Combat Air Patrol
CSF	Combined Striking Force
GM	Governments Marine
GVT.	Groep Vliegtuigen or Aircraft Group
GVT.(NEW)	A Reformed GVT (Author's Designation)
HMAS	His Majesty's Australian Ship
HMS	His Majesty's Ship
Hr.Ms.	Her Royal Majesty's Ship
IJA	Imperial Japanese Army
IJN	Imperial Japanese Navy
IJNS	Imperial Japanese Navy Ship
JAAF	Japanese Army Air Force
JNAF	Japanese Naval Air Force
KM	Koninklijke Marine or Royal Netherlands Navy
KMR	Koninklijke Marine Reserve or Royal Netherlands Naval Reserve
KNIL	Koninklijke Nederlandse Indische Leger or Royal Netherlands East Indian Army
KNIL-ML	Koninklijke Nederlands Indische Militaire Luchtvaart or Royal Netherlands East Indies Army Air Force (also ML)
KNILM	Koninklijke Nederlandse Indische Luchtvaart Maatschappij or Royal Netherlands Indies Air Company
KPM	Koninklijke Paketvaart Maatschappij, or Royal Packet Navigation Cpy.

ME	Marine Establishment; the main naval base for the Royal Netherlands East Indies Naval Squadron
MLD	Marine Lucht Dienst, or Royal Netherlands Naval Air Service
MS	Motor Ship
MVK	Marine Vliegtuig Kamp, or Naval Air Station
NAP	Naval Air Pilot
NAS	Naval Air Station
NCO	Non-Commissioned Officer
NEI	Netherlands East Indies
PatWing 10	Patrol Wing 10
RAAF	Royal Australian Air Force
RAF	Royal Air Force
REC-GROUP	Sub-formation of ABDA-AIR established to coordinate and control Allied reconnaissance aircraft and information
SS	Steamship
USAAF	United States Army Air Force
USN	United States Navy
USS	United States Ship
VVC	Vrijwillig Vlieger Corps, or Civilian Volunteer Flying Corps

Preface

On December 7, 1941, the Imperial Japanese Navy launched a massive carrier-based air strike against the United States Pacific Fleet, which lay at anchor in the naval base at Pearl Harbor, Hawaii. The attack was intended to prevent the Pacific Fleet's interference with Japan's conquest of colonial territories belonging to Great Britain and the Netherlands. At the same time, the American territories of Guam, Wake Island and the Philippines were targeted for invasion to guard the Imperial Japanese Army's flanks during these operations and to also prevent their use as forward bases for any subsequent Allied counterattacks.

The primary Japanese targets were the oilfields of the Netherlands East Indies, an immense colony that had been controlled by the Dutch for 300 years. Japan had waged a war of aggression on the Chinese mainland since 1932. A direct result of this prolonged conflict was a ban on all oil, petroleum and raw material exports to Japan from the United States, Great Britain and the Netherlands East Indies. As an island nation with few natural resources, Japan desperately needed these materials to continue the war. Without them, her military would almost certainly be forced into a premature peace with China — or worse yet, be forced to withdraw entirely.

When the Dutch East Indies government refused to resume oil shipments to Japan, even after intense diplomatic pressure throughout 1940 and 1941, the Japanese military drew up invasion plans to take by force what they could not obtain peacefully. Weak and isolated since the occupation of Holland by Nazi Germany in May 1940, Dutch colonial forces in the East Indies could not realistically hope to stand on their own. Yet, unwilling to bow to Japanese pressure and become a Japanese protectorate, they chose to fight.

When the Japanese did invade the East Indies in December 1941, they clashed with forces of the Royal Netherlands East Indian Army (Koninklijke Nederlandse Indische Leger or KNIL) and Royal Netherlands Navy (Koninklijke Marine or KM). Both Netherlands forces were extremely weak, and in an attempt to prepare for the coming Japanese invasion, they undertook a crash program to build their strength. With most of the world's major industrial powers already at war in 1940, only neutral America offered a viable source of military equipment. However, much of its defense industry was already committed to meeting the needs of its own last-minute rearmament programs. Most of what little production capability remained was dedicated to meeting the needs of Britain, which at the time stood alone against Germany.

As a result, Dutch efforts to procure weapons after the fall of Holland were not entirely successful, and its military was often forced to make do with equipment already rejected by U.S. forces. Although the majority of this material was of excellent manufacture, smaller firms that were sometimes undercapitalized produced much of it and many could not meet the large production demands and short timetables of the Dutch. When the Japanese invaded in December 1941, much of the equipment purchased and paid for in gold in advance by the Netherlands East Indies government had not yet arrived.

While the KM could obtain only small patrol boats from American firms, its supporting air arm was more successful at acquiring equipment it needed. The Marine Luchtvaart Dienst (MLD), or Naval Air Force, would play a dominant role in the early months of savage combat following Pearl Harbor. But while its American counterpart — Patrol Wing 10 of the United States Navy — has received ample recognition for its exploits over the years, accomplishments of the MLD have remained obscure.

While much of this oversight can be attributed to the language barrier (there are a number of strong sources on this subject available in Dutch), one can also look to historians who ignore the role of the East Indies in the volatile period leading up to Pearl Harbor. Others simply view the Dutch as a "minor power" that made little or no contribution to the Pacific War. Then there are those who seek to put blame (for which there is plenty to go around) for the early Allied failures immediately following Pearl Harbor on the shoulders of the Dutch, thus lessening their own accountability in the cold light of the postwar years.

But few realize the substantial role the MLD played in the first three months of combat in the Pacific War. With approximately 175 aircraft of all types, it greatly outnumbered both the American and British naval air reconnaissance forces combined in Southeast Asia. In fact, not only would the MLD play an active role in the Netherlands East Indies campaign, but the Dutch would also supply their American and British allies with generous amounts of spare aircraft, parts and equipment. Despite these facts, few English-language sources credit the MLD with the dominant role it played.

This volume seeks to rectify these omissions. Although it deals primarily with the MLD and its accomplishments, truncated operational histories of both American and Commonwealth forces have been inserted where relevant and necessary to present a full picture. Nonetheless, my primary goal is to set the record straight by presenting a factually accurate, but not necessarily politically popular, view of the proper role the MLD played in the defense of the Netherlands East Indies, Malaya and the Philippines.

Going a step further, this volume also seeks to dispel myths that the Dutch did not fight, that they passively gave up their immense empire, or that they simply stuck their heads in the sand and let their allies do the fighting. For however brief the East Indies campaign, the Dutch refused to simply "roll over" in defense of what for many Dutch colonials was the only home they had ever known. In the process, the MLD lost 75 percent of its force in barely 90 days of intense combat and preserved for itself a place in history, a history that is now being told — much of it for the first time.

1

The MLD: Equipment and Doctrine

THE MLD

The Marine Luchtvaart Dienst (MLD), or Naval Air Service, is the Dutch Naval Air Service. Initially formed in 1916 using interned German aircraft that had crossed the Dutch border in World War One, and volunteer officer crews from the surface fleet, the MLD was officially signed into existence by the Dutch Government on August 18, 1917. Since then, it has functioned as a separate force within the Royal Netherlands Navy (Koninklijke Marine or KM) throughout its long history. Although the MLD's origins were primitive, like all contemporary air arms, it quickly evolved into an advanced, highly trained force during the inter-war years.

Between the First and Second World Wars, its duties were rather mundane, although they gradually intensified throughout the 1930s as the threat of war with Japan in the Pacific loomed. Extensive day and night patrols were carried out across Dutch colonial territory in the Netherlands East Indies, mostly to investigate Japanese fishing vessels and foreign merchant ships. By the start of the Pacific War, no ship could enter the archipelago without being quickly sighted by an MLD plane. Once sighted, a nearby naval, or Gouvernementsmarine,[1] vessel would be directed to the scene so that the ship could be boarded and searched.

By the start of the Second World War, the MLD's primary duties included anti-submarine (A/S) patrols, convoy and fleet escort, air reconnaissance and minelaying. In the Far East, these were expanded to include helping the Hydrographic Service chart harbors and waterways, delivery of supplies to isolated outposts and the support of civilian police forces.[2] Operational doctrine called for the MLD to work closely with the fleet by relaying the position, course and speed of enemy ships. However, after the fall of Holland and the East Indies, there were few Dutch ships to support, so its role evolved into pure reconnaissance and A/S duties.

The MLD was a relatively small force within the KM when Germany invaded Holland in May 1940. Although funds had been authorized for increased personnel and new planes, the German invasion completely demolished a build-up of the naval air squadron in the Netherlands East Indies, where the bulk of the KM and MLD had traditionally been based. As a result, newly revived Dutch efforts to reinforce their military strength in the NEI and guard against a feared Japanese attack[3] were completely disrupted.

As a result, the East Indies Naval Squadron had to turn to other countries for assistance in order to continue the build-up. However, all branches of the East Indies military experienced continuing problems in these efforts. Germany had occupied most of Europe while Britain was fighting for its very survival and had no manufacturing capac-

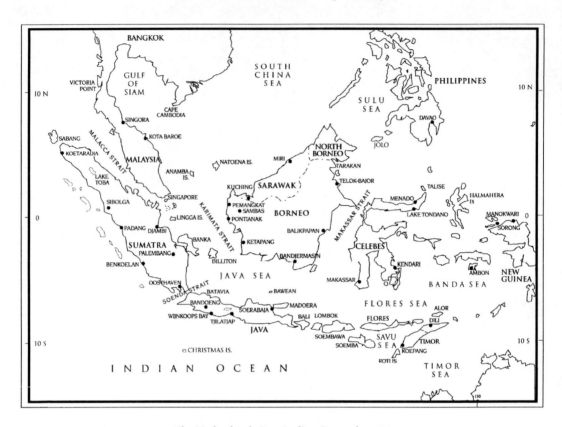

The Netherlands East Indies, December 1941

ity to spare for the Dutch. This left only the United States as a reliable source for heavy weapons, ammunition, large ships, aircraft and other military supplies, such as radio equipment, sights and related specialized equipment.

Unfortunately, the U.S. government initially proved hesitant to provide the Dutch with any kind of military support, modern weapons in particular. It feared the Dutch would follow the "French Model" in Indochina. Following the fall of France in June 1940, the Japanese placed intense pressure on the colony's government, which eventually allowed Japan's military to take de facto control of the territory. With Japan putting similar pressure on the colonial government of Governor-General Tjarda van Starkenborgh Stachouwer, the United States feared the Dutch would also bow to the pressure, wasting valuable resources that were needed for its own military build-up.

But while the Vichy French government actively collaborated with Nazi Germany, the Netherlands' Queen Wilhelmina escaped to London and formed a government-in-exile that would oversee Dutch efforts to continue fighting. With final say over all colonial decisions, this body played a key role in thwarting Japanese demands for greater economic and political control in the East Indies.[4] And as Governor-General Starkenborgh's government demonstrated its resolve to remain independent of Japanese control, the United States Government proved more willing to support the Dutch East Indies militarily.

As these restrictions loosened, the MLD proved particularly successful in obtaining aircraft and equipment from the United States. Although its own military was in the midst of a major build-up prior to the Japanese attack on Pearl Harbor, the United States Navy did not consider reconnaissance aircraft to be a top priority. This left the Consolidated and Sikorski plants free to fill Dutch orders without reducing American military demands. However, many of the aircraft the Dutch purchased still failed to arrive before the fall of the East Indies.

PLANES AND EQUIPMENT

Before the new equipment arrived, the MLD operated an obsolescent fleet of indigenous Fokker seaplanes and German Dornier flying boats.[5] In addition, there were a small number of modern German and Dutch flying boats sprinkled throughout. After the German invasion of Holland, acquisition of spare parts and replacement engines for the older aircraft was impossible. As a result, it became extremely difficult for the MLD to maintain its fleet of aging seaplanes.

To strengthen and modernize the MLD, the Dutch government between 1937 and 1940 authorized funding for 78 large seaplanes and 22 torpedo-carrying seaplanes. At the core of this appropriation were additional Do. 24Ks and the new Fokker T.VIII torpedo bomber, which was still under development. After May 1940, the Dutch were forced to turn to the United States for aircraft and equipment, which yielded fairly positive results for the MLD by the start of the Pacific War. All transactions in the United States were conducted by the Netherlands Purchasing Commission (NPC), which was formed by the Netherlands government-in-exile in June 1940 to continue the build-up of Dutch forces in the Far East.

Fokker T.IV

The most numerous among the large MLD seaplanes were 10 twin-engine T.IVa floatplanes. Featuring all-metal construction and two large floats under the fuselage, the T.IV had been designed as a torpedo/horizontal bomber and reconnaissance plane in the mid-1920s. The T.IV was also the first long-range seaplane acquired by the MLD, allow-

Ten Fokker T.IVa seaplanes were still in service with the MLD in December 1941 (photograph courtesy of San Diego Aerospace Museum).

ing it to effectively patrol the broad expanses of the East Indies archipelago on a regular basis for the first time.

Twelve Fokkers originally reached Morokrembangan in 1927, where they were designated as "T" class flying boats to distinguish them from other MLD seaplanes. The original aircraft were the T.IV version, featuring open cockpits and exposed gun positions. Numbered T-1 through T-12, all of these aircraft were written off and taken out of service in 1939 and 1940. The only exception was T-1, which was lost in an accident on October 16, 1937.

Based on the success of these first 12 aircraft, the MLD ordered a second batch of improved T.IVa models, which featured enclosed cockpits, gun positions and more powerful engines. Six (T-13 through T-18) were ordered in January 1935; these were followed by another half dozen aircraft (T-19 through T-24) beginning in January 1937. Of this group, T-13 was lost in a landing accident on October 12, 1937, while T-14 was lost on May 26, 1941. Shortly after the arrival of this group, the remaining T.IVs were upgraded to T.IVa status by MLD workshops on Java.

In December 1941, the remaining T.IVs were operating with *GVT.11* and *GVT.12* under the command of 1st Lieutenant J. Craamer and 1st Lieutenant B.J.W.M. van Voorthuijsen[6] of the Royal Netherlands Naval Reserve. Throughout the East Indies campaign, several of these planes were used for bombardier training; most were modified shortly after the outbreak of war to carry three depth charges and assigned to fly A/S and reconnaissance patrols along the north coast of Java and over the Java Sea. The surviving planes were destroyed on Java on March 2, 1942, to prevent their capture.[7]

Fokker T.VIII

This was a highly successful twin-engine, twin-float design that was intended to replace the T.IV. First ordered by the MLD in 1938, the first T.VIII was built to a Dutch government requirement that called for a long-range, high-speed seaplane that could function in both the horizontal and torpedo bomber role. It featured mixed wood and fabric construction, although later all-metal models were specifically built for service in the Far East. However, it was the aircraft's long-range, heavy payload and superior handling characteristics in the torpedo-bomber role that made it attractive to MLD forces in the East Indies.

Despite teething problems through the seaplane's test period, the MLD placed an order for 36 Fokker T.VIIIs. The first five aircraft were of the early mixed construction model; assigned the serial numbers R-1 through R-5, they were ordered in September 1938. A second batch, given the serial numbers R-6 through R-24, was ordered in January 1939. R-25 through R-36 were ordered in February 1940. Although most were intended for units in the East Indies, the outbreak of war in Europe in September 1939 delayed their delivery, and none was delivered as the Dutch government acted to build up its military forces in Europe.

Only the first 11 aircraft were delivered prior to the German invasion of Holland. Eight of these aircraft escaped to England in May 1940, where they operated with the RAF as 320 Squadron (Dutch) until replaced by newer aircraft. R-12 through R-36 were captured by the Germans while still under construction and flown by Kreigsmarine units in the Mediterranean. One of these aircraft was later stolen and flown to England by a Dutch pilot on May 6, 1941.

Fokker C.VII-W

There were a limited number of Fokker C.VII-W reconnaissance and training aircraft ("V" planes). Twelve of these seaplanes were originally shipped to the Netherlands East Indies in 1928 and 1929. Although their numbers were depleted by age and attrition, those few that remained were primarily used for torpedo launch and bad-weather flight training. Although it appears that most or all of the remaining aircraft were retired from service by 1941, it is possible that some still flew in ancillary or training roles during the Japanese invasion. They would have been destroyed in the fighting or just prior to Java's surrender in March 1942.

Fokker C.XI-W

The remaining Fokkers in the NEI were eight two-man C.XI-W floatplanes ("W" planes), of which 15 had originally been acquired in the mid-1930s. By December 1941 their numbers had been reduced to the aircraft W-1, W-4, W-8, W-10, W-11, W-12, W-14 and W-15 through a series of landing accidents and combat losses inflicted by the Germans during their invasion of Holland.

Designed for shipboard service, the C.XI-W entered service in 1938 in the reconnaissance role. It had stressed wings for catapult launches and a range of 453 miles. Although primarily designed as a cruiser plane, the KM carried out a series of tests in the late 1930s to evaluate the ability of the C.XI-W and other single-engine seaplanes to operate aboard Dutch destroyers and *Flores*-class gunboats based in the NEI. However, these tests were not particularly successful, as the destroyers were unable to use their "X" mounts while carrying the aircraft.

Operationally, they flew only off the Dutch light cruisers *De Ruyter* and *Java*[8] throughout the East Indies campaign, except during the battle of the Java Sea, when all were put ashore. The light cruiser *Sumatra* carried two aircraft when she reached Java in late 1941, but they were transferred ashore when that ship entered extended overhaul. A fourth light cruiser, the *Tromp*, was also equipped to carry two C.XI-Ws, although she apparently shipped only a single floatplane prior to the war. This plane was badly damaged in November 1941, and it is unknown if it was ever replaced. Many of these aircraft were lost during Japanese air raids on Java; MLD ground crews destroyed the remainder when Java fell in March 1942, as they did not have the necessary range to reach Australia or Ceylon.

Fokker C.XIV-W

There were also 10 Fokker C.XIV-W floatplanes ("F" planes) on Java that had been developed as advanced training and light reconnaissance planes to replace the Dutch military's aging Fokker C.VII-W seaplanes. At the time of Pearl Harbor, the remaining Fokkers were the remnants of 24 aircraft (F-1 through F-24) delivered to the KM in Holland and the East Indies between May and December 1939.

Eleven aircraft survived the German invasion of the Netherlands and eventually reached England. The MLD shipped 10 of these aircraft (see Appendix 4) to the Netherlands East Indies later that year for operations with its flight training school. Aircraft F-3 remained in England for operations with 320 Squadron (Dutch). It is unclear how many of those sent to the East Indies were lost during Japanese air strikes on Java, but all surviving machines were destroyed on Java to prevent their capture when the island fell to the Japanese in March 1942.

Only six of the ten Do. 15 "Whales" remained operational with the MLD flight training school in December 1941 (photograph courtesy of San Diego Aerospace Museum).

Dornier Do. 15 "Whale"

The MLD and Germany's Dornier aircraft factory had a long history. Their relationship started in the 1920s when the Dutch placed orders for 41 Dornier Do. 15 "Whales" for use in the East Indies in a long-range reconnaissance role. They were intended to supplement and eventually replace the T.IVs. The first five arrived on Java in 1926 and operated as "D" class seaplanes. The arrival of the Do. 15s in the Far East was significant, as their endurance and sturdy construction allowed the MLD to effectively patrol the broad expanses of the NEI by air for the first time.

Although highly valued by the MLD for their long range and ability to land on and take off from short waterways, production of the Do. 15 ceased in 1931 due to the worldwide depression. With Germany's occupation of Holland, the MLD found it extremely difficult to maintain the aging seaplanes due to a lack of spares. It appears that at least one (D-42) was cannibalized for spare parts in 1940 to keep the others flying. Most of the remainder were retired from service in the late 1930s with their engines being used in the construction of motor torpedo boats for the KM's East Indies Naval Squadron.

Six of the last ten remaining "Whales" were still operational in December 1941, although newer Dornier Do. 24K-1s had long since phased them out of front-line service. They were used primarily as advanced trainers by the MLD flight training school. Numbered D-41 through D-46, these were the newer Do. 15F model. It featured more powerful engines, a longer wingspan, more streamlined fuselage and keeled hull (as opposed to flat), which provided for enhanced flight characteristics, stability and sea-handling qualities.

Dornier Do. 24K

Commonly referred to as "X-boats" (because of their serial numbers, which were numbered X-1 through X-36), the Do. 24K-1 was a large, rugged seaplane specifically designed for long-range reconnaissance and air-sea rescue in the broad expanses of the

A prewar photograph of the Do. 24K-1 flying boat X-15; note the absence of a dorsal turret and armament (photograph courtesy of Nol Baarschers).

East Indies. The Dutch initially approached Dornier with the request for a new flying boat to replace their aging Do. 15 "Whales," from which the Do. 24 grew. It was a tri-motor flying boat with a heavy hull, good defensive armament (in later models) and a maximum range just under 3,000 miles. The prototype was delivered in 1937, followed by 11 German-built production models in 1937 and 38.

After delivery of the first six aircraft, the Netherlands Ministry of Defense placed orders totaling 72 flying boats to help offset the increased Japanese threat to the NEI. The first 36 would be the Do. 24K-1 with the 875 horsepower Wright-Cyclone engine. Although 15 percent lighter than the Jumo Junkers 600 horsepower 205C diesel engine, which would later equip Luftwaffe Dorniers, the Wright-Cyclone provided 50 percent more power. It was also in widespread service on the KM's Fokker T.IV seaplane and the twin-engine Martin 166, an export version of the USAAF Martin B-10 medium bomber then in service with the ML, or Militaire Luchtvaart (Royal Netherlands Army Air Force).

Beginning with the 37th Dornier, production shifted to the Do. 24K-2. The main improvements on these planes included the addition of the Wright-Cyclone 1,100 horse-power engine and larger fuel tanks for increased endurance. With the added power, the K-2 was extremely maneuverable and could effectively operate from the short waterways that the MLD often encountered around its undeveloped secondary bases.

Although all the flying boats of both versions featured armament in three Alkan dorsal turrets, the first 12 Do. 24K-1s were armed entirely with Colt-Browning 7.7mm machine guns license-built by FN-Browning in Belgium. Beginning with X-13, a rapid-fire Hispano-Suiza Model 404 20mm cannon replaced the machine gun in the dorsal turret. It is unknown whether the first 12 planes were ever retrofitted with the heavier armament after their arrival in the Far East.

In 1939 the number of KM seaplanes on order was reduced to 48 in order to free up funding for the ML, which at the time was acquiring the first of its Martin bombers. However, on June 16, 1939, the MLD placed orders for another 13 flying boats. Nine months later it followed up with an order for 12 additional seaplanes on March 12, 1940.

Top: On the step! At full power, time to liftoff for the Do. 24K-1 was only 17 seconds, although it took 27½ minutes to reach 16,500 feet (photograph courtesy of André de Zwart). *Bottom:* Beginning with X-13, a Hispano-Suiza 20mm cannon replaced the 7.7mm Colt-Browning machine gun in the Do. 24K's dorsal turret (photograph courtesy of André de Zwart).

Only 36 Do. 24K-1s reached the East Indies before the German occupation of Holland. Two years after her arrival on Java, X-4 was lost in a night landing accident with her entire crew on April 13, 1940. The loss of X-2 followed on November 13, 1941, while taking off at Morokrembangan, further reducing the number of operational planes to 34 by December 1941. Both were operating as training aircraft with the MLD's flight training school at the time of their loss.

A 37th flying boat, the X-37, arrived on Java in 1940, but its engines proved defective. The first of the new K-2 series, X-37 had completely different engines than the Do. 24K-1s already in service. And because the MLD in the East Indies had yet to receive any spare engines for this model, it remained inactive throughout the Japanese invasion as replacements could not be obtained from Germany or occupied Holland. In the meantime, ground crews rebuilt the Dornier into a command plane for the commander of the MLD.

When German forces overran Holland, they seized 13 Do. 24K-2s in various stages of construction at the Aviolanda Factory. They also captured enough materials to complete 16 more. At the same time, they seized a number of Wright-Cyclone engines and spares that were destined for use in the East Indies. The plant's production line quickly reopened under German control, allowing them to complete X-38 and X-39 almost immediately, which the Kriegsmarine subsequently put into service along with the others as they rolled off the line.[9]

These losses aside, all front-line MLD squadrons in the NEI were able to convert to the Do. 24K-1 between the outbreak of war in September 1939 and the Japanese attack on Pearl Harbor in December 1941. In turn, the older Do. 24K-1s (those with the lowest numbers) were replaced with newer aircraft (those with higher numbers) as the outbreak of war drew nearer.

By December 1941, the operational front-line planes were spread throughout the East Indies to cover strategic ports and waterways leading into and out of the Netherlands East Indies. The basic MLD formation was the three-plane GVT (Groep Vliegtuig or Aircraft Group). Eight groups totaling 24 planes, with a small number of newly arrived PBY-5 Catalinas, formed the backbone of the MLD's first-line reconnaissance strength. The remaining 11 Dorniers formed a small reserve pool at Morokrembangan, the MLD seaplane base at Soerabaja.[10]

Dornier losses were heavy, with no fewer than 28 of the original 34 lost in action or through accidents (two of the X-boats, X-2 and X-4, are not considered war losses, as both were lost in training accidents before the outbreak of war). Only six survived the East Indies campaign and subsequent evacuation of Java in March 1942 to fight another day. As their losses mounted and new American-made PBY Catalinas became available, the Do. 24K was gradually phased out.

Consolidated PBY-5 Catalina

American-built planes eventually made up a substantial portion of the MLD. As part of an emergency plan to build up the MLD, 48 Consolidated Model 28–5MNE Catalinas ("Y" boats) were ordered by the Dutch in 1940 to replace their Do. 24Ks. With a fuel capacity exceeding 14,000 gallons, the Model 28–5 could stay in the air for up to 22 hours. So in addition to easing maintenance issues, it was an ideal patrol aircraft to survey the vast expanses of the Netherlands East Indies.

Essentially the export version of the USN's PBY Catalina patrol bomber,[11] this order consisted of 36 PBY-5 seaplane variants, which were to be followed by 12 more aircraft. The German seaplanes, although tough and reliable, were becoming extremely difficult to maintain in the absence of spare parts following the occupation of Holland. The first two aircraft were scheduled to reach Java in August 1941, with the remainder of the order following in lots of four, four, six, six, six and six respectively, with the final two PBYs arriving in March 1942.[12]

Y-87 failed to reach Java before the Dutch surrender in March 1942 (photograph courtesy of San Diego Aerospace Museum).

Although the first two PBYs arrived at Morokrembangan on September 5,[13] and a total of 36 arrived before the fall of Java, they did not replace the Dorniers on a large scale until war losses mounted. This was mostly due to the severe shortage of trained aircrews. The remaining 12 PBY-5A Catalinas still on order failed to arrive before the Japanese landed on Java.[14] They were later delivered to the MLD forces operating from the Indian Ocean island of Ceylon. From here, they flew search-and-rescue missions for the remainder of the Pacific War as 321 Squadron (Dutch), attached to the Royal Air Force at China Bay (near Trincomalee) on the Indian Ocean island of Ceylon.

The first 15 aircraft reached Morokrembangan by mid-October 1941 and were being readied to phase out the older Dorniers. But although the MLD still faced a critical shortage of aircraft, it very nearly lost a substantial portion of the remaining PBYs before they ever arrived in the East Indies.

Due to a dramatic miscalculation in American production priorities, the British were under the impression that they would receive at least 155 PBYs between July 1941 and April 1942.[15] However, in early July they learned that no Catalinas were allocated for British delivery until May 1942, putting Britain in a severe bind. This was because by late 1941 the Battle of the Atlantic had reached a fever pitch as German submarines routinely mauled British supply convoys sailing to and from North America. As a result of these growing losses, the RAF and Coastal Command squadrons desperately needed long-range aircraft to help stem the losses.

Locked out of the existing production timetables, the British attempted to obtain the MLD PBYs that were in the process of being delivered to the NEI. They first raised the issue in September 1941 with the Dutch government-in-exile. The British need was so great that they initially considered offering the Dutch 100 P-40E Kittyhawk fighters — which the Dutch had unsuccessfully tried to obtain from the British earlier — in exchange for 18 of the 36 Catalinas that the Dutch had on order. However, it appears that the fighters

Y-38 or Y-39 being prepared for duty shortly after their arrival at Morokrembangan on September 3, 1941. In the background is a Do. 24 (photograph courtesy of Institute for Maritime History).

were either not available, or the RAF would not agree to the transfer, as the offer was apparently never presented to the Dutch.

On September 24 a delegation from the British Air Ministry met with Vice Admiral J.T. Furstner, the Dutch Minister for Naval Affairs in London, to officially raise the issue of obtaining 18 of the 21 MLD PBYs that had not yet reached Morokrembangan. Although the British sought to convince him that their presence in the Atlantic desperately outweighed Dutch needs in the NEI, Furstner refused their request due to the limited number of front-line flying boats then operating in the East Indies. As detailed earlier, the PBYs were needed to replace the MLD's aging Dorniers, which were becoming difficult to maintain.

In response, the British tried an end run by appealing directly to Admiral Helfrich in a face-to-face meeting at Batavia on October 10. If they could change his mind, they clearly hoped to influence Admiral Furstner's stance. This time, it appears that Helfrich raised the issue of trading the PBYs for a number of Bristol Beaufort torpedo bombers in return. These would come from Australian-produced stocks, of which some 270 aircraft would be available sometime between June and August 1942. After a series of internal exchanges, this proposal was rejected when the British deemed that none of the Beauforts could be spared.[16]

Thus arriving in Batavia empty handed, the British argument once again hinged on convincing the Dutch of the critical nature of the Atlantic Theater. They also voiced their belief that the MLD did not have enough pilots and flight crews in the East Indies to man the aircraft. Helfrich replied that the MLD did have ample manpower and that he would need all of the aircraft in the event of war with Japan. Nonetheless, he agreed to the transfer if the London government concurred that the Atlantic Theater had higher priority than the build-up of his forces in the NEI.

Throughout the process, the British Air Ministry sought to obtain a quick transfer of the MLD aircraft, which were scheduled for delivery to Java at a rate of 10 per month. As 15 PBYs had already reached Morokrembangan, it was deemed imperative that their request be approved before any of the remaining 21 aircraft departed. The Air Ministry correctly foresaw that it would be all but impossible to secure Dutch agreement for their request once the Catalinas had departed the Consolidated Aircraft factory in San Diego, California, for delivery to the Far East.

One major sticking point to the transfer was that both the Australian and Dutch governments believed that approximately 200 PBYs would be delivered to the RAF by mid-1942. As a result, the Dutch felt that the MLD seaplanes were not as critical as implied. The British countered with production figures that showed 282 PBYs were scheduled for delivery between December 1, 1941, and June 30, 1942. With the exception of the 36 Dutch aircraft, and another 50 allocated to Canada (most of which were later obtained by the British Air Ministry as well), all of the remainder were slated for USN and USAF units.

In the meantime, the Dutch government continued to debate the request. Its decision was made easier in mid-October when the Japanese government's civilian Cabinet resigned, leaving Japan in control of its military, which advocated the removal of western colonies from Asia through military action. As a result of this sudden change in the Far East's political landscape, the British recognized the sensitivity of the situation and decided to back off their request for a week or so to see how things wrinkled out. For their part, the Dutch promptly delayed any decision on the matter until December 16. In the meantime, deliveries to Java continued, and the attack on Pearl Harbor abruptly ended the discussion.

In the end 35 of the 36 Catalinas eventually reached Java, where no fewer than 27 of the aircraft were lost.[17] These losses include a Dutch PBY destroyed in the attack on Pearl Harbor, three Catalinas loaned to the Royal Navy at Singapore shortly after the outbreak of war and five more loaned to the United States Navy in January 1942. Still, because of the Catalina's lighter armament and twin-engine arrangement, Dutch crews greatly preferred the heavier, albeit older, Dorniers with their 20mm cannon, third engine and eight self-sealing fuel tanks.

Training Aircraft

During the military build-up in the East Indies between May 1940 and December 1941, the Dutch government purchased a number of training aircraft. Forty-eight Tiger

Table 1— East Indies Volunteer Flying Clubs

- NEI Flying Club, Andir (Java)
- Batavia Flying Club, Kemajoran (Java)
- Soerabaja Flying Club, Morokrembangan (Java)
- Semerang Flying Club, Benteng River (Java)
- Djojakarta Flying Club, Djojakarta (Java)
- Malang Flying Club, Singosari (Java)
- Balikpapan Flying Club, Balikpapan (Borneo)
- Medan Flying Club, Medan (Northern Sumatra)
- South Sumatra Flying Club, Palembang (Southern Sumatra)

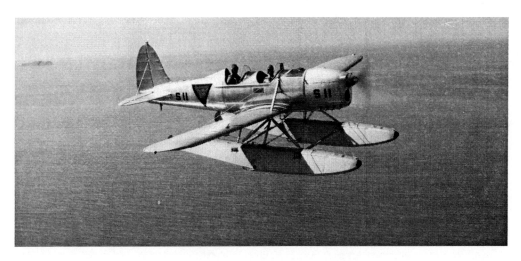

An MLD Ryan STM-S2 primary trainer over Soerabaja (photograph courtesy of San Diego Aerospace Museum).

Moth primary trainers were purchased from Australia, including 33 for the ML and 15 for the MLD. Eleven of these planes were allocated to the East Indies Volunteer Flying Club, a group of nine government-subsidized volunteer clubs formed in May 1941 to help train young men aged 17–20 as reserve pilots.

In addition to the Tiger Moths, the volunteer flying clubs had five Bückner Jungmann primary trainers that had been acquired from Germany before the war. They were joined by two Piper Cub light aircraft. Many of the reserve pilots called up by the MLD immediately prior to the start of the Pacific War received their primary flight training through these volunteer flying clubs.

Following the occupation of Holland, the MLD also ordered 48 Ryan primary trainers, or "sport aircraft," for MLD flight training in the East Indies. Assigned serial numbers S-11 to S-58, half of these planes were the STM-2 land configuration model, and the remainder were STM-S2 floatplanes.[18] The first three Ryans reached Java in November 1940 and were followed by 12 more in January 1942. A total of 108 aircraft eventually reached ML and MLD forces throughout 1941.

The MLD aircraft were immediately sent to Perak Airfield outside Soerabaja and Morokrembangan, the primary seaplane base on Java. Although considered trainers, a number of Ryan floatplanes were sent to Borneo following the outbreak of war to fly reconnaissance missions and patrol the island's various harbors. A number of Ryans were lost during the East Indies campaign, but 34 survived to be evacuated to Australia in March 1942, where they were bought by the Australian government and transferred to the RAAF.

Aircraft on Order

The MLD still had a large number of planes on order when the Japanese attacked. They were all American models, most of which never arrived before the fall of the NEI. These were later dispersed among the various US allies. The largest order consisted of 80 Douglas DB-7B and DB-7C light bombers, which the MLD intended to use as torpedo bombers in an anti-shipping role. The KM reserved for them the serial numbers D-47

Top: Four KNILM Sikorsky S-43 seaplanes operated under MLD control during the NEI campaign (photograph courtesy of San Diego Aerospace Museum). *Bottom:* The MLD ordered 24 VS.310 Kingfishers, but Java fell before their arrival, and 18 of the planes were instead delivered to the RAAF (photograph courtesy of Craig Busby).

through D-126. Of these, 48 were eventually bought by the Netherlands Purchasing Commission and constructed by Douglas; however, the MLD received only six planes just a week before the fall of Java.[19]

Only one DB-7 ever got into the air, with the remainder being destroyed by the Dutch or captured by the Japanese. Japanese photos show that at least one of these planes was captured or assembled from the parts of destroyed planes and taken to Japan for testing. The USAAF took over the remainder of the order and distributed it to the RAAF and Soviet Union under the Lend-Lease Program. The wreck of one Australian bomber was found in the New Guinea jungle in the 1980s, complete with MLD serial number and RAAF insignia painted over Dutch markings and camouflage.

The MLD also placed an order for 48 twin-engine Sikorski S-43 seaplanes,[20] a mil-

Two MLD VS.310s being prepared for transport to the NEI by Dade Brothers shipping company of Long Island (photograph courtesy of Cradle of Aviation Museum).

itary version of the same type of aircraft then in service with KNILM and numerous other civilian airlines around the world. This aircraft was intended to serve in a transport role, most likely to help maintain its extensive chain of isolated seaplane bases throughout the NEI. It is unclear whether these aircraft were actually ordered by the Netherlands Purchasing Commission or the MLD simply placed an option for them between the fall of Holland and the attack on Pearl Harbor. In any event, none was delivered prior to the fall of Java, and the order lapsed.

Also on order were 24 Vought-Sikorsky VS-310 Kingfishers.[21] The Kingfisher was a modern, single-engine floatplane designed to operate either from land or as a catapult-launched shipboard aircraft. It first flew in 1938, and the Dutch order followed in 1940. The Kingfishers were intended to replace the KM's older single-engine Fokker floatplanes, which were also becoming difficult to maintain in the absence of spares. The Kingfishers were to be delivered with six spare engines, six constant-speed propellers and 20 percent spare parts and tool kits. Ordnance equipment, including weapons, would be delivered with the aircraft.

Dutch officials urgently requested these aircraft during a fact-finding mission to Java by several American military officers in early August 1941.[22] On August 25, the White House approved the diversion of these aircraft from existing USN orders, although the Dutch government still had to pay for them up front. Dutch purchasing officials accepted the aircraft, numbered V-1 through V-24, on December 31, 1941. They were immediately put aboard three merchant vessels[23] at New York and routed to the East Indies.

However, Java fell before they arrived, and all three ships were diverted to Australia, still carrying their cargo. Upon their arrival Down Under, 18 were eventually transferred to the RAAF by way of the USAAF's 5th Air Force, which had assumed ownership of the Kingfishers from the Dutch upon their arrival. However, the fate of the remaining aircraft is unclear, although at least two reportedly found their way onto the battleships USS *Arkansas* and USS *New Jersey*, which were operating with the Atlantic Fleet in early 1943.[24]

The Dutch military had also appealed to the American military mission for 24 twin-engine Beechcraft C-45 Expediter aircraft. They were ordered for the MLD for use in training seaplane pilots,[25] but the Japanese invasion also prevented their delivery. After the fall of Java, they were delivered (serial numbers A-1 through A-24) to a combined MLD and ML flight school that had been set up at Jackson, Mississippi, where training of Dutch pilots and flight crews continued until 1944.

THE KNILM

KNILM (Koninklijke Nederlands Indische Luchtvaart Maatschappij or Royal Netherlands Indies Air Company) was the government-subsidized East Indies airline. Starting service in 1928, the civilian airline operated a diverse mixture of land, sea and amphibious aircraft along an expansive network of air routes connecting the East Indies to Europe, Australia, New Guinea, Asia and Japan. Shortly after the start of the Pacific War, many of the airline's pilots, aircrews and ground personnel were drafted by the MLD and hastily retrained on military aircraft.

The land pilots were forced to quickly learn the intricacies of seaplane operations. In addition to seaplane flight instruction, their training included the basic regulations and rules of seamanship regarding harbor navigation, water currents, jetties, buoys and anchorages. They also had to learn advanced theories governing how and where to land depending on wind direction and force, wave motion, swell and water depth. In addition, flight crews and ground personnel accustomed to land operations learned how to service seaplanes on the water, fuel them from barges and carry out maintenance without the benefit of a dock.

In addition to its fleet of Douglas, Fokker and Lockheed land aircraft, KNILM also operated a fleet of seaplanes that was vital for the airline to effectively serve all parts of the East Indies.[26] These included four-engine Sikorski S-42B flying boats and twin-engine Sikorski S-43 and Grumman G.21a seaplanes.[27] During the campaign, these aircraft maintained a steady—albeit gradually diminishing—series of passenger, mail and resupply flights among Java, the East Indies, Malaya and Australia.[28] The seaplanes also flew a number of very dangerous long-range missions to maintain contact with isolated colonial outposts in Dutch New Guinea.[29]

The primary KNILM terminal was located at Semplak on Java. Although free from air attack until mid-February, the airline would lose many planes there as Japanese fighter sweeps over the island increased. Minor hubs were scattered throughout Sumatra, Borneo, Celebes and the Flores Islands. There were also a number of primitive terminals located in Dutch New Guinea; many of these areas had no airstrips and were serviced by the airline's seaplanes.

Flying alone along these hazardous air routes, the unarmed civilian airliners' best defense was to avoid combat. But as the Japanese ploughed through the East Indies, they could not help but encounter KNILM aircraft. So that by the time KNILM received permission to evacuate its remaining planes to Australia on February 19, 1942, heavy losses had already been suffered. Of the 30 land and seaplanes operated by the airline on December 7, 1941, no fewer than 18 were lost. Among the civilian flying boats lost were one S-42 (flagship of the KNILM seaplane fleet), two S-43s and three of four Grumman G.21 "Goose" flying boats.

BATTLE DOCTRINE

For its part, the MLD was a well-trained organization, with its primary function being to provide the fleet with air reconnaissance, photography, gunnery spotting and general support as needed. As would be expected, the level of cooperation between the air and surface arms was extremely high. After more than two decades of close cooperation, the KM and MLD had developed a very efficient system with extensive radio contact exchanged directly and efficiently between aircraft and ships. All prewar exercises carried out by the Dutch revolved around this organization. The system was sound and worked to a very high degree of precision.

But when the Allies formed a multinational command (called ABDA for the American-British-Dutch-Australian nations, which it represented) in January 1942, the British assumed strategic command of Dutch forces in the area. They insisted that all Dutch and Allied aircraft operate under a single command. The reasoning was that the Allies would have a central "clearing house" through which all air reconnaissance information would efficiently pass for distribution to Allied commands.

However, the ABDA system backfired due to inherent weaknesses in language, an inefficient command structure and overall lack of coordination and preparation on the Allies' part. It created huge logjams of information, which often failed to reach other departments of the Allied command structure on timely basis. By that time though, they were often too old to be of much value. In his postwar memoirs, Dutch Admiral Conrad Emil Lambert Helfrich wrote,

> "An urgent report previously received in 10 minutes now sometimes took up to six hours. I no longer knew what the aircraft were doing, neither did the ships [of the surface fleet] nor the base commanders. And vice versa. We were groping in the dark."[30]

With the strategic air network used to guide the Dutch fleet ripped away, its ships were forced to operate blind. The damage was only slightly minimized by reconnaissance being carried out according to the strategic directives of ABDA. However, the problems previously described still existed. So in the end, the only reliable reconnaissance came from the floatplanes carried aboard the Allied cruisers. Unfortunately, these light aircraft were far too short-ranged to effectively do the job. After a fierce debate in Washington, the Dutch were put in command of REC-GROUP, an ABDA sub-command that included control of all the alliance's valuable reconnaissance aircraft. This decision was partially based on the fact that the MLD commander, Captain G.G. Bozuwa, had superior knowledge of Dutch territory. Politics also played a role, as the Dutch government put intense pressure on President Roosevelt after being all but shut out of ABDA's top leadership positions. This arrangement was extremely frustrating to Admiral Helfrich, as virtually all fighting south of the Philippines was taking place on Dutch territory.[31]

Bozuwa assumed command of REC-GROUP on January 16 and held this position until ABDA was dissolved on February 25. Captain P.J. Hendrikse assumed command of the MLD until his death on March 3, 1942. Bozuwa also technically had control of all reconnaissance units in Malaya, but no British aircraft came under ABDA control until February 7. This was because Air Chief Marshal Sir Richard E. Peirse (the senior RAF commander in Malaya) and General Sir Archibald Wavell (supreme commander of ABDA) allowed RAF and RAAF units that were nominally under Bozuwa's command to disobey ABDA orders in order to satisfy national interests.[32]

SPY GAMES

The MLD's build-up of aircraft did not go unnoticed by the Japanese, who had a large, well-entrenched espionage network throughout most of the East Indies. In turn, Dutch counterintelligence was quite sophisticated after years of successfully combating internal threats posed by Indonesian nationalist and communist groups. Building on this expertise and their many local informants, Dutch intelligence agencies were able to easily identify and control most of the Japanese operatives. Nonetheless, Japanese agents were still able to easily track the MLD build-up through readily available sources, such as newspapers, radio stations and public announcements.

Most of these spies operated through the Japanese embassy at Batavia, although Dutch, American and British codebreakers— at Bandoeng, Manila and Singapore, respectively — were able to intercept and decode their consular radio transmissions as early as the mid-1930s.[33] However, Japanese embassy personnel maintained the benefit of being able to communicate with Tokyo via weekly diplomatic pouches, which could not legally be opened or searched by the Dutch.[34]

As a result, the Japanese were well informed of Dutch military strength through these reports, which often went into great detail. In one lengthy radio transmission from Batavia to Tokyo dated October 25, 1941,[35] embassy personnel reported extensively on Dutch military and civilian air strength, including the number of Dorniers and PBYs at Morokrembangan, Menado and Ambon. This included information on the arrival at Morokrembangan from the United States of two PBYs in early September 1941 (probably Y-38 and Y-39), which were followed by three more in late October (probably Y-52, Y-53 and Y-54).

The same report also detailed that the Netherlands Purchasing Commission had recently signed $24,000,000 worth of contracts in the United States for the delivery of a large number of "two-motored medium weight bombers of the B type." These would have been B-25 Mitchell bombers for the KNIL that did not reach Java before the Dutch surrendered. The report further revealed that the Dutch East Indies government had recently passed a supplementary appropriation bill releasing 14,340,000 guilders for the purchase of a fleet of torpedo bombers. These were the 80 Douglas DB-7 aircraft described earlier. However, the report failed to mention that another 51,000,000 guilders had also been appropriated for the purchase of 48 large seaplanes. These would have been the Sikorsky seaplanes already detailed.

From this report, the Japanese High Command also learned that the bulk of new aircraft were received and assembled at either Soerabaja or Bandoeng, where large supply depots existed. Their operatives also reported the existence of the government-subsidized civilian flying clubs, and that there were approximately 40 student pilots in each class at both Batavia and Soerabaja. There had also been an increase in the number of aircraft accidents (particularly with the army air force bombers), leading an operative to speculate that military training operations had picked up in order to man the new aircraft and those on still on order.

While some of the more sensitive information was undoubtedly gleaned from actual espionage, the bulk of it came from radio broadcasts and daily newspapers on Java. In many cases the Dutch public relations machine, which shifted into top gear following the invasion of Holland in 1940, readily released information on the strength of their military forces. Their reasoning for doing so was twofold.

First was the desire to reinforce civilian morale (both European and Indonesian) regarding the strength of Dutch military forces. Although all branches of the armed forces in the NEI were critically weak, this highly effective propaganda campaign misled many civilians into believing that their military was much stronger than it was. As a result, they were shocked when the Japanese easily overran the NEI. On a purely cosmetic level, the Dutch government needed to cast an impression of European power to the Indonesian people. To let nationalist groups see weakness on the part of the Dutch would have further amplified their cries for independence.[36]

Second, it was critical for the Dutch military to create an impression of strength in order to hold the Japanese at arm's length for as long as possible. After the invasion of Holland, the Dutch government liberally promoted its military build-up in an effort to delay a Japanese invasion of the NEI. Each day gained was another in which Dutch forces in the NEI could be reorganized and strengthened. Nonetheless, it was a dangerous game that involved a delicate balancing act between revealing too much information and, perhaps, not enough. In the end it did not matter, as the Japanese were strong enough to overwhelm the Dutch at every turn.

2

Cold War Clashes:
The Build-Up to War

MOROKREMBANGAN

The primary MLD base in the Netherlands East Indies was MVK (Marine Vliegtuig Kamp, or Naval Air Station) Morokrembangan at the Marine Establishment (Naval Base) at Soerabaja on eastern Java. One of the largest seaplane bases in the world, it was a large complex purpose-built for amphibious operations in 1923. Before the base became operational on July 30, 1925, all previous naval air operations had been carried out from the ML air base at Tandjoeng Priok, outside Batavia on the western end of Java. The new location was also more convenient, since the KM's East Indies Squadron also operated from Soerabaja.

Located just outside Soerabaja on the southwestern edge of Morokrembangan, Perak was the city's primary civilian airfield. All MLD land-based primary flight training was also carried out here. It had two 3,000-foot runways and a KNILM hangar that were also used by the Dutch military throughout the East Indies campaign to provide the port, naval and seaplane bases with air cover. Although its facilities and ground personnel were officially under naval jurisdiction, the ML traditionally provided all of the fighter aircraft operating from Perak. The KM went so far as to order six Fokker C.V-D fighters in 1927; however, they were instead delivered to ML units in the East Indies.[1]

Located on the north coast of eastern Java on the mouth of the Krembangan River, the ME was sheltered by the large island of Madoera. Just west of the naval base lay Soerabaja's vast commercial port, which handled thousands of civilian merchant ships annually. MVK Morokrembangan lay a short distance west of the commercial port, although the distance between it and the ME was not far.

Although the KM regularly dredged it, the harbor at Soerabaja was still shallow. Bare and exposed at low tide, a series of mudflats dotted the harbor and was deceptively concealed just beneath the surface at high tide. A channel leading to the seaplane base was usable at all times and clearly marked. However, without charts or local knowledge of the channel, it was impossible to know which side of the buoys to stay on. If one strayed off the step, the penalty usually involved having to be pulled off the flats by one of the base's small harbor boats.

In 1939 and 1940, MVK Morokrembangan received a series of substantial modifications and renovations as the Dutch government attempted to strengthen the country's armed forces. These efforts yielded a large number of new hangars, ramps, workshops and barracks. By the outbreak of the Pacific War, Morokrembangan had 24 hangars, concrete ramps, expansive workshops, transport cranes, underground fuel tanks and powerful radio facilities that let it easily communicate with distant corners of the East Indies and KM ships that were at sea.

Top: Morokrembangan (with Perak Airfield in the background) was the largest and best-equipped seaplane base in the Pacific outside Japan or Hawaii. *Bottom:* Powerful radio facilities let Morokrembangan communicate with aircraft and base personnel at the farthest reaches of the NEI (photographs from *Soerabaja 1900–1950* [2004], courtesy of Asia Maior Publishers).

The base also received its first floating dock in 1932, further increasing its ability to maintain and service seaplanes operating from the base. And although none of the MLD aircraft taking part in the East Indies campaign was amphibious, the MLD was still able to pull them out of the water quite easily for major repairs and comprehensive overhauls. This was done using hoists or special trailers built by the Braat Steelworks in Soerabaja that were towed by Caterpillar tractors.

But despite all of these facilities, Morokrembangan was far from ideal in more than one respect. In addition to the mudflats described earlier, pilots were forced to negotiate and compensate for fast-moving currents during landings and takeoffs, which made their job that much more difficult. Its location almost directly adjacent to the ME also often put air traffic near or directly in the middle of sea traffic entering and leaving the naval base and commercial port. As a result, the area was always congested. And finally, its close proximity to the ME ensured that Morokrembangan would consistently remain a prime target for any land, air or sea attacks against Soerabaja. But in spite of these drawbacks, it was a well-built complex that many aviation experts regarded as the largest, best-equipped and most modern seaplane base in the Far East outside Japan.

FLIGHT TRAINING SCHOOL

Prior to May 1940, most MLD pilots,[2] aircrews, officers and enlisted men were trained either at the De Mok and De Kooy seaplane bases or Willemsoord Naval Base in Holland. Pilot trainees first learned to fly in standard land-configuration planes before making the transition to seaplanes. Primary, intermediate, advanced and formation flight

Ryan STM-S2 trainers in formation with Fokker T.IVa seaplanes attached to the MLD flight training school at Morokrembangan (photograph courtesy of San Diego Aerospace Museum).

training took place in Holland. As most seaplane pilots were assigned to units in the East Indies, a majority of the cadets were then transferred to Morokrembangan for operational training.

After the occupation of Holland, the MLD relocated all flight training to Java and initiated an extensive network of training programs at Morokrembangan. In addition to primary, intermediate and advanced seaplane flight training, they also included technical studies for all branches of the MLD. Besides training personnel for the East Indies, a number of Dutch personnel evacuated from Holland were sent to Java to complete their flight training before returning to Europe.

The MLD Flight Training School operated a total of 10 Dornier Do. 15 "Whales" (not all operational), 1 Fokker T.IV, 6 Fokker C.VII-W, 10 Fokker C.XI-W, 40 Ryan ST and 5 Tiger Moth primary trainers. In addition, a small number of T.IVs were transferred from active service to the school. The STM-2 (land) primary trainers were based at Perak and the STM-S2 floatplanes went to Morokrembangan. Many of these aircraft were lost as the Japanese began bombing Java on a regular basis. As a result, the school was shut down in mid-February 1942 and transferred to Australia to avoid further losses of personnel and equipment.

Flight training in the East Indies greatly accelerated after the fall of Holland and was extremely intense. Prior to the attack on Pearl Harbor, there were approximately 60 European and Indonesian cadets undergoing training. Although the ML transferred four flight instructors to the school, they proved too few for the task at hand. As a result, the quality of training for many of the students suffered.[3]

To improve the pace and quality of its flight training program, the MLD hired 12 American flight instructors from the United States in 1941. Although all were civilians, they appear to have been ex-military or reserve pilots from the ranks of the USN and USMC.[4] It is unclear how many were seaplane pilots as most were engaged in primary flight training. Soon after their arrival at Morokrembangan, the Americans dubbed the giant seaplane base "Little Pensacola" after the naval air station in Florida where many had undergone their own flight training.[5]

X-3 is serviced while attached to the flight training school at Morokrembangan; note the Fokker T.IVs moored immediately behind (photograph courtesy of André de Zwart).

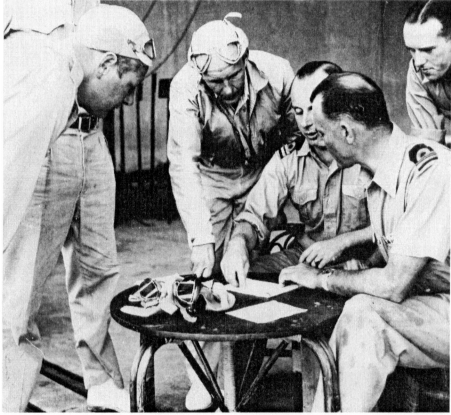

Top: As the threat of war with Japan grew, the MLD initiated a full-scale flight training program that included both European and Eurasian cadets (photograph courtesy of San Diego Aerospace Museum). *Bottom:* Three of the American flight instructors hired by the MLD in 1941 (l to r): Lt. John Russel (USN), Unknown (standing), William Eddy (civilian), Lt. Willard Reed (USMCR), Lt. 1st Class K. Holtz (MLD) and Sub-Lt. F. Beugeling (MLD) (photograph courtesy of Institute for Maritime History).

Primary flight training began on the Ryan land trainers, followed by additional primary training on the Ryan seaplanes. Trainees then graduated to more advanced seaplane flight training on the Fokker C.XIV-W, Fokker T.IV and Dornier Whale.[6] They completed operational training on the new Do. 24K-1s as these planes became available. A number of MLD pilots trained at Morokrembangan and Perak were later transferred back to England to fly Anson and Hudson aircraft with Dutch forces in exile attached to British Coastal Command.

To facilitate the substantial increase in the numbers of pilots and flight personnel undergoing training, the MLD recalled the Fokker T.IV seaplanes of GVT.11 from patrol duties at Balikpapan in mid-August 1940. The squadron's reconnaissance duties over the Makassar Strait were taken over by ML Martin bombers operating from airfields on Borneo. It appears that the Fokker crews were transferred to one of the new GVTs then being formed with the Do. 24s.

In a short time, the trainees, many of them reservists or teenagers just out of high school, had to absorb a vast amount of complicated information. Not all of it involved the mechanics of flight, but also how to differentiate weather formations, identify storm fronts and analyze water conditions to gauge landing conditions. These grueling flight and navigational exercises went on 24 hours a day, supplemented by continuous bombing and gunnery training. The latter took place either on a floating dock anchored in the Madoera Strait or the decommissioned destroyer *Lynx*, whose grounded hulk lay beached on a sandbar near the ME.

In contrast to their American and British counterparts, many regular MLD pilots in the Far East were older than average.[7] This can be attributed, at least in part, to the MLD being a small, highly skilled peacetime force. Turnover in these types of close-knit organizations is rarely high in any country's military. In addition, funding throughout the 1930s strictly limited the growth of the MLD, dictating that it remain a small force dominated by career men.

Like their American counterparts, combat experience among MLD flight crews was virtually nonexistent. Although many had logged large numbers of flight hours prior to the outbreak of war, it was still "on-the-job training" when the shooting started. Three KNIL fighter pilots were sent to Britain for training and operational experience in late 1940. However, two of them were killed in action in 1941, and only one returned to Java. Five more pilots were en route to Europe when the Japanese attacked Pearl Harbor, and they were recalled.

For their part, the British scattered a handful of experienced veterans throughout most of their air units. However, the most experienced were sent to combat zones in Europe and Africa. This meant that the bulk of the aircrews in the Far East were composed of young, inexperienced personnel straight out of training schools in Australia, East Africa, New Zealand and Rhodesia.[8]

The German invasion of Holland also cut off the MLD from its traditional source of personnel. As the total number of Europeans in the East Indies, women, children and senior citizens included, numbered fewer than 300,000, this forced the MLD to compete with the KM and KNIL for qualified technical recruits in a severely restricted pool of applicants. Although Eurasians and Indonesians were eligible to join the KM in every branch and capacity, few met the rigid educational requirements required to become pilots.[9] As a result, the MLD was left with a substantially older, albeit well-trained, core of seaplane pilots.

In addition to courses for regular and reserve officers, training centers for air gunners, radio operators and mechanics also existed. An MLD mechanics and workshop training college for Indonesian recruits at Makassar was also expanded. A number of these men were evacuated before Java fell and formed the bulk of Dutch ground crews throughout the war.

One of the largest training programs was for radio operators. Although all its planes were in direct contact with shipboard and shore-based radio stations, one of the most severe shortages the MLD faced was a lack of trained operators. As radio equipment became standard on MLD planes throughout the 1930s, the first wireless operators were trained in Holland and shipped to Java to form the core of a specialized training program for aircraft and shore radio operators.

With the expansion of the MLD and occupation of Holland, this program was expanded, and a number of militia recruits trained. Still, the shortage remained so severe throughout the fleet that in early 1941, Admiral Helfrich ordered the formation of a separate communications branch of the MLD to meet the East Indies Squadron's needs.[10] Since the MLD had a surplus of junior officer pilots at that time, a number of these recruits were retrained as radio operators. To fill yet another void, all radio operators were also cross-trained as air gunners and flight medics.

Although men and material consistently remained in short supply, evacuees from occupied Holland and civilian volunteers from South Africa provided the MLD with a solid core. As seen earlier, from May 1941 on the MLD could also draw from the ranks of the VVC (*Vrijwillig Vlieger Corps*) or Volunteer Flying Corps, for new pilot trainees. These young men flew DH.82a Tiger Moth,[11] Büchner Jungmann[12] or Piper Cub[13] training aircraft on weekend training flights. These reserves formed a valuable personnel resource for the East Indies air forces.

A contingent of navy pilot trainees had been evacuated from Holland in May 1940.

After a brief period in England, they were transported to Java by ship, arriving in Batavia on November 21, 1940. They underwent advanced flight training at Morokrembangan before returning to England to form the nucleus of the Royal Air Force's 320 Squadron (Dutch). They did not return to the Pacific and flew from British air bases throughout the war.

In addition to its comprehensive training facilities and workshops, all supplies, spare parts, engines and reserve aircraft were housed at Morokrembangan. There were also a number of older planes, including the older "D" and "T" planes, many of which were reactivated for duty in late 1941. Throughout the campaign, damaged seaplanes of all nationalities also came into Morokrembangan for overhaul and

The crew of X-8; note the Indonesian crewman at a time when USN flight crews were strictly racially segregated (photograph courtesy of Nol Baarschers).

The crew of X-15 relaxes atop its plane at Bima Harbor in March 1939; at least two crewmen drink milk from coconuts (photograph courtesy of Nol Baarschers).

repairs, while new Dutch PBYs from the United States arrived to be made ready for operational service. Large numbers of American seaplanes from the Philippines also moved in and out of the base as the campaign progressed.

Morokrembangan remained free from air attack until February 3, 1942. The first attack was heavy, with 72 bombers and 44 fighters hitting the ME and nearby air bases. Allied fighters were unable to stop the attack, and that day at least 15 MLD planes were shot down or destroyed on the water. From that point Morokrembangan remained a prime target for the Japanese as they returned time and again to claim more MLD planes in an effort to reduce Allied air power.

SECONDARY BASES[14]

There were four main secondary bases throughout the NEI, including MVK Priok at Tandjoeng Priok outside Batavia on western Java, MVK Ambon, MVK Tarakan and MVK Prapat on Lake Toba in Central Sumatra. Although all were officially considered major hubs, with the exception of Tandjoeng Priok, they were little more than built-up advance bases that were capable of carrying out major maintenance on MLD aircraft. For example, MVK Prapat was completed only just before the outbreak of war and had only a concrete ramp and barracks for aircrews. As with Morokrembangan, all were equipped with Caterpillar tractors and specially built trailers that let the seaplanes be easily removed from the water.

Activated on December 24, 1918, MVK Priok was substantially smaller than the main air station at Morokrembangan. Although closed upon the completion of Morokrembangan, Priok was refurbished and reactivated in 1940, as the MLD was rebuilt and strengthened. Situated just west of the civilian harbor, it featured two hangars capable of housing

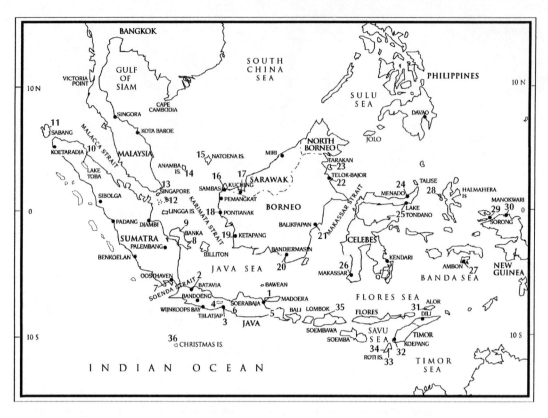

MLD Seaplane Bases December 1941. Legend: (1) MVK Morokrembangan; (2) MVK Priok; (3) Tji-latjap; (4) Lake Tjileuntje; (5) Lake Grati; (6) Brantes River; (7) Oosthaven; (8) Tandjoeng Pinang; (9) Klabat Bay; (10) Lake Toba; (11) Sabang; (12) Poelau Sambo (Riouw Archipelago); (13) NAS Selatar (Singapore); (14) Anambas Islands; (15) Natoena Islands; (16) Sambas; (17) Kuching; (18) Pontianak; (19) Ketapang; (20) Bandjermasin; (21) Balikpapan; (22) Telok-Bajor; (23) Tarakan; (24) Menado; (25) MVK Kalkas (Lake Tondano); (26) Makassar; (27) MVK Halong (Ambon); (28) Ternate; (29) Sorong; (30) Manokwari; (31) Kalabhai (Alor Island, Lesser Soenda Islands); (32) Koepang; (33) Roti Island; (34) Benooid Bay (Roti Island); (35) Bima (Soembawa, Lesser Soenda Islands); (36) Christmas Island.

four flying boats, an underground fuel tank and a number of workshops; at maximum capacity, MVK Priok could handle 10–20 large seaplanes. Although small it benefited from the reliable, well-organized transportation network that the island of Java offered.

The primary seaplane base in the eastern East Indies was MVK Halong, on the island of Ambon. Completed in 1939 and situated on the northern shore of Ambon's enclosed inner bay, it was the largest MLD seaplane base after Morokrembangan and served as the headquarters for Captain P. J. Hendrikse, who commanded all MLD and Allied reconnaissance operations in that part of the archipelago. MVK Halong consisted of three large hangars, three underground fuel tanks, workshops and a number of barracks that were still under construction when the island fell to the Japanese in January 1942. The island was also a support base for the KM with powerful radio facilities and naval base that in reality served as little more than a staging point for Dutch submarines.

A naval air station for the MLD since the 1920s, MVK Tarakan was modernized in 1940 and capable of supporting two GVTs. Improvements included the construction of large barracks for flight and ground crews, an electric plant, maintenance workshops and

The Dorniers of GVT.4 moored in Bima Harbor, March 1939 (photograph courtesy of Nol Baarschers).

two underground aviation fuel storage tanks with a capacity of 220,000 gallons each. In late 1941, it received a small floating aircraft dock and expanded facilities that let it carry out simple aircraft repairs. But despite its status as a major support hub for MLD operations in the northern NEI, Tarakan in fact remained little more than a well-equipped support base.

There were also three lesser-developed support bases. The first was Kalkas, which had been established on the southeastern edge of Lake Tondano on Northern Celebes in October 1941. It featured a small workshop, and two squadrons could operate from the base. The ML was supposed to have provided air cover for the base from Kalawiran Airfield, situated some three and a half miles southwest of Lake Tondano near the town of Langoan. However, it appears that a shortage of fighter aircraft meant that none were ever deployed to the airfield during the East Indies campaign. This would contribute to the tragic losses suffered by two MLD squadrons at Kalkas on December 26, 1941.

At the same time, Balikpapan on the east coast of Borneo, and Pontianak in southern Borneo, allowed MLD patrols to effectively patrol the South China Sea and Makassar Strait. Of the two, Balikpapan was the oldest. Although officially rated as a support base, it could support the operations of two squadrons and was able to provide them with routine maintenance and other repairs thanks to a floating dock that been towed to the port from Java between September and December 1939. Pontianak had become operational only in 1940, but like Kalkas on Lake Tondano, it featured a small workshop that allowed minor aircraft repairs and maintenance.

In addition, the MLD had 51 remote bases scattered throughout the NEI.[15] Usually situated near isolated settlements, they included the Riouw Archipelago, the Talaud Islands, Ternate and Morotai in the Moluccas Islands and Sorong, New Guinea. The MLD also reached a prewar agreement with the British government to establish a seaplane base on Christmas Island, 300 miles south of Java in the Indian Ocean. Although fully stocked, the MLD never had adequate strength to use this base during the East Indies campaign.

MLD pilots also had another 153 auxiliary bases on their charts.[16] Of these, 43 were undeveloped staging points for the most part. Although rare, some had skeleton ground crews and radio facilities that let them communicate with Morokrembangan. However, all contained hidden fuel and ordnance dumps, providing adequate stopover points for refueling, repairs and rest for the aircrews. The remainder were little more than primitive jungle campsites situated on secluded rivers and lakes that had been established for the dispersal of aircraft if required.

The MLD could also count on a number of so-called "Guaranteed Depots" to help maintain its air operations in remote parts of the archipelago. These were supply depots strategically located at various civilian oil company facilities, ports and seaplane bases. Stocked and maintained in conjunction with civilian oil companies, they contained fuel, oil and other supplies that MLD aircraft would require in order to maintain air operations.

All the seaplane bases were serviced in one way or another by a wide variety of small boats. These included fast motorboats for personnel transport, boats for refueling seaplanes in the harbor, specialized ordnance boats for "bombing up" planes and "crash boats" to rescue survivors or to take off wounded. At Morokrembangan, the MLD operated small harbor boats, which resembled miniature tugboats. These maneuverable boats had a cockpit forward with a towing bit placed amidships. This design allowed the coxswain to put the seaplane in tow wherever he wanted.[17] Although few of these boats were standardized, no base could effectively function without them, and their destruction seriously limited the efficiency of an MLD base.

The lifeline provided by these forward bases was possible thanks to large supplies of fuel, oil and ordnance stocked before the war and supporting aircraft tenders of the Governments Marine. The Governments Marine (GM) was a civilian naval force similar in organization and function to the United States Coast Guard. As a state police force, its peacetime duties included police work, customs and drug interdiction, although in times of war, it came under the operational control of the KM.

Militarized in September 1939, GM patrol boats and auxiliaries were put under the operational command of the East Indies Squadron. Seven of the larger patrol boats—*Arend*, *Bellatrix*, *Fazant*, *Merel*, *Poolster*, *Reiger* and *Valk*—were converted and assigned to the MLD for use as seaplane tenders. Carrying aviation fuel, oil, spare parts, supplies, ammunition and powerful communications equipment, they provided an invaluable network of mobile support bases that allowed a GVT to simply relocate when threatened. It appears that a small number of single-engine Fokker floatplanes were also attached to *Arend* and *Valk* in a utility role, and the two ships were equipped to operate a single aircraft as part of their normal complement.

This broad network of seaplane bases let the MLD maintain a high degree of operational efficiency and mobility both prewar and throughout the East Indies campaign. It also let the Dutch keep a wide eye on what the Japanese were doing as they moved toward Java. The militarized seaplanes of KNILM, which used its prewar civilian hub facilities, patrolled those areas of the NEI that the MLD could not cover.

Japanese strategy centered on neutralizing these bases, and it proved effective. Throughout the campaign, the GVTs lived a nomadic existence, being harried from base to base. One squadron operated from 5 different bases in 15 days. Flying 16- to 18-hour

Fazant was one of seven Governments Marine patrol boats converted for use as MLD seaplane tenders in 1939–40 (photograph courtesy of Jan Klootwijk).

missions for days on end added to the strain for Dutch air crews. Although the MLD tried to rotate squadrons out of the line, this was not always possible. As the war converged on Java, there soon were no safe places left for them to hide.

ANTI-AIRCRAFT DEFENSES

A primary reason for the overwhelming success of Japanese air strikes on Java was clearly the Allies' lack of fighter aircraft. Another was the weak state of Dutch AA defenses across the board. Although their weapons were of excellent manufacture and quality in general, there were simply too few available to make much of an impact. The KNIL's decision to parcel them out in penny packets in order to provide important facilities with some semblance of air defense only served to further dilute their effectiveness.

In December 1941 the KNIL, which was responsible for AA defenses throughout the East Indies, could count on the services of only four heavy AA batteries. These were composed of one 105mm and three 80mm AA batteries. They were supported by 104 Bofors 40mm AA guns that had been acquired from Sweden between December 1936 and December 1939. The KNIL had also ordered a substantial number of Rheinmetal 20mm light AA cannon from Germany, although only small numbers of these weapons reached the NEI prior to May 1940. The Swedish firm of Bofors was the primary manufacturer and distributor of the heavy pieces, although the acquisition of 75mm AA guns from this firm had also been disrupted by the war in Europe.

Because of the importance of these targets, the heaviest AA weapons were concentrated at Soerabaja, Batavia and Bandoeng, capital of the East Indies government and traditional headquarters of the Dutch military's high command. As the seat of power, Bandoeng had 20 80mm AA guns to defend it.[18] At the same time, Soerabaja had eight 80mm batteries deployed throughout the city and port.[19] The civilian and naval ports at Tandjoeng Priok were allocated a total of four 80mm and six 40mm guns.[20] The naval air station was defended by four 40mm AA.[21]

The remaining weapons were parceled out in small numbers. As a primary airfield on east Java, Perak was allocated four 105mm and four 40mm AA guns.[22] Being in such close proximity to the airfield, Morokrembangan benefited from their firepower as well, although the seaplane base had only a single battery of two 20mm cannons for its own defense.[23] Air defenses at all of these facilities were typically supplemented by 7.7mm and 12.7mm machine guns, although they were virtually useless against anything other than strafing fighters. In most cases, the latter were the only air defense at larger MLD support bases in the outlaying territories.

The Dutch fully realized this deficiency as early as June 14, 1940, when the NPC presented a list of needed armaments to the United States Treasury Department's Procurement Division. No longer able to procure additional weapons from its traditional European suppliers, the KNIL, which was responsible for AA defenses throughout the NEI, requested permission to purchase substantial numbers of AA guns with ammunition, rangefinders, searchlights and related equipment from either the United States Army or American arms factories. This equipment included:

In response to this and other urgent requests from the NEI government, the United States Army dispatched a military mission to Java to review Dutch military defenses and ascertain their actual military needs firsthand. As might be expected, the Dutch cooperated fully with the members of the mission and provided a detailed look into the state of their defenses and provided a comprehensive list of their requirements. In the following chart, it is interesting to note that the KNIL's AA requirements increased dramatically from their initial needs just two months earlier.

As is clearly seen, the Dutch needs for their AA defenses alone were massive, and they had little time to rebuild or strengthen them. A great deal of this deficiency can be attributed to the United States' early refusal to sell weapons to the Dutch out of fear that

Table 2: AA Weapons Requested by the KNIL, June 1940[24]

1 battery (four 90mm AA guns): to be delivered with fire-control apparatus, electric-transmission system and 13-foot range finder, four spare barrel liners and 38,040 high-explosive shells.

13 batteries (four 80mm AA guns each): to be delivered with 21 fire-control directors, each with a fire-control apparatus, electric-transmission system and 13-foot range finder. They would also come with two spare guns, a small number of spare barrel liners and munitions cases and 37,440 high-explosive shells.

• 5 batteries (three Bofors 40mm AA guns each): to be delivered with 15 telephones. 15- x 7-foot rangefinders. 1,500 cartridge holders and 30,000 high-explosive shells.

• 17 batteries x (two Bofors 40mm AA guns each): to be delivered with 68 spare barrel liners, 20 fire-control systems, 3,400 cartridge holders and 68,000 high-explosive shells.

• 32 batteries (two Bofors 40mm AA guns each): to be delivered with 128 spare barrel liners, 32 telephones, 32 7-foot rangefinders, 6,400 cartridge holders and 128,000 high-explosive shells.

• 16 batteries (two Hispano-Suiza 20mm AA guns each): to be delivered with 64 spare barrel liners. 130- x 3-foot rangefinders, 384,000 high-explosive shells and 76,800 armor-piercing shells.

• *In the event that Bofors 40mm weapons were unavailable, the Dutch also indicated a willingness to accept 37mm AA weapons with simplified fire control systems.*

Table 3: Dutch AA Requirements, August 1940[25]

Equipment	Total Needs	On Hand	Number Requested	Remarks
90mm Mobile Mount	60	—	60	Urgently requested for
— Extra gun barrels	60	—	60	defense of naval bases
— Fire-control sets	15	—	15	important military facilities
—13-foot rangefinders	18	—	18	and use by KNIL.
— HE shells with mechanical fuses	41,500	—	41,500	
80mm Fixed Mount	28	28	—	For defense of naval bases,
—13-foot rangefinders	8	—	8	and important military
— Fire-control sets	9	2	7	facilities; rangefinders and fire control sets urgently needed.
40mm Mobile Mount	140	40	100	
— Complete fire-control set	70	—	70	Urgently requested for
— 7-foot rangefinders	77	32	45	defense of naval bases, and
— 3-foot stereoscopic equipment for observing tracer fire	75		75	important military facilities.
— Ammunition (tracer)	680,000	80,000	600,000	
20mm Mobile Mount —1-watt rangefinders (stereoscopic picture type)	160	30	130	Urgently needed
— 3-foot stereoscopic equipment for observing tracer fire	80 80	—	80	
— Ammunition HE/Tracer	1,200,000	200,000	1,000,000	70,000 ordered in USA; delivery expected August 1941
Armor Piercing	400,000	—	400,000	

the East Indies government would fold under Japanese pressure and become little more than a quasi-protectorate within the Japanese Empire. So although the United States did agree to supply AA weapons to the KNIL, it did so too late for most of the orders to be filled. So whether through human delay or unavailability of the requested equipment, the Dutch in December 1941 faced a crippling shortage of weapons and equipment that time and again would lead to tragic losses for the MLD.

Nonetheless, the Dutch AA forces did receive a small number of reinforcements in early 1942. In the first week of February 1942, several British AA units that had been evacuated from Singapore reinforced the KNIL batteries. These units included the 21st Light Anti-Aircraft Regiment with nine 40mm AA guns and the 77th Heavy Anti-Aircraft Regiment with nine 3.7" weapons. Unfortunately, the latter were hampered by a shortage of ammunition after the merchant ship *Derrymore* was sunk during the evacuation of Singapore while carrying a cargo of 3.7-inch shells.

The British guns also arrived on Java with the only radar set in the East Indies. This equipment was set up on the island of Madoera, just north of the ME. However, the British did not fully trust the Dutch or their Indonesian troops and did not allow them to come near the installation. Nor, it appears, were they willing share information on how it functioned, lest it fall into the hands of the Japanese through Indonesian spies. Although the radar set was not functional during the first Japanese raid on Java, it remained online throughout the rest of the campaign.

NEUTRALITY AND MOBILIZATION
IN THE NEI

The MLD went on its first war footing when Italy invaded Albania on April 7, 1939. Although there was little threat of the conflict spilling over into the East Indies, Captain K.W.F.M. Doorman, commander of the MLD forces in the NEI, ordered two squadrons at Morokrembangan to bases in the Makassar Strait and Riouw Archipelago, where they initiated neutrality patrols on April 13. The squadron operating in the Riouw Islands was supported by the seaplane tender Hr.Ms. *Bellatrix*, which in turn, was under the command of the gunboat Hr.Ms. *Flores*.

On September 8 of that year, the GM patrol vessels *Sirius*, *Fazant* and *Reiger* were ordered into the ME, where they were converted into MLD seaplane tenders. Three weeks later they were put under the operational control of the ME naval commander and MLD reconnaissance commander of the eastern East Indies at MVK Halong on Ambon. They joined *Bellatrix*, *Arend* and *Valk*, which had been militarized and converted for MLD service several months earlier. In this capacity, all of the tenders transported fuel, munitions and supplies, in addition to carrying out minor aircraft repairs and changing out motors during overhauls.

Immediately prior to the outbreak of widespread war in Europe, Captain Doorman received orders to maintain no fewer than eight GVTs in active service at all times. At least two of the squadrons were assigned to the East Indies Squadron in a reconnaissance capacity. Two more were based in the Moluccas Archipelago (operating from Ambon), with single squadrons based in the Riouw Islands and at Tandjoeng Priok, Tarakan and Balikpapan. Although most of these aircraft were Do. 15s or Do. 24s, the last two squadrons flew Fokker T.IVs.

When Germany invaded Poland in September 1939, the MLD had 78 large seaplanes in service with its East Indies squadron. These included 26 Dornier Do. 24, 19 Dornier Do. 15, 17 Fokker T.IVa, nine Fokker C.XI-W and seven Fokker C.VII-W aircraft, the last seven dating from the mid to late 1920s.[26] Front-line strength of the fleet air arm in the NEI consisted of nine GVTs operating a mixture of modern Do. 24s, which were slowly replacing the obsolescent T.IVs.

The Dutch planes immediately began flying neutrality patrols over the East Indies to prevent the war from creeping into their territory. Most of the flights were around Sabang in the Malacca Strait, over the Soenda Strait and along the west coast of Sumatra. GVT.2 (X-11, X-12 and X-13) also began flights over the southern Makassar Strait and South China Sea, while GVT.4 (X-19, X-20 and X-2) set up operations at Ambon and initiated regular patrols over the eastern half of the East Indies.[27] These patrols were soon intensified as the combatants began operating in and around NEI waters.

Following the outbreak of war, 19 German merchant ships sought refuge in NEI waters. As Holland and the NEI were still neutral, all were interned.[28] However, British forces kept close tabs on them, leading to several violations of Dutch territory. The first occurred on September 6 when a seaplane from a British cruiser attacked the German merchant ship *Franken*, and on at least two other occasions Royal Navy ships illegally entered Dutch waters. Then in April 1940 a Dutch aircraft fired warning shots against another seaplane operating from an RN armed merchant cruiser near Makassar. The British plane had entered Dutch territory to reconnoiter the German merchant ship *Scheer*, which lay interned in the harbor.[29]

Seven months later, on November 16, the German battleship *Graf Spee* stopped the Dutch merchant ship *Mapia* in the Indian Ocean near Durban, South Africa, and inquired about her cargo. Although the German captain let the neutral freighter go, it was feared that the raider was moving toward the East Indies. To ensure Dutch neutrality, the MLD began a series of patrols along the sea-lanes around Sabang harbor in Northern Sumatra. Although these flights were eventually discontinued, renewed reports of German armed merchant cruiser activity would again spark a week of intense reconnaissance patrols between Dutch New Guinea and the island of Celebes in early 1941. By that time though, Germany and the Netherlands were at war. As a result, the Dutch airmen actively sought out the German raiders, but without success.

On December 13, *Bellatrix* reported an unidentified Japanese tanker entering Dutch waters through the Lombok Strait. Even at this early stage, the Dutch were fearful and uncertain of Japanese intentions toward the East Indies and took steps to keep the tanker under observation. KM HQ on Java immediately ordered Captain Doorman to carry out reconnaissance patrols over the area using aircraft operating from southern Java and the Lesser Soenda Islands. However, before the patrols could be organized, the Japanese ship disappeared and was not seen again.

In response to Japan's continued war on the Chinese mainland, the United States banned all copper and brass exports to the Japanese in January 1941. As an island nation with few natural resources of its own, these items were absolutely vital if Japan was to continue its war in China. Without them, its war effort would slowly grind to a halt. The final blow came when the Dutch followed the American lead and stopped all oil exports from the East Indies. With its vital resources cut off, and surrounded by what it regarded as enemies, Japan made ready to fight.

Although Japan had openly coveted control of the East Indies since the First World War, it had been reluctant to act while the Dutch homeland remained unoccupied. However, with many of Holland's strongest allies under Nazi occupation, and the remainder fighting for their existence, Japanese nationalists felt strong enough to act in early April 1940 when the IJN was put on "Increased Readiness"[30] in preparation for an invasion of the East Indies beginning May 1, 1940. At the same time, senior fleet officers were ordered to prepare for war against England and the United States, as the Japanese military believed that neither country would idly stand by while Japan blatantly committed such an aggressive act of war.[31]

Beginning the first week of April 1940, the Dutch received a series of reports that warned of the Japanese plans. The bulk of this information came from a sympathetic high-ranking German officer inside the Abwehr;[32] he also warned of the pending German invasion of Holland,[33] which was confirmed by similar signals from the Vatican as well. In response the KM assembled the East Indies Squadron off the coast of Borneo, and the MLD intensified reconnaissance flights over the South China Sea, Makassar Strait and Moluccas. Tensions rose even higher when it was learned that a large concentration of Japanese ships had assembled at the island of Formosa, which was assumed to be the departure point for any invasion of Dutch territory.

It is unknown whether a formal invasion plan was ever drawn up, but from records found in Kriegsmarine archives, it appears that Japan planned a lightning strike against the East Indies in conjunction with the pending German invasion of Holland. As their final decision rested on German invasion plans, the Japanese pushed the Germans for specifics on their invasion plans throughout the first two weeks of April. However, on

The Japanese operated some 500 civilian fishing and pearling boats throughout the NEI, secretly mapping installations and taking harbor soundings (photograph courtesy of National Archives of Australia).

April 17 Vice-Admiral Nobutake Kondo, the IJN's Deputy Chief of Staff, ordered his forces to stand down as the Japan Cabinet still wanted to avoid war with the United States and Great Britain by pursuing a policy of negotiation.[34]

So instead of an overt invasion, the IJN took steps to intensify covert intelligence operations throughout the East Indies. A large fleet of approximately 500 Japanese fishing boats— manned by some 4,000 civilians, reservists and active-duty personnel — was assigned to these operations.[35] To support this fleet, the Japanese set up entire fishing communities and fisheries throughout the NEI, which allowed their ships to move at will. In some instances, Japanese submarines resupplied them.

As a result, the fishing boats were able to move freely. In the process, they often flagrantly violated Dutch territorial waters and fishery regulations to "fish" and dive for pearls near important military installations. When stopped and searched, many were often found with sophisticated sounding equipment, well-detailed charts of various harbors throughout the East Indies and powerful radio equipment capable of transmitting all the way to Japan.

In areas where Dutch rule was weak, the crews of these fishing boats often landed on smaller islands to bully the civilians and steal food. They also engaged in opium trafficking, shipments of which were relayed to them by other Japanese ships outside Dutch territorial waters. Powerful crime syndicates with top military ties undoubtedly operated these operations, as this type of activity was also rampant in the occupied areas of mainland China and Manchuria.[36]

The sheer size of this fleet and its movements caused tremendous intelligence concerns for the Dutch fleet. To help police their movements, a naval squadron including the light cruiser *De Ruyter* was deployed off Celebes, and her shipboard seaplanes were extensively used to locate and monitor the Japanese fishing boats. At the same time, an

MLD group was sent to the Lesser Soenda Islands archipelago, while submarine divisions were deployed to Ambon and the port of Bima on Soembawa Island. But even with the help of the Governments Marine and intensified air patrols by the ML, there was still much space left for the Japanese to operate.

In February 1941 a large Japanese naval task force assembled off northern Indochina. At the same time, the Imperial Japanese Army began stockpiling war supplies throughout Indochina and Formosa. Alarmed by this build-up, Admiral Helfrich ordered all Dutch ships to concentrate in the southern half of the South China Sea. He also ordered all warships under repair or in overhaul to be ready to put to sea within 24 hours of receiving orders.[37]

On February 11, Dutch merchant ships in Chinese and Japanese waters were ordered to head south for safer waters. That same day, Admiral Helfrich also closed all Dutch harbors to Japanese shipping. The Dutch clearly expected a Japanese invasion in the immediate future. They believed there would be a direct attack on Java itself, and all available warships concentrated at Soekadana Bay on Western Borneo to intercept such a thrust. Here, shallow water prevented Japanese submarine attacks, and the MLD carried out a series of intensive, long-range patrols to the north; cruiser floatplanes searched the immediate area.

However, the anticipated attack never materialized, and eventually the Dutch state of readiness lapsed as it became clear that Japanese attention for the time being was focused on Indochina. Tensions, which were already high following the oil embargo, had been taken almost to the breaking point. At the same time, the Japanese were now well aware that the Dutch were prepared to resist any invasion of the NEI. This led to the start of an intense cold war in which both sides knew there was no turning back a full nine months before Pearl Harbor.

Hr. Ms. *De Ruyter* launches one of her Fokker C.XI-W floatplanes (photograph courtesy of Institute for Maritime History).

Natives pose in front of X-9 at an unknown MLD seaplane base, most likely in New Guinea or Borneo (photograph courtesy of Institute for Maritime History).

These activities by the Japanese finally convinced the Dutch to openly participate in joint defensive planning sessions with the Australians and British. They had previously not done so to avoid provoking the Japanese. At one of these joint meetings, a RAF staff officer from Singapore requested, and was granted, permission to tour various Dutch bases throughout the East Indies with an eye toward Commonwealth forces using them in the event of war. The Dornier X-9 then spent a week ferrying him and an ML officer between the ME and the bases at Ambon, Lake Tondano, Tarakan and Balikpapan before returning to Soerabaja.

As the Allies solidified their defensive plans, the Dutch and Japanese engaged in a number of provocative incidents. On May 6, a Do. 24 sighted a suspicious motorboat without a national flag operating in the Dutch-owned Riouw Archipelago, just south of Singapore. As the seaplane circled, its crew identified the boat as being Japanese and repeatedly issued orders for it to leave Dutch territorial waters, all of which were ignored. In an effort to stop and search the ship, the X-boat pilot then attempted to land nearby. As he did the Japanese skipper attempted to ram the seaplane, leading Dutch gunners to fire several rounds across the Japanese ship's bow.[38]

Some time later, a Japanese officer sent a highly fictionalized account of this encounter to his superiors in Tokyo. His version not only claimed that the Dutch had deliberately fired on the fishing boat first, but also that British troops had also landed on Java as part of a plan to take the NEI into British custody as a protectorate.[39] Although the report failed to induce the war he sought, this officer helped to further intensify the Dutch-Japanese cold war.

In another incident[40] off western Borneo, the crew of a Japanese fishing vessel lined the railing of their vessel and challenged an MLD seaplane to fire on them. They clearly hoped to provoke an international incident, but the plane's commander refused to play along. Nonetheless, the Japanese political pressure brought about by these actions was tremendous. Anxious to avoid inflaming the situation, the Dutch government agreed to use its seaplanes only for reconnaissance and to cease the practice of stopping and searching Japanese fishing boats at sea. Almost immediately, the fishing boat crews were apparently ordered to routinely ignore orders from MLD aircraft to leave Dutch territorial waters when discovered.[41]

Later that month Dutch planes sighted the Japanese cargo ship *Zuyo Maru* in the Halmahera Sea with a suspicious deck cargo. However, no ships were close enough to intercept, and contact was lost. On the 22nd, however, the Governments Marine patrol boat *Arend* stopped and boarded the *Asahi Maru* in Dutch waters off New Guinea. But nothing was found, and *Arend* was forced to let the ship and her laughing master go about their business.

As tensions mounted between the Dutch and Japanese, the NEI government stepped up military relations with its American, Australian and British counterparts. From May 15 to 20, three MLD Do. 24s flew from Morokrembangan to Darwin and back via Koepang in an exercise designed to strengthen military ties between the two nations. Although the Dutch had participated in a series of joint defense planning sessions with the Americans, Australians and British at Manila, Singapore and Batavia in 1940 and 1941, they had up to this point refrained from overt military cooperation.

These planning sessions resulted in the creation of a series of classified inter-Allied codes for Anglo–Dutch–United States Radio Communications. They were issued to Allied land and seaplane flight crews throughout the Far East in May 1941 and included standardized operating procedures, radio call signs and a detailed list of reconnaissance signals. An Anglo–Dutch–United States table of lettered coordinates was also distributed in August 1941.

The Dutch then participated in a two-day operation between July 23 and 25 with American and British aircraft. Each nation executed a series of reconnaissance flights throughout its respective operational areas, which had been previously established at the American-Dutch-British talks at Singapore in 1941. Although the primary goal of the operation was to familiarize the aircrews with the above protocols, it also proved helpful in helping determine logistics and equipment needs at various allied air bases throughout the Far East. As a result of this operation, a RAF seaplane base was established at Sabang harbor on Malaya's western coast.

Meanwhile, Japanese fishing boats continued intensify their espionage operations throughout the NEI. In response to a rash of intrusions into the Dutch territorial waters, Admiral Helfrich ordered GVT.7 to the MLD base at Pontianak, Borneo, with the tender *Poolster* on September 24. From there, the squadron flew reconnaissance patrols in the area of the Natoena, Anambas and Tambelan Islands until transferred to Tarakan on December 6.

On September 28 an unidentified X-boat reported a suspicious ship in the Ceram Sea. Believing it to be a Japanese spy ship trespassing in Dutch waters, the KM sent out two destroyers to investigate. However, by the time they reached the area, the vessel had disappeared, and they were recalled.

Numerous operations such as these continued until November 23, 1941, when the

Royal Australian Navy (RAN) requested Dutch help in locating one of its cruisers, which had gone missing while en route from Singapore to Fremantle, Australia. At the time, no one knew the German merchant cruiser *Kormoran* had sunk HMAS *Sydney* on the 19th. Although there were no survivors from *Sydney*, German sailors later testified that the Australian captain had let himself be drawn within range of the merchant cruiser's guns and torpedo tubes. In an action lasting approximately one hour, both ships received mortal damage and drifted out of sight of the other before sinking.

Sydney went down without a word and was declared overdue when she failed to enter port. However, a full-scale search-and-rescue mission began in earnest only when merchant ships started to rescue survivors from *Kormoran*. Although *Sydney* failed to answer repeated signals, it was hoped that her transmitter had been damaged and she was making for a port in the NEI.

In response to a RAN request for immediate assistance, Admiral Helfrich deployed the light cruiser *Tromp* to the Soenda Strait with orders to follow *Sydney's* last known course. At the same time, he ordered MLD units from Morokrembangan, Tandjoeng Priok and Tjilatjap to sweep the Indian Ocean between Java and Christmas Island. Despite intensive sweeps along all possible paths of the Australian ship and heavy damage to *Tromp's* C.XI-W floatplane during the operation, they found nothing, and all units stood down several days later. To this day the exact cause of *Sydney's* loss remains unknown.

Between September 1939 and December 1941, MLD aircraft flew more than 3 million miles in an effort to preserve Dutch neutrality and keep Japanese espionage activities under control. In the process, they maintained a regular Dutch air presence throughout a territory the size of Western Europe and helped secure a border perimeter totaling some 7,800 miles.[42] Perhaps more important, they also provided raw flight crews and reservists with invaluable operational experience under wartime conditions, thus preparing for what they would soon encounter.

But despite being successful for the most part, these neutrality patrols inflicted tremendous wear and tear on the MLD's aircraft and equipment. And while the MLD had the facilities, personnel and expertise to maintain regular overhauls during peacetime operations, a shortage of certain spares and engines made the German-built Dorniers and older Fokkers increasingly difficult to maintain. As a result, the number of mechanical accidents and aircraft losses rose accordingly with the outbreak of war as the MLD struggled to maintain its cohesion in the face of savage Japanese air attacks that would grow more intense with each passing month.

3

December, Part I:
The MLD Goes to War

The MLD's wartime bases stretched over an immense area, from Singapore in the west to Java in the south, New Guinea in the east and Tarakan in the far north. From these bases, the Japanese drove the MLD back to Morokrembangan. Diagrams of MLD deployments can be found in the appendices of this book.

As part of prewar Anglo-Dutch agreements, the Dutch, British and Americans were allocated separate spheres of influence. In the Dutch area, MLD planes provided air reconnaissance in the northern East Indies. However since the British Royal Air Force was critically short of reconnaissance aircraft, the MLD was also asked to transfer two squadrons of Dorniers to Singapore's Seletar Naval Air Station at the start of war. The British need for reconnaissance planes being acute, GVT.8 was placed under British operational control before hostilities started. The Dutch also promised the transfer of a second squadron of unmanned reconnaissance aircraft to Seletar that would be manned by RAF personnel.

All MLD reconnaissance squadrons had been deployed prior to the war, allowing them to immediately undertake extensive patrols. It was these squadrons that saw some of the first action of the war. Shortly after the shooting started, GVT.3 replaced GVT.8 on December 10. From Singapore, GVT.8 deployed to Kuantan, Malaya, while GVT.1 flew into Kuching, Borneo. From these bases, the two squadrons flew reconnaissance patrols along the Kuantan-Pulo Laut-Kuching line. A primitive seaplane base at Sedanau on Natoena Island served as an intermediate refueling point.

To the northeast, GVT.2 and GVT.5 patrolled the Talaud-Morotai-Sorong line. GVT.2 was based at Sorong, New Guinea, while GVT.5 deployed to Ternate. The converted GM patrol boat *Reiger* served as a tender for both squadrons at Sorong. A third squadron was also scheduled for deployment to Kalkas seaplane base if necessary. Reconnaissance over the western approaches to the Java Sea and Batavia area was provided by GVT.16 at Tandjoeng Priok. The squadron also served as a reserve for those operating out of Kuantan and Kuching.

Plans also called for GVT.7 to fly air patrols over the far northern reaches of the East Indies out of Tarakan. Army bombers flew the missions until the MLD was able to deploy a squadron to the area. Afterwards, Dutch seaplanes flew air reconnaissance and strike missions from the island until the Japanese occupied it in January 1942.

By the first week of December 1941, imminent signs of war were clear all across the Pacific. Although Japanese diplomatic efforts remained unchanged on the surface, a tense air lingered. Not only had regular airline flights from Japan to the western colonies stopped, but her merchant fleet had also vanished from Allied harbors. Then, American, British and Dutch reconnaissance planes reported large Japanese troop convoys moving

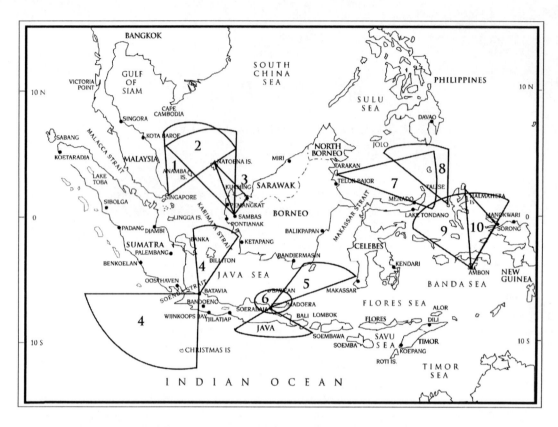

MLD Operational Areas December 1941. Legend: *Area 1*: GVT.8 (X-16, X-17, X-18) based NAS Sele-tar; patrols over South China Sea and Gulf of Siam. *Area 2*: GVT.4 (X-13, X-14, X-21) based Sambas; patrols over South China Sea. *Area 3*: GVT.1 (X-15, X-35, X-36) based Sambas; patrols in area between Sambas, Kuching and Natoena Island. *Area 4*: GVT.16 (Y-51, Y-56, Y-57) based Tg. Priok; patrols over Indian Ocean, Java Sea, Karimata and Gaspar Straits. *Area 5*: GVT.6 (X-28, X-29, X-31) based MVK Morokrembangan; patrols over Java Sea and south coast of eastern Java. *Area 6*: GVT.11, GVT.12, GVT.13 and GVT.14 based MVK Morokrembangan; A/S patrols in area around Soerabaja. *Area 7*: GVT.7 (X-32, X-33, X-34) based Tarakan; patrols over Celebes Sea. *Area 8*: GVT.5 (X-26, X-27, X-28) based Ternate (Moluccas); patrols over Celebes Sea and sealanes south of the Philippines. *Area 9*: GVT.17 (Y-58, Y-59, Y-60) based MVK Halong; patrols over Molucca Sea and Halmahera Sea. *Area 10*: GVT.2 (X-11, X-12, X-25) based Sorong; patrols between bases at Morotai and Ambon.

south. Although Japan had made no formal declaration of war, there was little doubt among the Allied commanders that their final destinations were Allied territories through-out the Pacific.

On December 1, X-10 of GVT.2 encountered a Japanese fishing vessel near Sorong, New Guinea. Well aware that large numbers of Japanese spy ships disguised as fishing boats had long operated in the region, the Dutch pilot circled the ship several times at wave-top level as his crew carefully examined it. He then initiated a dangerous game that involved cutting off the Japanese ship every time it tried to change course. In the process, X-10 clipped the fishing vessel's mast, bringing down its wireless antenna. In return the Dornier's wing was badly damaged, forcing it to retire to Morokrembangan for repairs and being replaced by X-25 from the reserve pool.

Under normal circumstances, the accident would have caused an international inci-dent with dire consequences for the seaplane's pilot. But fortunately for the sake of his career, war was just around the corner, and the attention of his superiors was fixed on other issues. It is interesting to note that the Japanese apparently never filed a protest, probably because doing so would have invited a Dutch demand for an explanation of what the ship was doing in the area in the first place. The fact that war was only a few days away also likely played a role.

MALAYA

Japan's invasion of Malaya got under way on the morning of December 4, as 19 transports carrying more than 26,000 troops from the 5th Infantry Division and the 56th Infantry Regiment departed Hainan Island. The heavy cruiser *Chokai* and destroyer *Sagiri* with the 3rd Destroyer Flotilla and the destroyers of the 12th, 19th and 20th Destroyer Divisions support escorted them. The 7th Cruiser Squadron and 11th Destroyer Division departed at the same time with orders to provide the convoy with distant cover. The following day a second, smaller convoy departed Saigon escorted by the light cruiser *Kashii* and frigate *Shimushu*. This group comprised seven transports carrying units of the 143rd Infantry Regiment.

The commander of the main Japanese convoy, Vice Admiral Jisaburo Ozawa, had received orders to proceed southwest. He was to skirt the coast of Indochina and rendezvous with a second, smaller convoy some 100–150 miles off Cape Camao in the Gulf of Siam. If sighted before joining the second convoy, Ozawa was to maintain a course as if his destination were Bangkok and await further orders. Upon linking up, the Japanese convoys would turn south and make their final run across the Gulf of Siam for invasion points throughout Thailand and Northern Malaya.[1]

At 0130 Java Time[2] on December 4, Dutch sources at Menado on the island of Celebes reported that a convoy of 8 transports, escorted by 20 warships, was set to depart from the Japanese naval base on Palau Island with the intention of landing troops somewhere in the Northern East Indies.[3] This force actually consisted of 7 transports escorted by the light cruiser *Nagara*, 22nd Destroyer Division and the 11th Seaplane Carrier Division under the command of Rear-Admiral Kyuji Kubo. Kubo departed Palau on December 8 and landed a 2,500-man battalion at Legaspi on the Philippine island of Luzon on the night of December 11–12.

As the invasion forces moved on Malaya, they received air cover from aircraft of the Imperial Japanese Army's 3rd Air Division. This formation consisted of the 3rd Flying Battalion (one fighter and two bomber regiments), 7th Flying Battalion (one fighter and three bomber regiments), 10th Flying Battalion (one fighter and one bomber regiment), 12th Flying Battalion (two fighter regiments), 15th Independent Air Regiment (two reconnaissance squadrons) and the 83rd Reconnaissance Regiment (three reconnaissance squadrons).[4] These units totaled 465 aircraft, including 196 fighters, 203 bombers and light attack planes and 66 reconnaissance and utility aircraft.

They were supported by elements of the Imperial Japanese Navy's 11th Air Fleet. The 21st, 22nd and 23rd Air Flotillas operated more than 430 fighters and bombers from air bases throughout Southern Indochina, Formosa and Palau. These flotillas consisted of elements of the Kanoya, Genzan and Mihoro air wings. In addition, Japan had 80 or so short-range reconnaissance seaplanes aboard surface ships operating in the South China Sea and Gulf of Siam, including the converted seaplane tenders *Kamikawa Maru* (14 aircraft), *Sanyo Maru* (8 aircraft) *Sagara Maru* (8 aircraft) and *Sanuki Maru* (8 aircraft).

Table 4: IJA 3rd Air Division[5]
(Headquartered Southern Indochina)

3rd Flying Battalion
Operational Area: Southern Indochina, South China Sea, Western Borneo, Burma, Malaya, and Northern and Southern Sumatra and Western Java.
    59th Sentai (24 × Ki-43 "Oscar")
    27th Sentai (23 × Ki-43 "Oscar")
    75th Sentai (25 × Ki-48 "Lily")
    90th Sentai (30 × Ki-48 "Lily" and Ki-30 "Ann")

7th Flying Battalion
Operational Area: Southern Indochina, South China Sea, Western Borneo, Burma, Malaya, Northern and Southern Sumatra and Western Java.
    64th Sentai (35 × Ki-43 "Oscar"
    (6 × Ki-27 "Nate")
    12th Sentai (21 × Ki- 21 "Sally")
    60th Sentai (39 × Ki-21 "Sally")
    98th Sentai (42 × K-21 "Sally")

10th Flying Battalion
Operational Area: Southern Indochina, South China Sea, Western Borneo, Burma, Malaya, Northern and Southern Sumatra and Western Java.
    77th Sentai (27 × Ki-27 "Nate")
    31st Sentai (24 × Ki-30 "Ann")
    62nd Sentai (22 × Ki-21 "Sally")
    70th Sentai (8 × Ki-15 "Babs")

12th Flying Battalion
Operational Area: Southern Indochina, South China Sea, Western Borneo, Burma, Malaya, Northern and Southern Sumatra and Western Java.
    1st Sentai (42 × Ki-27 "Nate")
    11th Sentai (39 × Ki-27 "Nate")
    81st Sentai (9 × Ki-15 "Babs")
          (7 × Ki-46 "Dinah")

15th Independent Flying Unit
Operational Area: Southern Indochina, South China Sea, Western Borneo, Burma, Malaya, Northern and Southern Sumatra and Western Java.
    50th Independent Squadron (5 × Ki-15 "Babs" / Ki-46 "Dinah")
    51st Independent Squadron (6 × Ki-15 "Babs" / Ki-46 "Dinah")

83rd Independent Flying Unit
Operational Area: Southern Indochina, South China Sea, Western Borneo, Burma, Malaya, Northern and Southern Sumatra and Western Java.
    71st Independent Squadron (10 × Ki-51 "Sonia")
    73rd Independent Squadron (9 × Ki-51 "Sonia")
    89th Independent Squadron (12 × Ki-36 "Ida"
    12th Transport Squadron (Kawasaki Ki-56 "Thalia")
          (Kawasaki-Lockheed Type LO Transport "Thelma")

The purpose-built seaplane carriers *Chitose* (24 aircraft) and *Mizuho* (24 aircraft) added another 48 fighters.[6]

    While on a routine reconnaissance patrol in the South China Sea on December 6, X-21 of GVT.4 sighted what it reported to be a camouflaged minelayer at 0915.[8] The pilot reported the vessel to be making approximately 7 knots northeast of the Southern Natoena Islands at 3° 45' North, 110° 18' East with a SSW course. The Dutch crew also reported four deck guns covered by canvas tarps. Aside from a momentary glimpse of scattered crew on the bridge, not a soul was seen aboard the ship as X-21 leisurely circled at low

Top: Although less well-armed than the JNAF "Zero," the JAAF Nakajima Ki-43 "Oscar" was equally maneuverable (photograph courtesy of San Diego Aerospace Museum). *Bottom:* Although being phased out by the "Oscar," the obsolescent Nakajima Ki-27 "Nate" was a formidable opponent for Allied flying boats (photograph courtesy of San Diego Aerospace Museum).

altitude. Admiral Helfrich ordered the Dornier to maintain contact with the Japanese ship, which it did until oncoming darkness forced the Dutch plane to break off and return to base at 1630.

This ship was likely the Japanese auxiliary minelayer *Tatsumiya Maru*, which had been ordered to lay a secret minefield off the coast of Malaya and east of Tioman Island to coincide with the pending air strike on Pearl Harbor. The minefield would help screen Japanese landings in Northern Malaya and Thailand against expected counterattacks from British Royal Navy warships based at Singapore. However, after the departure of X-21, the minelayer's captain became concerned about his ability to execute the mission after being sighted; with this in mind, he laid his mine barrage some 18 miles further

Table 5: IJN 11th Air Fleet, December 8, 1941[7]

21st Air Flotilla
Operational Area: Eastern Netherlands East Indies, including Menado, Kendari, Ambon, Koepang and
   Java.
  1st Group (headquartered at Takao, Formosa)
    72 × fighters (18 detached to Indochina)
    24 × fighters in reserve
    6–9 × reconnaissance aircraft
  Kanoya Air Group (headquartered at Taighu, Formosa)
    54 × bombers (18 detached to Formosa)
    18 × bombers in reserve
  Toko Air Group (headquartered on Palau)
    12 × flying boats
    4 × reserve flying boats

22nd Air Flotilla
Operational Area: Western Netherlands East Indies, including southern Sumatra, Banka Island and
   western Java.
  Genzan Air Wing (headquartered at Saigon, Indochina)
    27 × bombers
    9 × reserve bombers
  Mihoro Air Wing (headquartered at Saigon, Indochina)
    27 × bombers
    9 × reserve bombers

23rd Air Flotilla
Operational Area: Central Netherlands East Indies, including Tarakan, Balikpapan, Bandjermasin,
   Makassar, Bali, eastern/central Java.
  Takao Air Group (headquartered at Takao, Formosa)
    54 × bombers
    18 × reserve bombers
  3rd Group (headquartered at Takao, Formosa)
    72 × fighters
    18 × reserve fighters
    6–9 × reconnaissance aircraft

north than originally ordered, putting the spread just north of Tioman, rather than to the east of the island.[9]

Later that same morning, X-17 of GVT.8 was operating out of Seletar when its crew sighted a Japanese ship in the Gulf of Siam at 1105 (Java Time).[10] The pilot reported the ship's position as being northwest of the Anambas Islands at 4° 33' North, 104° 56' East moving south at 14 knots. She flew a Japanese battle flag, and her decks were crowded with soldiers, giving every appearance of being a fully loaded troop transport. However, when the MLD plane appeared overhead, the transport immediately reversed course to the north.[11] The Dutch plane shadowed this vessel as well until being forced to return to base when fuel ran low.

Admiral Helfrich ordered both squadrons to send out planes at first light the next morning to resume surveillance of the two Japanese ships. However, neither was able to regain contact, and the Japanese slipped away. In the meantime, X-13 of GVT.4 encountered a Japanese flying boat over the South China Sea, and the two seaplanes warily circled each other before continuing on without incident. The tension was building, and both sides undoubtedly knew that it would only be a matter of hours before the first shots of the Pacific War were fired.

Meanwhile, British and Australian aircraft from Singapore were also flying a series

Extremely maneuverable and heavily armed, the primary fighter of the JNAF was the Mitsubishi A6M "Zero" (photograph courtesy of San Diego Aerospace Museum).

of reconnaissance patrols over the South China Sea and Gulf of Siam. Although poor weather precluded flight operations on December 4–5, three Hudson bombers from 1 Squadron (RAAF) departed from the airfield at Khota Bharu in northern Malaya mid-morning of December 6. Flying separately, two of these aircraft reported a large Japanese convoy some 200 miles off the coast of Malaya. This was Vice-Admiral Ozawa's main force, which had joined *Kashii's* smaller convoy and was now making its final run for points in Thailand and Malaya.

The first Hudson reported two minesweepers and a transport. It later found the main body of 25 transports with an escort of one battleship, five cruisers and seven destroyers. Another Hudson sighted a second convoy of 21 transports, escorted by two cruisers and 10 destroyers. Although Japanese floatplanes from the seaplane tender *Kamikawa Maru* attempted to intercept, the Hudson's superior speed allowed it to pull away. Another Hudson from Khota Bharu followed late that afternoon but was unable to locate the convoy and returned home.

To follow up on these reports, the Royal Air Force's 205 Squadron, operating from Seletar, sent out PBY FV-S to carry out a night search over the Gulf of Siam. The flying boat departed at 1830 but apparently made no contact with Seletar for several hours. As a result, the squadron ordered PBY FV-W into the air at 0200 on the morning of December 7.

Apparently flying over the aforementioned *Tatsumiya Maru* without sighting her in the fog and darkness, Flight Officer P.E. Bedell located a large convoy off the coast of Southern Indochina shortly before dawn. He then proceeded to dodge in and out of the clouds to avoid the convoy's fighter escort while his radio operator sent a series of detailed reports back to Singapore. Finally, at 0820 an E13A1 "Jake" floatplane from the *Kamikawa Maru* intercepted the PBY 20 miles WNW of Pajang Island (south of Phu Quoc on the coast of southern Indochina).

Piloted by Ensign Eiichi Ogata, aircraft ZI-26 surprised the flying boat and put a short burst into the hull, causing Bedell to turn away from the convoy. As Bedell retired to the south, Ogata proved unable to match the PBY's superior speed and could not make another attack, although he continued to trail behind and monitor its movements.

Twenty-five minutes later, a patrol of six Ki-27 "Nate" fighters from the Japanese Army Air Force's 1st Sentai bounced the PBY.

Despite taking defensive fire from Bedell's gunners, one of the fighters immediately set the flying boat afire on its first pass. The other four "Nates" then attacked the PBY, which exploded under the weight of their combined efforts. It appears that the radio was damaged almost immediately, as Seletar suddenly lost contact with the PBY with no indication of what happened during the short fight. As a result, it was not until after the war that the world learned of the PBY's fate. In any event, Bedell and his crew become the first casualties of the Pacific War in an attack that took place several hours before the attack on Pearl Harbor.[12]

As Bedell's PBY was being destroyed, Admiral Helfrich ordered MLD aircraft to once again observe and monitor the Japanese ships sighted the previous day. Although the troopship could not be found, X-18 of GVT.8 reported a transport north of the Anambas Islands at 0920. Sighted at 4° 34' North, 105° 30' East, she held a 010° northerly course with a speed of 13 knots. Although unidentified, it appears that ship was the *Tatsumiya Maru* headed home after completing her minelaying mission off Tioman Island.[13]

As the Japanese convoys moved south, both the British and Dutch were gripped by inaction. The most obvious offensive weapons available at this stage were 15 Dutch submarines based at Soerabaja and Singapore. But although the British had a number of these boats under their operational control, they were unwilling to initiate a war without assurances of support from the United States, which refused to commit its Pacific Fleet to the defense of Singapore. So with Britain's resources stretched to the limit by fighting in Europe and Africa, she could simply not afford to initiate a war in the Pacific — even to defend against a Japanese invasion.

The Dutch were dependent on British assistance if they hoped to prevail in a war. At the same time, the KM was also undoubtedly cautious about another large-scale deployment in light of its two prior naval deployments in May 1940 and February 1941. It was a time when the wrong move could have serious consequences, and Helfrich had to be certain before moving his forces. The Dutch and Japanese were also engaged in what amounted to an intense cold war at the time, and the KM did not wish to provoke the Japanese with any semblance of offensive action that might provide them with political justification for a "defensive" attack against the NEI.

And finally, the hidden submarines were the Allies' most potent naval weapon at this stage of the coming conflict. Had the Japanese discovered their presence prior to the outbreak of war, their effectiveness would have been greatly reduced in the face of alert anti-submarine defenses. So although a submarine line had been deployed in the South China Sea to intercept the Japanese, the Allied boats were ordered to re-deploy to points off the coast of Malaya, Borneo and Sumatra.

THE FIRST MLD LOSSES

The MLD suffered its first loss before the war even started. Y-44 was lost with her entire crew in a landing accident at Tandjoeng Pinang at Banka Island on December 6. However, the first war loss suffered by the MLD came during the Japanese attack on Pearl Harbor the following day.

The strike on Pearl Harbor commenced just before midnight on December 7 with word of the attack reaching the Dutch High Command in the city of Batavia on West

Java around 0300 Java Time on December 8.[14] At 0533, Admiral Helfrich signaled the following message to all KM and MLD units: "America and England at War with Japan" and subsequently ordered all Dutch merchant ships at sea to make for the nearest friendly port. At 0630 that morning, General Hein Ter Poorten, Commander-in-Chief of the KNIL, issued a general mobilization order to all Dutch ground units and called up those reserves not already in uniform. At 0700, the governor-general of the Netherlands East Indies, Dr. A.W.L. Tjarda van Starkenborgh Stachouwer, made a formal declaration of war in a terse radio announcement.[15]

Meanwhile, three new Dutch PBYs— Y-68, Y-69 and Y-70 — were en route to Java from the Consolidated aircraft plant at San Diego, California. All PBYs delivered to the MLD prior to the outbreak of war crossed the Central Pacific in groups of three using a civilian and military air route that staged through Hawaii–Wake Island–Guam–Manila. They were ferried across the Pacific by contracted civilian crews from Consairways, a subsidiary American airline of the Consolidated factory. MLD flight crews would meet the planes at Manila and fly the Catalinas down to Java.[16]

Although all three planes were supposed to remain together during flight, this particular formation had become separated. While Y-69 and Y-70 continued ahead, Y-68 was ordered to remain at Pearl Harbor for several days. Its crew was to await the arrival of Lieutenant-General Ludolph van Oyen, head of KNIL-ML forces in the NEI, who was returning to Java after wrapping up an official visit to Washington, DC, where he had requested additional military aid. He would reach Honolulu via Pan Am clipper and join Y-68 for the remainder of the trip.[17]

When the Japanese attacked Pearl Harbor, Y-68 sat in a large hangar at Ford Island Naval Air Station. Y-69 and Y-70 had proceeded ahead and were already at Midway Island. As a result, Y-68 was destroyed on the ground when a bomb blast toppled one of the hangar's huge doors onto her wing, damaging the PBY beyond repair.

Y-69 and Y-70 had already departed Midway for Wake Island at 0600 local time when word of the Pearl Harbor attack reached the island. Both planes were immediately recalled and landed back at Midway later that day. It quickly became clear that the Japanese were moving all across the Pacific, and the status of the prewar air route was unclear. As a result, both planes were ordered to remain at Midway where the island's Marine Corps commander immediately seized them and their cargo. Although they had no bomb or gun mounts, they were pressed into service alongside 12 USN VP-21 Catalinas that were operating from Midway at the time.

As *VP-21* ground crews worked to make the Dutch PBYs ready for war patrols, Vice-Admiral Chuichi Nagumo's carrier strike force retired from the area around Hawaii. To cover his withdrawal and minimize the chance of counter air strikes from Midway, Japanese planners of the Pearl Harbor raid had detailed a small surface force, composed of the destroyers *Ushio* and *Sazanami*, to shell the airfield.[18] But although given the rather grandiose designation *Midway Destruction Unit,* their mission would be considered little more than a nuisance raid by the American military at the time.

Supported by the naval tanker *Shiriya, Ushio* and *Sazanami* departed Japan at the same time as Admiral Nagumo's force and made their way independently to Midway. They arrived off the island on the night of December 7 and opened fire at 2131. Encountering only uncoordinated resistance from Marine shore batteries, *Ushio* fired 108 5-inch rounds, and *Sazanami* 193, in a bombardment lasting 54 minutes. Although the runway was undamaged, they did hit a number of oil tanks and shore installations, including the Pan

American Airways radio center, knocking off-line the island's only communications with the outside world. In return, the Marines claimed damage to one of the destroyers, although this is unconfirmed. The force then returned to Japan by way of Kwajalein Island.

The bombardment also set afire a hangar at the seaplane base in which a VP-21 PBY was lost. Shrapnel also badly damaged Y-69. The next morning ground crews counted more than 300 holes in its wings and fuselage that required 334 patches to repair.[19] Following extensive repairs by naval personnel, Pan American Airways mechanics and civilian contractors, the PBY was test flown on December 17 and returned to Pearl Harbor the following day by a reserve *VP-21* crew that was flown out for that purpose.[20] Y-69 returned to San Diego for overhaul and was later delivered to MLD forces in Australia in March 1942;[21] she and other surviving Dutch PBYs were then flown to Ceylon in a non-stop flight in May.

Following the Japanese bombardment, Y-70 was ordered back to Pearl Harbor on December 8, where the USN again seized it. It probably would have remained there if not for General van Oyen. The general reached Pearl Harbor immediately following the attack, only to find that the U.S. military had terminated all air traffic across the Pacific. And with Y-68 destroyed, van Oyen effectively found himself stranded in Hawaii before the arrival of Y-70 from Midway.

Although the seaplane was immediately impounded upon landing, van Oyen was able to secure the release of Y-70. However, the prewar ferry route remained closed, so the PBY took a longer, less-developed route through the southern Pacific via Christmas Island–Canton Island–Samoa–Australia before it flew on to Java. Although most frequently used by civilian flights to Australia and New Zealand, most of these bases had been completed only that year and were extremely primitive, isolated and poorly equipped. As a result, a damaged plane could be stranded for weeks while a spare part was located and flown in.

Nonetheless, now carrying General van Oyen, Y-70 staged through these primitive island bases and reached Morokrembangan without incident on December 27.[22] Upon their arrival, the PBY's entire Consairways ferry crew received the Dutch Flying Cross.[23]

WAR

Just hours after Pearl Harbor on December 8, X-27 of GVT.5 was on patrol out of Ternate when its pilot sighted a large concentration of fishing boats off Halmahera Island. A closer look revealed that one of the ships flew a "Rising Sun" on the bow, revealing its Japanese ownership. With orders to clear Dutch waters of all Japanese fishing craft, the X-boat set down on the water and taxied to the Japanese craft. An armed party of naval troops, which the plane carried for such an occasion, then boarded the fishing boat and interned it and the crew.

The first war action for the MLD came in the Bougainville Strait on December 8, when X-12 of GVT.2 sighted a Japanese convoy composed of the 161-ton schooner *Koukoku Maru* towing four small sailboats, which were apparently pearl-diving boats. X-11 immediately strafed and bombed the schooner, near-missing her with four 100-pound bombs, but observed no damage before the plane had to turn for home. Believing that the ships carried infiltrators to be put ashore in Dutch New Guinea, the squadron commander, 1st Lieutenant W. J. Reijnierse, ordered X-11 to find the convoy again the next morning.

X-11 found the convoy again on the morning of the 9th and attacked *Koukoku Maru* with four 100-pound bombs, near-missing her once. It then called in X-25, which was on its morning patrol. When X-25 arrived, it found the schooner had lost speed and was leaking oil. X-25 too dropped four 100-pound bombs, hitting it directly amidships once. *Koukoku Maru* erupted in a blast of flame, killing 10 crewmen and leaving a column of black smoke to mark its position as the planes returned to Sorong.

Soon after, the base radio operator picked up a report from the Y-47 of the approach of enemy planes. With no air cover or AA defenses, the planes of GVT.2 immediately scrambled and scattered so as not to be caught on the water. The anticipated air attack never materialized, and the planes returned to Sorong several hours later. X-11 then made a final reconnaissance flight over the *Koukoku Maru*, which it found abandoned and afire; the Japanese ship sank later that day. At the same time, X-12 flew to Ambon to reload with bombs.

On the 10th, X-18 of GVT.8 sighted a surfaced submarine while on patrol out of Sele-tar. The submarine immediately crash-dived upon sighting the approaching seaplane. The Dutch pilot did not attack as he could not ascertain the identity of the submarine and was afraid of attacking a friendly vessel. Although the submarine could have been a Dutch boat operating under British operational control, she did not attempt to flash any Allied recognition signals. At the time, there were no fewer than 18 Japanese submarines operating in the South China Sea to screen the landings in Malaya.[24]

Later that day, GVT.3 replaced GVT.8 at Seletar, and the squadron returned to Morokrembangan for routine maintenance and overhaul of its aircraft. For the rest of December, *GVT.3* flew patrols over the South China Sea and attacked Japanese fishing boats in the area. The squadron also evacuated a number of women and children from Tarempah Island in the Poelau Archipelago.

On December 12, the MLD made good on its prewar promise and transferred three unmanned MLD Catalinas—which the Dutch did not have crews for—from the reserve pool at Morokrembangan to the Royal Air Force at Singapore.[25] The Catalinas were ferried from Morokrembangan by skeleton British crews to the Seletar where they reinforced 205 Squadron. Their arrival allowed two elderly Royal New Zealand Navy Singapore III flying boats to be transferred to Fiji. But even with their arrival, the British need for recon-naissance aircraft remained critical throughout the Malaysian and NEI campaigns.

Later that day, GVT.16 was ordered to provide A/S support for SM-1, a large convoy leaving Singapore for the Indian Ocean via the Soenda Strait. That day, four British and three American merchant ships left Singapore escorted by the Dutch light cruiser *Java* and the destroyers *Evertsen* and *Van Nes*. Also in escort were the Australian armed mer-chant cruiser *Kanimbla* and the British destroyers *Stronghold*, *Encounter* and *Tenedos*. In conjunction with planes of the ML on southern Sumatra, PBYs of GVT.16 provided A/S cover for the convoy until it dispersed south of the Soenda Strait on December 16.

X-22 of GVT.3, flown by 1st Lieutenant G.F. Slotje, claimed the MLD's first aerial kill of the war. The X-boat was operating out of Poeloe Samboe, Sumatra, on December 13 when it encountered what the crew reported as three Japanese fighters near Kuantuan. X-22, with its 20mm cannon, drove them off, claiming one heavily damaged. Villagers claimed to have seen the damaged plane crash into the sea, although this was never confirmed. Nonetheless, Machinist Mate Leo Willems was decorated for this action. The "fighters" were actually G3M "Nell" bombers of the Mihoro Air Wing, which was oper-ating out of Southern Indochina.

LANDINGS ON BORNEO

With their operations in Malaya securely in hand, thus adequately protecting their flank, the Japanese now undertook the invasion of the East Indies. Their plans called for a series of southward pincer movements down through the eastern and western halves of the archipelago. The western pincer would commence operations from Camranh Bay in Southern Indochina with the goal of securing British Borneo, western Dutch Borneo and southern Sumatra.

The eastern pincer would commence operations from the port of Davao on the southern Philippine island of Mindanao. This port would be occupied in late December and would serve as the springboard for the invasion of the eastern East Indies. It would also protect the Japanese flank against counterattack from the Philippines during their East Indies campaign. Moving south from Davao, Japanese troops would then secure eastern Borneo, Celebes, Ambon and the Lesser Soenda Islands. Loss of the Lesser Soendas cut off Allied air reinforcements from Australia.

As each primary invasion point was secured, subsidiary operations would branch out in supporting movements to secure oil fields, refineries, airstrips and seaports that would protect the flanks of the next stage of the operation. Priority was placed on putting captured airfields back into use as soon as possible in order to maintain air cover during every stage. Using captured airfields on Celebes, Borneo and Southern Sumatra, the Japanese anticipated complete air supremacy over the entire East Indies by February 1942. At that point, they would be in position to carry out a simultaneous invasion of Java on both its eastern and western ends.

Action grew heated as the Japanese intensified their air operations over the South China Sea in an effort to cover an invasion convoy that departed Camrahn Bay on the morning of December 13. Under the command of Admiral Shintaro Hashimoto, it consisted of 10 transports bound for Miri, North Borneo, with troops of the 2nd Yokosuka Special Naval Landing Force and 124th Infantry Regiment. In close escort was the light cruiser *Yura* with the 12th Destroyer Division and *Subchaser 7*. The tender *Kamikawa Maru* provided air cover and A/S support.

The 17th Cruiser Squadron, screened by the destroyers *Fubuki* and *Sagiri*, provided additional support against a possible Royal Navy sortie from Singapore.[26] The 2nd Division/3rd Battleship Squadron, 1st Division/4th Cruiser Squadron further reinforced them from northeast of the Natoena Islands with the 6th Destroyer Division and 2nd Section/8th Destroyer Division. A line of submarines was also deployed between Natoena Island and the coast of Borneo.

On the 14th, GVT.1's X-15 and X-35 encountered three enemy fighters flying cover for this convoy near Natoena Island while on a reconnaissance patrol out of Pontianak.[27] The flying boats claimed one Japanese plane shot down, but this claim was also unconfirmed. The following day the squadron's third aircraft, X-36, suffered engine failure while on a reconnaissance flight over the South China Sea and was forced to set down on the open water south of the Natoena Islands. It was eventually towed to the MLD base at Pontianak for repairs.

These aircraft presented a threat to Japanese invasion forces, and they were quick to respond to their continued operations. On December 16–17, H6K "Mavis" four-engine flying boats attached to the Toko Air Wing at Palau began a concentrated campaign to hunt down and destroy the MLD forward bases. Although the Japanese hit all across the

East Indies, they directed initial attacks on MLD bases throughout the eastern half part of the NEI, particularly Sorong, Ternate and Menado. As the campaign progressed, they would also be joined by other seaplane units, which moved from Palau to Davao and Jolo in the southern Philippines as those points were occupied.

A "Mavis" flying boat from the Toko Air Wing attacked Sorong at 1030 on the 16th. The Japanese pilot concentrated on the seaplane tender *Arend*, which had just delivered a load of aviation fuel. The bombs missed by a quarter-mile, and X-12 and X-25 scrambled to intercept. However, the faster Japanese plane soon outran the Dorniers and disappeared in the clouds as the Dutch planes reached 8,000 feet.[28]

However, the squadron commander of GVT.2—1st Lieutenant W.J. Reijnierse—believed the Japanese plane would return the next morning, so he conceived a plan to intercept the raider. At 0830 the following day, X-12 and X-25 took off and patiently circled in the clouds while X-11 remained on the water to act as "bait." At 0905 the crew of X-11 heard an approaching aircraft and taxied out for takeoff. But the engines quickly faded and X-11 returned to her anchorage.

Then at 0950, a four-engine Kawanishi flying boat suddenly appeared over the base. Without the benefit of radar direction, neither X-12 nor X-25 had been able to find the raider in the clouds, allowing it to approach the base undetected. The Japanese seaplane dropped three bombs near X-11 from 5,000 feet and disappeared. Again, the Dutch planes returned to Sorong empty-handed.

The Japanese also raided the Anambas Islands on the 16th. Although the MLD had a support base on Anambas, it was not at Terempa, where a small village was heavily bombed; the Japanese returned again the following day and heavily strafed Terempa. Dutch authorities initially put casualties at 40 dead and 100 wounded, although this figure was later revised to 65 dead.[29] Unable to provide adequate air cover for the squadron's aircraft, and fearful of additional attacks, the MLD ordered GVT.3 to abandon Anambas as a base and retire south to Tandjoeng Pinang in the Riouw Archipelago. In the process, the squadron evacuated the island's European civilians and a group of interned Japanese.

At the same time, the Japanese convoy landed its troops at the western Borneo ports of Miri, Seria and Lutong before dawn on the 16th. Although the Allies were unable to mount a response that day, ML and MLD aircraft struck back with a series of heavy air attacks throughout the 17th.

Operating from Tarakan, GVT.7 (X-32, X-33, and X-34) loaded 440-pound bombs and took off to bomb oil wells the British had been unable to destroy before withdrawing into the interior of Borneo. Nine miles north of Miri, they sighted a small group of three ships off Lutong, which they reported as an anchored merchant ship, one small torpedo boat and a large cruiser, which steamed independently approximately one mile ahead of the others.[30] While X-34 bombed the oil fields, X-32 and X-33 attacked the convoy in the face of light AA fire at 0650.

Attacking out of heavy cloud cover at just under 15,000 feet, X-32 dropped six 500-pound bombs on the cruiser. In reality, it was the 1,950-ton destroyer *Shinonome* of the 12th Destroyer Division. Although one bomb hung in X-32's rack, five dropped, resulting in two direct hits and one near miss. Apparently one of them ignited ready ammunition in one of the destroyer's aft turrets, causing a huge plume of white smoke to billow up 5,000–6,000 feet. Within one minute of this explosion, *Shinonome* lost way and heeled over as she went down by the stern, taking along her entire crew of 228 officers and men within five minutes.

The seaplane tender *Arend* was the target of a *Toko Air Wing* "Mavis" on December 16 while delivering aviation fuel to *GVT.2* at Sorong, Dutch New Guinea (photograph courtesy of Jan Klootwijk).

X-33 followed up on this attack five minutes later. She dropped four 500-pound bombs on the merchant ship *Hiyoshi Maru*, which was being escorted by the minesweeper *W-7*. However, these bombs missed by some 65 yards. Although the Dornier's tail gunner reported seeing black smoke emitting from the transport's stern, *Hiyoshi Maru* suffered only minor damage. The two Dorniers then regrouped and returned to Tarakan several hours later.

Shinonome's loss has been the subject of some confusion. Although Japanese monographs list her as a victim of air attack, most English sources attribute her loss to a Dutch mine, despite Miri being a British territory that was well north of any Dutch minefields. The British apparently never laid any mine barrages in the area. This belief was probably due to the fact that *Shinonome* went down out of sight of *Hiyoshi Maru* and *W-7*, neither of which saw X-32's bomb run. So when their repeated radio calls went unanswered, they assumed that a mine had sunk her.[31]

Other older sources report that *Shinonome* had been torpedoed by X-33. Although the MLD had ordered large numbers of torpedo bombers before the war, none ever arrived. Nor was the Do. 24 designed or equipped to carry torpedoes, and there are no documented cases of it doing so in the Pacific or European theaters. And finally, since Dutch and Japanese records are in agreement, this appears to conclusively settle the debate concerning the loss of *Shinonome*.

As X-32 and X-33 turned for home, they realized that X-34 was no longer with them. Despite repeated radio calls to X-34, it did not respond, never returned to Tarakan and was presumed lost. Although X-32 and X-33 spent the following day searching for the downed aircraft, they sighted nothing and returned to base empty-handed. Meanwhile, X-7 replaced X-34 from the reserve pool at Morokrembangan.

Several weeks later, a radio report from an isolated Dutch outpost in the interior of Borneo finally shed light on the fate of X-34. On her return flight from Miri, an F1M "Pete" from *Kamikawa Maru* intercepted her. In lonely engagement at 8,000 feet, the Japanese floatplane damaged X-34 so badly that 2nd Lieutenant A. Baarschers, KMR was forced to crash-land on a small river in central Borneo.[32]

Machinist Mate T.G. van der Beek and Seaman D. Floris were killed. However, the plane's remaining three crewmen — Baarschers, Sergeant-Pilot J.M. van Halm and the Dornier's wireless operator, Seaman K.A. Roon — survived the crash. They hiked 120 miles through the jungle for three weeks to reach Moeara Teweh, a small town on the upper end of the Barito River on the northern coast of Borneo. However, the Japanese had already occupied the city as part of their invasions of Tarakan and Balikpapan and captured the airmen. After the war the MLD learned that all three were eventually decapitated on August 27, 1942.

Meanwhile, on the 17th, the KNIL commander at Medan in northern Sumatra signaled that a Japanese parachute drop had taken place east of him and that an attack on the city was imminent. He urgently requested a reconnaissance plane to confirm the report. Admiral Helfrich immediately dispatched a PBY from GVT.16 to Lake Toba in Central Sumatra.

After flying a number of missions over Medan and the surrounding area, the PBY saw nothing and was withdrawn. However, as the Japanese pushed down the Malay Peninsula, the Dutch feared infiltrators would cross the Malacca Strait to Sumatra, so the seaplane was again sent to Lake Toba on December 20. It flew missions along the east coast of Sumatra north to the RAF seaplane base at Penang on the west coast of Malay until the end of the month, but reported little or no Japanese movement.

Meanwhile, the Japanese were also moving forward in the eastern half of the East Indies. On the afternoon of December 16, 14 transports carrying approximately 5,000 troops of the 33rd Infantry Regiment and 146th Infantry Regiment departed Palau for Mindanao. They were given close escort by the 2nd Destroyer Flotilla, which was supported by the 5th Cruiser Squadron, the light carrier *Ryujo* and the seaplane carrier *Chitose*. A lone destroyer, the *Shiokaze*, screened this distant covering force. As the convoy neared Mindanao, *Ryujo* launched a small air strike, while seaplanes from *Chitose* scouted the harbor.

The first Japanese troops began landing on both sides of the city before dawn on December 20. Although Davao was held by 2,000 troops of the Philippine Army's 2nd Battalion, 101st Infantry Regiment, the Japanese met only moderate resistance, which was soon broken, giving them complete control of the city, its port and airfield by 1500 on December 20.[33] Heavily outnumbered by the Japanese force, the American commander withdrew his battalion to high ground positions outside the city and dug in. However, the Japanese were interested in occupying Davao only for the present time and made no attempt to pursue them.

With the Davao invasion force safely ashore and well in control, the IJN immediately withdrew many of its forces from the area. These included eight transports and four destroyers along with *Ryujo* and *Chitose*, which all retired to Palau to refuel in anticipation of supporting the upcoming invasion of Jolo Island. Refueling quickly, the warships immediately sailed and rejoined the Jolo convoy on February 24 as it moved toward the island.

The Japanese wasted no time in moving on Jolo. Located some 300 miles southwest of Davao, it would serve as a support base and provide air cover for the invasion of the East Indies. The Jolo invasion force was planned to depart Davao immediately, but a lone Filipino machine gun detachment inflicted so many casualties on one of the IJA units before being wiped out that it had be replaced by the IJN's Kure 2nd Special Naval Landing Force at the last minute.[34] A surprise air raid by USAAF B-17s on the morning of December 22 further delayed the operation and inflicted four casualties on the destroyer *Kuroshio* through strafing.

Nonetheless, nine transports departed Davao for Jolo later that day carrying the Kure 2nd SNLF and the IJA's 143rd Infantry Regiment. *Jintsu* and the 15th Destroyer Division gave close escort with air cover and A/S support provided by *Ryujo, Chitose* and *Shiokaze*. This force landed at Jolo on the evening of December 24; encountering weak resistance from 300 poorly armed Philippine Constabulary, the Japanese were in control of Jolo city and its airfield by the next morning.[35] Upon securing the island, a forward seaplane base was immediately set up, and the Japanese were now ready to begin their invasion of the East Indies.

4

December, Part II: The USN Evacuates the Philippines

PATROL WING 10
ABANDONS THE PHILIPINES

As the Japanese prepared to drive into the Netherlands East Indies, the MLD began receiving unexpected, although welcome, reinforcements in mid-December. Between December 13 and December 24, Patrol Wing 10, the USN's only airborne reconnaissance unit in the Far East, began withdrawing from the Philippines to Java.[1] The Wing had experienced heavy losses since the outbreak of war and desperately needed relief from the relentless waves of Japanese fighters and bombers that prowled almost at will over the Philippines.

Although PatWing 10 had been flying reconnaissance missions over Camrahn Bay since April 1940, it had suffered no losses until the outbreak of the Pacific War.[2] However, the bulk of General Douglas McArthur's air power in the Philippines had been destroyed on the ground on the first day of war. This immediately gave the Japanese near complete air supremacy, and the PBYs of PatWing 10 paid the price. With losses totaling 10 of the Wing's 28 planes in the war's first week, Admiral Thomas C. Hart, the USN Asiatic Fleet commander, ordered Captain Frank D. Wagner to evacuate his remaining Catalinas south to Morokrembangan.

The evacuation began during the night of December 13–14, with messengers alerting the aircrews to prepare for evacuation from the Philippines immediately. By 0430, the first five planes were away, and the Wing's remaining flyable PBY's and two J2F "Duck" utility planes followed. The seaplane tenders USS *Heron*, *William B. Preston*, *Childs* and *Langley* followed, bound for the Dutch port of Balikpapan, where they would refuel and proceed onto Java.[3] So abrupt was the departure that the runners missed two of the camouflaged PBYs in the darkness. Somehow sleeping through the noise, their crews woke up the next morning to find all but a few of their squadron missing.

From Balikpapan, *Langley* proceeded to Menado, where she provided a refueling stop for PBYs heading south. As the tender negotiated the harbor, *Langley* was greeted with a low flyover by the Dorniers of GVT.5, which was operating from MVK Kalkas. As the Dutch planes circled, the tender was suddenly attacked by a four-engine Japanese flying boat,[4] which the crew had thought to be Dutch as it approached.[5] The bombs dropped 50–100 yards to port and the plane then disappeared, giving the Dutch seaplanes no chance to intercept.

The PBYs en route from the southern Philippines were to have refueled at Lake Ton-

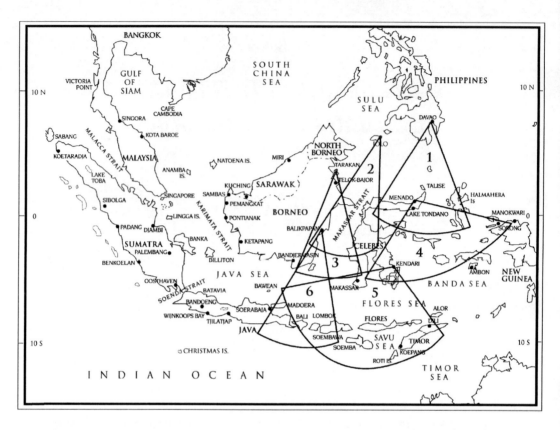

Japanese Air Superiority December 1941–Janaruy 1942. Legend: (1) Sphere of Japanese air superiority provided by JNAF units operating from Davao as of January 15, 1942. (2) Sphere of Japanese air superiority provided by JNAF units operating from Jolo as of January 15, 1942. (3) Sphere of Japanese air superiority provided by JNAF units operating from Tarakan as of January 15, 1942. (4) Sphere of Japanese air superiority provided by JNAF units operating from Menado as of January 15, 1942. (5) Sphere of Japanese air superiority provided by JNAF units operating from Kendari as of January 15, 1942. (6) Sphere of Japanese air superiority provided by JNAF units operating from Balikpapan as of January 15, 1942.

dano, but the report of this attack worried Captain Wagner. Fearful of additional air attacks, he ordered the planes to divert to Balikpapan instead. However, a PBY flying on one engine and the two single-engine floatplanes did not have enough fuel to reach Balikpapan and diverted to Menado. En route, the "Ducks" were forced to land on the open sea and refuel from jerry cans their pilots carried aboard the planes. After refueling, it was too late to continue into Menado, so the three seaplanes flew to Kalkas for the night as *Langley* cleared the area. They landed an hour and 40 minutes after the Japanese bomber attacked *Langley*.

Meanwhile, some of the Wing's ground personnel were taken out aboard the seaplane tender *Childs*, which left Luzon on the night of December 14 with all the spare parts and aircraft engines she could carry. A number of men were also evacuated aboard the MS *Maréchal Joffre*, a fast Vichy French passenger ship that had been interned in Manila on December 14. Upon being boarded, her crew was given five minutes to decide where their loyalties lay. Those who declared for Vichy were taken ashore and interned. In all, 63 crewmen stayed aboard to operate the ship.

Among *Maréchal Joffre's* crew the boarding party found a diverse setting that would have made a perfect backdrop for a Humphrey Bogart movie. One crewman, it was discovered, was an operative for an American intelligence agency in Manila. He was covertly funneling information on Japanese shipping that he gathered during the ship's frequent layovers at Saigon. However, other crewmen were less dedicated to the Allied cause.

On the other end of the extreme was a ship's officer who had the engine's main injection needles in his cabin and was prepared to throw them overboard. Without them, the Americans would be unable to move the ship. However, he was caught off guard by the boarding party and was unable to disable the *Maréchal Joffre*. Another unknown crewman attempted to destroy the ship's auxiliary switchboard. Concerned about the situation, Admiral Hart ordered Captain Wagner to send the ship south as soon as possible.

Meanwhile, staging through the southern Philippines, Borneo and Celebes, the first nine Catalinas of PatWing 10 arrived over Soerabaja on December 20. Despite staging through Dutch territory on the trip down, no one had bothered to inform authorities on Java as to the time of their arrival. As the PBYs flew over the naval base in formation, sirens sounded all over the city and the Dutch put out an air raid alert and notified nearby airfields.

After briefly taking fire from Dutch AA,[6] the planes set down in the channel leading to Morokrembangan. However, the pilots did not realize that the channel was very shallow and inundated with mudflats. This made it extremely easy to run aground if one did not know the harbor, or deviated from the center of the channel, which was clearly marked with buoys. As a result, five of the American PBYs ran aground shortly after putting down.[7] A tenth PBY from Balikpapan landed safely the following day.

In total, PatWing 10 brought ten PBYs, two J2F "Ducks," four OS2U "Kingfishers" and one SOC "Seagull" utility plane south to Java in its evacuation of the Philippines. In addition, the USN added four seaplane tenders, which like the GM vessels would offer tremendous flexibility for operations across the East Indies. But despite the large percentage of aircrews brought out aboard the seaplanes and tenders, PatWing 10 left some 500 ground personnel behind. With no way to evacuate them, the majority of these men were captured when the Philippines fell.

Ashore, the men of PatWing 10 found the MLD personnel at Morokrembangan to be extremely generous. The Dutch made available the tremendous resources offered by the base, including its comprehensive machine shops, hangars and other facilities. Still free from air attack at that time, the seaplane base provided an excellent opportunity to service and overhaul the planes, many of which had not been out of the water since the outbreak of hostilities.

During their stay at Morokrembangan, the American enlisted men and NCOs were quartered in an empty hangar on the seaplane base. Some officers lived in regular quarters on base, but most were housed at the Oranje Hotel in Soerabaja. After their tour in the Philippines, the Americans found Soerabaja to be a welcome respite. Not only did the Dutch serve mess four times a day, but there was always plenty of beer. In addition, the Dutch offered a rest camp at Tretes, high in the mountains of Central Java. A prewar resort, the Commodore Hotel made an excellent rest facility.

Although enamored with Soerabaja, the stay at Morokrembangan was brief for many of the new arrivals. On December 23–24, eight PatWing 10 PBYs left the base in two four-plane sections, bound for Ambon where they joined the PBYs of GVT.17. There, Captain

Wagner established his HQ and began reconnaissance operations over the northern and eastern parts of the archipelago.

On Christmas Day, the four American seaplane tenders also departed for ports throughout the East Indies and Australia.[8] The men who remained at Morokrembangan were periodically rotated among the active squadron and tender crews so that all the American airmen could have leave on Java. For those not fortunate enough to be on Java, most spent the next few months being harried from remote island base to remote island base before finally being withdrawn to Australia.

Action remained brisk off western Borneo as the Americans moved south. On the 17th, while on patrol out of Seletar at Singapore, X-20 sighted a Japanese motor schooner off the Badas Islands and attacked it with bombs and heavy strafing. When the Dornier finally turned for home, the schooner was heavily afire and sinking. This boat apparently belonged to a fleet of fishing vessels that was intercepted and their crews interned by the Dutch minelayer *Willem van der Zaan* in the Riouw Strait several days later.

That same day, a four-engine Kawanishi "Mavis" flying boat again attacked Ternate, which had already been abandoned as a primary base following the Japanese raids on December 16. The "Mavis" dropped two bombs on the GM patrol vessel *Poolster*, both of which missed. X-30 of GVT.5 then appeared just as the Japanese plane retired. After a 25-minute pursuit at full throttle, the MLD plane caught up to the Japanese plane and a brief firefight ensued in what might very well have been the first dogfight in history between flying boats.

Unable to seriously damage the other with their machine guns, the two flying boats traded fire with their single 20mm cannons. X-30's tail gunner then got lucky and hit the Mavis's starboard, inboard motor and shredded an aileron with his 7.7mm machine gun. However, the fight abruptly ended when the Japanese plane's 20mm cannon shot out X-30's middle engine and electrical system. Unable to continue, X-30 broke off and returned to Ternate. After temporary repairs, she flew to MVK Ambon on two engines for advanced repairs.

On December 18 X-35 of GVT.1 engaged nine "Nells" from the Mihoro Air Wing in the Api Passage near Natoena Island. In a fight off the Borneo coast, X-35 took several hits to her center engine before breaking off the action. Afterwards, the Japanese reported engaging a British flying boat that eventually broke off the action and dove into a cloud with white smoke trailing from one of its engines.[9]

In support of their western Borneo operations, the Japanese maintained a series of strong air raids against British and Dutch installations along the island's northwest coast. On the 19th, six "Nells" from the Genzan Air Wing in southern Indochina and one Kawanishi H6K "Mavis" flying boat heavily bombed the port city of Kuching. Although there was no major military damage, some 100 civilians were killed, and the local airfield's entire fuel supply was destroyed.

At the same time, nine "Nells" from the Mihoro Air Wing raided Pontianak. They caught GVT.1 on the water, including X-36, which lay in drydock undergoing repairs. The seaplane had been towed to the base after engine trouble forced the pilot to make an emergency landing in the South China Sea south of Natoena Island several days earlier. A series of strafing attacks by the bombers further damaged the Dornier's middle engine. In exchange, a trio of Dutch Buffalos intercepted the formation and shot up one of the "Nells" so badly that it was forced to ditch in the sea 20 miles south of its base at Hanoi on the return flight.

The raid itself lasted approximately 45 minutes, in which time the Japanese dropped some 50 bombs, destroying the fuel depot and burning an oil company warehouse. Civilian and military casualties numbered 81 dead and 290 wounded.[10] But although damage to the seaplane base and surrounding facilities was severe, all three Dorniers of GVT.1 escaped destruction. However, X-35 and X-36 were forced back to Morokrembangan (both on two engines) for repairs later that day. X-6 temporarily replaced them until they rejoined GVT.1 on December 23.

The action continued when X-20 and X-22 of GVT.3 encountered a pair of Kawanishi "Mavis" flying boats on the 20th. The fight ended when both sides broke off and headed for home. In the running engagement X-22 suffered extensive damage but was able to return to the MLD support base at Tandjoeng Pinang for local repairs. X-20 was involved in another fight in the same area three days later. Again, neither side suffered any mortal damage. These encounters with Japanese bombers and flying boats became increasingly frequent on the patrols to the north as the Japanese exerted their air power over the East Indies.

The GVTs were constantly on the move. On December 20, GVT.16 (Y-51, Y-56, Y-57) became operational and moved to Tandjoeng Priok on western Java to fly reconnaissance over the Indian Ocean, Java Sea, Karimata and Gaspar Straits. The following day, GVT.2 moved its three X-boats from their prewar base at Sorong, New Guinea to Babo, New Guinea. From here, the squadron flew to Lake Tondano in northern Celebes on the 23rd.

As GVT.2 descended on Kalkas, X-6 of GVT.1 (which had replaced X-36 after she departed for repairs at Morokrembangan) sighted a Japanese convoy north of Tandjoeng Datoe and her pilot reported one cruiser, two destroyers, four transports and one tanker. As the X-boat shadowed the convoy on the morning of the 23rd, a Japanese fighter intercepted her and damaged the aircraft. The boat's commander, 2nd Lieutenant W.C.L. Nuver, was also slightly injured while pulling out of a power dive he used to help evade the Japanese plane. As the Dornier turned for home, X-35 (2nd Lieutenant P. Jaapies) took over.

This was another invasion convoy under the command of Admiral Hashimoto, whose forces had taken Miri, Seria and Lutong the previous week. Bound for Kuching some 300 miles to the south, six transports departed Miri on December 22 carrying two battalions of the 124th Infantry Regiment. Again, the convoy received a close escort from *Yura*, 12th Destroyer Division (minus *Shinonome*) and the minesweepers *W.3* and *W.6*. Seaplanes from *Kamikawa Maru* provided air cover. The light cruiser *Kinu* with the heavy cruisers *Kumano* and *Suzuya* provided distant cover with the destroyers *Fubuki* and *Sagiri*. They were further reinforced by the 2nd Division/7th Cruiser Squadron, which was screened by the destroyer *Hatsuyuki*.

As the convoy neared Kuching, X-35 established contact with the Dutch submarine *K-XIV*, which was on patrol in the area and informed her of the convoy's position. With light signals, the X-boat signaled: "Eight Enemy Ships About 50 Nautical Miles North of You, Course 210, Speed About 10 Knots." She then flew off to get another sighting that was also reported to *K-XIV*. In a third signal, the flying boat informed the submarine that two floatplanes had been catapulted off and that the convoy escort has assumed an anti-submarine formation.

One of the floatplanes was off *Kamikawa Maru*, while the other belonged to *Yura*. X-35 engaged both planes and led them away from the submarine, allowing it to close on the convoy unmolested from the air. Later that night, *K-XIV* attacked the convoy off Kuching, sinking or heavily damaging four transports. This action was a clear example of what the MLD and Dutch surface fleet trained for. Had the MLD been allowed to remain with its parent organization, Japanese losses to Dutch submarine and surface ships would undoubtedly have been much higher.

As for X-35, *Kamikawa Maru's* floatplane claimed to have shot her down in a running air fight at 1,000 feet. However, these records are in error as X-35 returned to base, although with heavy damage to its center engine. Its hull and fuel tanks were also heavily holed, so that when the seaplane landed back at Singapore, it immediately had to be beached to prevent it from sinking. The next day, X-35 flew to Morokrembangan for repairs. These repairs were completed on December 27, and the seaplane rejoined the squadron at Tajan on the coast of Borneo.[11]

December 23 turned into a busy day for the MLD. That afternoon, two X-boats encountered a Japanese fighter patrol off Pontianak but held their own. And for the second time, there was an attack on Dorniers near Sorong, but the flying boats drove off the Japanese without loss.

At the same time, GVT.8 moved to Tandjoeng Priok from Morokrembangan, from where it flew convoy escort between the Soenda Strait and Singapore and reconnaissance missions over the Indian Ocean, Java Sea, Karimata and Gaspar Straits. But despite this flurry of action, the 23rd was also notable as the date the MLD launched its first major counterattack against the Japanese.

THE MLD GOES ON THE OFFENSIVE

On the morning of December 23, the planes of GVT.2 (X-11, X-12 and X-25) and GVT.5 (X-26, X-27 and X-30) were making plans to attack Davao, which had been occupied by the Japanese on December 20. Under the command of 1st Lieutenant W.J. Reijnierse, GVT.2 was based on a small lake near Babo, New Guinea, when it landed while GVT.5, under the command of 1st Lieutenant H.V.B. Burgerhout, KMR, set up reconnaissance operations at a small secondary base on Talisei, a small island off the northern tip of the Minahassa Peninsula.

Although Davao officially fell into the American sphere of operations, Admiral Helfrich ordered both squadrons to attack shore installations and shipping in the harbor because he correctly assumed that it would be the springboard for an invasion into the East Indies. As long as the Japanese occupied it, his northern flank would be threatened. Also, the USAAF had no air units capable of hitting back, as the only heavy bombers in the Philippines had already been withdrawn to Australia due to a lack of air cover. Although, as already noted, when B-17s from Australia did eventually bomb the port, they had to cross 4,000 miles and stage through Java.

Because the MLD command considered Babo too exposed for the operation, GVT.2 was ordered to Lake Tondano, where it arrived at the Kalkas seaplane base on the 22nd. However, the base was not suited for large-scale operations, and GVT.2's arrival severely strained base resources. The loading of fuel and 500-pound bombs took place on the lake throughout the night of December 22–23 amid a pouring rainstorm. The operation proceeded slowly as there was only one motorboat and two praus available at the base to service the seaplanes. At the same time, these craft also had to offload the personal effects and squadron gear of the new arrivals.

The mission's operational plan called for GVT.2 to depart Lake Tondano at 0200 on the 23rd. GVT.5—which had remained at Talisei due to the inadequate facilities at Lake Tondano—would follow 30 minutes later. The altitude, airspeeds and respective courses of the two squadrons were coordinated so GVT.5 would arrive over Davao five minutes ahead of GVT.2. The two squadrons would then attack in separate waves. However, the slowness of fueling and arming the seaplanes at Kalkas delayed their departure, so GVT.2 did not lift off the water until 0300. According to plan, GVT.5 followed 30 minutes later.

The Dorniers of GVT.5 formed up about a mile north of Talisei and set a course for Davao at an altitude of 13,000 feet. Although Lieutenant Burgerhout aboard X-30 commanded GVT.5, his most experienced bombardier was the pilot of X-26. Because of this, X-26 assumed the lead, with X-27 trailing slightly behind to port and X-30 to starboard in a tight V formation. Prior to takeoff, Burgerhout carefully briefed his flight crews;[12] they were to execute their bomb runs at all costs, while the pilots of the trailing planes were not to not drop their bombs until they saw X-26 do so. They were to scatter only if attacked by Japanese fighters.[13]

Although the squadron's aircrews were inexperienced in formation flight at night, the mission started well. They initially encountered calm seas, moderate winds from the east and scattered clouds that allowed the pilots to retain visual contact in the moonlight. However, north of Tahoena Island, GVT.5 encountered strong headwinds and heavy

The MLD thought the secondary seaplane base at Kalkas to be out of range of Japanese attack until the raid of December 26 (photograph courtesy of the Australian War Memorial).

clouds that plunged the sky into darkness. X-30 quickly dropped back out of sight, and X-26 soon followed.

Unable to see the water or each other, all three planes were forced to proceed on instruments independently. Approximately 20 miles north of the Kawio Islands, the wind died down around 0500, and the crewmen could see small patches of sea as visibility improved. Just before 0600, the pilot of X-27, Ensign F.W.J. Sürink, sighted X-30 north of Tanica Point, and the two planes formed up. However, there was still no sign of X-26, and they continued on alone.

X-27 and X-30 arrived over Davao at 0600 and found the harbor full of shipping, including both warships and merchant vessels. Initially, AA fire from shore batteries was light, but quickly intensified as the Dorniers set up their attack. X-27 dropped her bombs on a group of large seaplanes moored near the beach and claimed to have left many wrecked or burning.[14] These were nine Kawanishi H6K "Mavis" flying boats belonging to the Toko Air Wing, which had arrived from Palau on December 21. X-30 dropped her six 440-pound bombs on a large warehouse complex, leaving its warehouses and quays in a mass of flames nearly 1,000 feet in diameter.

X-27 was then bracketed by a barrage of flak and suffered damage to her starboard engine, which developed a severe oil leak and soon quit. Without the power of her third engine, X-27 quickly fell behind X-30 as both Dutch seaplanes flew over the harbor and turned over Davao to evade the AA fire, which was now becoming very heavy. At this point, X-27 encountered a number of Japanese floatplanes flying a CAP over the harbor.

With the departure of *Chitose* and *Mizuho* to Palau for refueling, the primary air defenses for Davao Harbor now rested with the air group from the seaplane tender *Sanuki Maru*. Upon dropping anchor in Malalang Bay on December 21, her eight "Pete" floatplanes immediately began flying CAP and A/S missions over those ships still remaining in the bay. Although four floatplanes were on patrol over Davao that morning, only two "Petes" were in position to intercept the MLD aircraft.

Even then, one apparently could not reach the Dutch planes' altitude and thus remained some 2,000–3,000 feet below throughout the subsequent air fight.[15] However, the second "Pete" hung on its propeller and climbed quickly. These were likely aircraft II-B-04 and II-B-06, which later reported shooting down two Dutch flying boats that day. As the Japanese closed on the Dornier from astern, the rear gunner signaled the letter "J" to the rest of the crew to alert them.[16]

There was no time for anything else. The pilot of II-B-04 made three aggressive passes on X-27, rupturing her hull and fuel tanks, allowing fuel to pour into compartments 3, 4 and 5. For his troubles, the rear gunner was also seriously wounded in the leg before the "Pete" disappeared. The dorsal gunner claimed to have shot it down, but this is unconfirmed.

X-30's gunners also claimed to have shot down a Japanese floatplane on the way out of the harbor. But since II-B-04 was the only Japanese aircraft to see action that day, it can be safely assumed that this was the same plane. Although II-B-04 returned to *Sanuki Maru*, the "Pete" overturned and capsized while landing due to a large hole in its centerline float.[17] Although Japanese records officially list her as an operational loss, the real reason can almost certainly be attributed to damage suffered in her action with X-27 and X-30 over the harbor.

Meanwhile, X-27 struggled to stay in the air as X-30 steadily pulled away. With her fuel tanks punctured, the port and center engines were not getting an adequate fuel flow, severely reducing their power output. Combined with the loss of her starboard engine, the plane quickly descended to 7,500 feet from an altitude of 11,000 feet. With only 25 gallons of fuel left in her tanks, there was considerable doubt as to whether X-27 would make it out of Davao Harbor, much less return to Lake Tondano. A sergeant pilot then thought of pumping loose fuel back into the X-boat's only undamaged tank using a bilge pump. Although it was not enough volume for the plane to gain altitude, it did allow Ensign Sürink to clear the harbor.

As X-27 and X-30 retired, they passed X-26, which was beginning its bombing run. Dodging in and out of the intense AA fire, X-26 attacked what its pilot reported to be a light cruiser. However, the Japanese ship reportedly reversed course at the last moment, and all six of the flying boat's 500-pound bombs missed forward of the bow by approximately 100 feet.

Five minutes later, GVT.2 arrived over the harbor right on schedule. Although it had encountered the same weather front as GVT.5 while en route from Lake Tondano, these pilots were highly trained veterans of the peacetime MLD. In contrast to GVT.5, whose flight crews included a number of inexperienced reservists and pilot trainees, they had years of prewar experience in night-formation flying. This allowed them to remain together during the inbound flight and carry out their attack in a tight formation.

Although X-11, X-12 and X-25 encountered vicious AA fire while setting up their bomb run, they suffered little damage. In a brief attack, the squadron concentrated on the 19,209-ton tanker *Tonan Maru No. 2*, a converted whale factory ship that appeared to be in the process of refueling a heavy cruiser. X-11 claimed one direct hit on the tanker's bow with a 500-pound bomb and claimed two near-misses; both ships were reportedly in flames as GVT.2 turned for home.[18] The Japanese did not pursue, and the squadron landed at Lake Tondano around 0900.

Meanwhile, X-27 remained in serious trouble. Flying alone, its fuel-starved engines could not provide adequate power, and the plane settled lower with each mile. As it cleared the harbor, X-27 flew over another large Japanese cruiser escorted by a destroyer. Then, 20 miles south of the Kawio Islands, the plane passed a small Japanese convoy consisting of two destroyers and three merchant ships just two and a half miles off. Barely flying a few hundred feet off the water by now, the crew undoubtedly got a much closer look at the convoy than they desired. Still, X-27 did not break radio silence, which had been in effect throughout the entire mission.

Approximately 10 minutes later, with the convoy just over the horizon, X-27 gave up, and Ensign Sürink was forced to set down on the open sea. Force 6 weather conditions were in effect, and choppy waves and a strong north wind made for a rough landing.[19] Under peacetime, non-emergency circumstances, a landing in these conditions probably would have been a court-martial offense. However, Sürink had no choice but to try with a dead engine and two others generating a fraction of their normal output.

On the first attempt, X-27 hit the rough water with a huge crack and promptly bounced back high into the air. The Dornier's rugged construction was probably all that kept it from breaking apart. Once on the water, with its hull badly punctured, the plane began to slowly sink. The radio operator now broke radio silence as he frantically tried to raise one of the other planes. Fortunately, he was able to reach X-30, which immediately turned back.

Expecting the Japanese convoy to appear on the horizon at any minute, the crew was tense. As it waited, the pilots destroyed secret paperwork, code books and threw classified material overboard while the crew plugged the hull and cared for the wounded gunner. X-30 appeared overhead 45 minutes later and made a safe landing despite the rising seas. Its pilot later said that he would not have risked landing had it not been for the extremely poor condition of X-27.

After a rough transfer in rubber rafts, X-30 proceeded to Menado. But upon landing in the Bay of Menado, no one seemed to notice, though the Dornier's crew clearly saw some two dozen officers milling about a club located near the shore. After several unsuccessful attempts to contact them using a megaphone, he was about to have the seaplane's tail gunner fire a short burst in frustration. However, before he could give the order, a small motorboat appeared. After delivering the wounded man to a hospital, the plane returned to Lake Tondano late that morning.

Despite losing X-27, the Davao raid appeared to have been a success. A large warehouse complex was burned and a number of quays destroyed. GVT.2 claimed direct hits and near-misses on a 10,000-ton tanker and the heavy cruiser she was fueling. However, neither postwar Allied nor Japanese records confirm either of these hits. One MLD pilot reported after the war to have been told in a POW camp by a Japanese naval officer that the raid killed 500 Japanese. Whether true or not, the pilot neglected to mention that he had participated in the attack.

Upon landing at Lake Tondano, GVT.2 was immediately ordered to refuel and rearm for a strike against the convoy sighted by X-27 prior to its emergency landing. However, darkness fell before the planes could be readied, so the squadron commander pushed his strike back to the following morning. But before he could launch his pre-dawn air strike, Captain A.M. Hekking, the senior KM officer on Ambon, ordered him to instead fly a reconnaissance mission to relocate the convoy and report on its final destination and anchorage.[20] Based this report, GVT.2 would then coordinate its attack with bombers from Ambon.

With the aircraft of GVT.2 bombed up, an aircraft from GVT.5 was dispatched to patrol the area where the Japanese ships had been sighted. However, the Dornier sighted no trace of the convoy, so the planes of GVT.2 remained on the water throughout the day and night of December 24.

The only action that day occurred that afternoon when X-32 of GVT.7 sighted an unidentified Allied ship of approximately 6,000 tons near Tarakan while on a routine reconnaissance flight. Drawn to the ship by its funnel smoke, the Dornier encountered a lone "Pete" from *Kamikawa Maru*, which was observed to drop a bomb as it circled the ship. Although the ship's davits were fully extended, there were no signs of lifeboats or survivors in the water. As the X-boat neared, the Japanese pilot immediately abandoned his attack on the ship and set up on the Dornier.

A heavy dogfight ensued in which X-32 suffered moderate damage. Despite a number of weapons malfunctions that limited their firepower, the Dutch gunners apparently killed or wounded the Pete's observer, as return fire from the floatplane's rear cockpit machine gun abruptly ceased. At that point, the Japanese plane began circling tightly; X-32 could not stay with it and was forced to let the floatplane escape. Although the "Pete" made it back to *Kamikawa Maru*, the heavily damaged floatplane sank upon landing before the tender's crew could hoist it aboard.[21]

In Malaya, 205 Squadron lost another PBY on December 24 when a G3M "Nell" from the Mihoro Air Wing forced FV-Z to set down in the South China Sea following a 25-minute engagement, after which it blew up. The crew scrambled into a life raft and drifted for several hours until spotted by the pilot of FV-W/Y-54 the next day. After dropping supplies and additional lifeboats, he radioed their position, which helped the Dutch submarine *K-XII* rescue the British flight crew later that day. The survivors were then returned to Seletar.

Upon their return to base at Saigon, the Japanese flight crew claimed to have shot down a Dutch seaplane, but no MLD aircraft were lost in the area that day. Likewise, the Japanese list their air action as taking place on December 25, but this could possibly be explained by the fact that Japanese land, sea and air units operated and issued combat reports according to Tokyo Time, which was approximately 90 minutes ahead of Java Time.[22] This time differential could have pushed the action into the following day. Some 30 minutes later, the same bomber engaged another flying boat off the coast of Malaya without results, and the unknown Allied plane slipped away.

THE EMPIRE STRIKES BACK

With the exception of an inconclusive engagement between X-19 and a Japanese aircraft near the Anambas Islands, there was a brief lull in the action in the East Indies on Christmas Day. However, operations resumed on the 26th with tragic results for the Dutch planes on Lake Tondano. Immediately after the Davao raid, the Japanese deployed seven A5M "Claude" fighters and two B5M "Kate" torpedo/horizontal bombers from the light carrier *Ryujo* to Davao airfield.

They were reinforced that same day by 12 A6M "Zero" fighters and two C5M "Babs" reconnaissance aircraft from the 3rd Air Wing. These aircraft were to provide air cover over the harbor and interdict further Allied attacks. In retaliation for the Dutch raid, the Japanese also made plans to send a strike force against Lake Tondano, which they correctly suspected was the mission's starting point.

For their part, the Dutch were concerned about the possibility of a Japanese air attack on Kalkas after their raid on Davao. Japanese planes had already attacked the ports of Kema and Menado on December 16, leading MLD commanders to consider the possibility of a Japanese carrier in the area. However, reconnaissance flights of the surrounding seas showed no enemy activity in the immediate area. To be sure, X-30 left Kalkas at 0600 on the 26th to fly a reconnaissance mission over Davao to determine what ships were in the harbor.

Meanwhile, the remaining X-boats of GVT.2 and GVT.5 still rested peacefully at anchor at Kalkas, armed and fueled for an attack. However, it now appeared that their target would be an invasion convoy off the island of Jolo in the southern Philippines, where the Japanese had landed the previous day. In preparation for this mission, the pilots had begun warming up their engines at 0630.

But approximately 40 minutes later, the base received an urgent phone call from the port city of Kema. Located on the north coast of Celebes' Minahassa Peninsula, the caller reported six Japanese Zeros crossing the city in the direction of Lake Tondano. Just three minutes' flying time from the city, Kalkas could do little but sound the klaxons before the fighters arrived overhead at 0710.

The fighters belonged to the 3rd Air Wing, which had reached Davao two days earlier. Under the command of Lieutenant Toshitada Kawazoe, they had taken off from Davao some four hours earlier, led by one of the unit's C5M reconnaissance planes that provided navigation support for the mission. Sweeping out of the early-morning sky, three fighters stayed with the utility plane and flew top cover at about 6,500 feet while the remainder came in low to strafe the hapless, bomb-laden Dorniers on the water. Shortly afterwards the Zeros exchanged places, and the remaining three fighters also came down to strafe the base.

With no AA defenses, the only resistance came from the light machine guns and cannon aboard the flying boats themselves. With little to deter them, the fighters burned X-11, X-12 and X-25 of GVT.2 on the water, along with X-26 of GVT.5. They also burned a recently arrived four-engine Sikorski S-42B flying boat belonging to KNILM.[23] The motor sloop, which had provided the only efficient water transport for the base, was also heavily worked over.

At the time of the attack, X-30 was returning from its reconnaissance flight to Davao. It survived only because it was ordered not to approach the base. The pilot was able to remain clear of the retiring Japanese fighters and returned to Lake Tondano later that morning after the all-clear signal had sounded. Upon landing at Kalkas, her crew was immediately greeted by huge plumes of thick, black smoke as the five seaplanes burned on the water.[24] On the ground, they found 6 dead and 17 wounded, including the base surgeon.[25]

The raid was a complete surprise to the Dutch, who thought Kalkas to be out of range of land-based fighters, although they considered it exposed and too far north after the occupation of Davao.[26] However, despite the appearance of long-range Japanese reconnaissance planes over the base for a week, no attacks had followed.[27] This led the Dutch to believe that Lake Tondano was out of range of their aircraft. With no carrier in the area, the MLD leadership felt secure enough to remain there for a final mission. Had reconnaissance revealed a carrier in the area, or at Jolo, Kalkas would have been abandoned. Later investigation revealed that the fighters carried auxiliary fuel tanks that they dropped before commencing their attack.

The Dutch took a calculated risk at Lake Tondano by letting their planes linger too long in an exposed area.[28] The risk failed, and the MLD paid a heavy price for maintaining its offensive spirit. The raid was a costly setback.[29] Kalkas was abandoned as a base and the personnel of both squadrons evacuated, with only a small ground staff remaining.[30] X-30 took out GVT.5's aircrews and ground personnel, while Y-47 of GVT.18 flew in from Tandjoeng Priok to collect the survivors of GVT.2. The flight crews of both squadrons were then flown to Morokrembangan, where they reformed with PBYs and spent the next several weeks training on their new aircraft.

By now, the MLD had orders to carry out only night reconnaissance missions over Jolo due to heavy Japanese air activity. Despite these orders and the tremendous blow suffered at Lake Tondano, the MLD sent X-33 from GVT.7, still based at Tarakan, over Jolo early on the morning of the 27th. X-32 was still under repair following her fight with *Kamikawa Maru's* "Pete" two days earlier, so X-33 was the squadron's only available aircraft. Concentrating on cruisers in the harbor, the seaplane encountered no resistance in the air, but AA fire was intense.

As X-33 lined up for its bomb run, the Dornier suffered a heavy hit under the starboard wing. The plane stayed together as the pilot dropped his bombs and turned for home. Several floatplanes attempted to intercept but could not reach the Dorniers in time. Upon their return to Tarakan, the aircrews were given distressing news that six PatWing 10 PBYs from Ambon had preceded them, drawing off the bulk of the Japanese fighters. Attacking in two waves of three planes each, the American PBYs encountered extremely heavy flak and large numbers of enemy fighters. As a result, four of the American PBYs went missing.[31] Damage to X-33 was so severe that it had to return to Morokrembangan for major repairs the next day.

On the other side of the archipelago, X-19 of GVT.3 (flying out of NAS Samboe at Singapore) also saw action that day while on a reconnaissance flight over the South China Sea. It took four hits in a 90-minute fight with yet another "Nell" belonging to the Kanoya Air Wing while operating near the Anambas Islands. The bomber crew from the "Nell" claimed the Dutch flying boat was shot down, but X-19 returned home with little difficulty. In return, the Dutch gunners also claimed to have damaged the bomber before both planes broke off.

On December 27, X-15 of GVT.1 went missing south of Midai Island. At 1025, the squadron's base radio operator picked up a partial transmission: "Air Action 03 Degrees North, 107 Degrees, 48 minutes East...."[32] The message abruptly ended, and X-15 did not return to base. Despite searching those coordinates for two days, neither X-35 nor X-36 found

Nol Baarschers and the crew of X-15 when their plane was shot down by a G3M "Nell" near Midai Island on December 27, 1941 (photograph courtesy of Nol Baarschers).

any sign of the plane or its crew. It later transpired that X-15 had fallen victim to a "Nell" from the Mihoro Air Wing. The Japanese bomber was on a routine anti-shipping patrol when it encountered the Dutch seaplane and shot it down in a 21-minute fight in which the "Nell" suffered no damage.[33]

The bomber was one of nine Mihoro Air Wing aircraft flying reconnaissance and anti-shipping missions in the South China Sea that day. As the Japanese moved farther south into the Netherlands East Indies, they simultaneously increased their air activities, which were designed to interdict the movement of Allied warships and supply convoys among Borneo, Singapore and Java. At the same time, the 3rd Air Wing flew regular offensive reconnaissance and strike missions against Dutch Martin bombers and Buffalo fighters operating from airfields on Borneo.

The Japanese also continued to target MLD bases in New Guinea to prevent Dutch operations against their flanks. On December 28 they again hit the seaplane base at Sorong, killing three and wounding six; two days later they also targeted Babo for the first time and left 3 dead and 14 wounded, including a number of children. Although there were no Dutch losses in either raid, it did reinforce to both the MLD and KM high commands that the Japanese air presence over the East Indies was growing stronger and bolder the farther south it pushed.

Nonetheless, the MLD continued to fly daily missions despite this pressure. On December 29, GVT.1 received orders to find and airdrop supplies to British and Indian troops who had recently evacuated the town of Sinkawang in the interior of Borneo. The squadron's two remaining aircraft followed the column's approximate jungle route and dropped the supplies. This was the squadron's last mission, as it then rotated back to Morokrembangan and disbanded.

That same day, the Japanese made their first landing on Dutch territory. In the early-morning hours of the 29th, they sent a small force ashore in the Tambelan Islands, halfway between Borneo and Singapore in the South China Sea. The primary objective of the landing was part of the overall Japanese goal to eliminate the MLD's support bases and limit its ability to interfere with invasion convoys that were beginning to move southward. With the Tambelans occupied, the MLD was now without a crucial staging base that it needed to fly long-range reconnaissance over the South China Sea.

On the afternoon of December 31, X-32 received an urgent SOS from the American merchant ship *Ruth Alexander*. The 8,135-ton vessel had been attacked by Japanese bombers near Cape Mangkaliat and needed immediate assistance. When the Dornier arrived, *Ruth Alexander* was heavily afire and sinking. Her crew had already abandoned ship after losing one dead and four wounded; X-32 landed near three lifeboats and rescued 48 survivors, who were flown to Tarakan.

On the 31st the MLD rotated GVT.3 to Morokrembangan from Tandjoeng Pinang in the Riouw Islands. After being transferred from Seletar, it had flown reconnaissance missions from the archipelago over the coast of Malaya since December 12. The aircrews spent the next two weeks re-equipping with PBYs and conducting bombing and air gunnery exercises with their new aircraft.

The squadron's Dorniers underwent a comprehensive overhaul, their first since the start of the Pacific War. All three seaplanes were then to have entered the reserve pool. However, their state of disrepair from two months of constant daily flying without proper maintenance had taken a severe toll on the planes and their engines, for which spares were in short supply. Instead of entering the reserve pool, all three planes remained under repair and inactive for the rest of the East Indies campaign.

This last move ended the first month of war for the MLD. The Dutch were pleased with several aspects of the war, primarily the Dorniers' ability to absorb damage and conduct long-range missions. They had carried out several demanding missions successfully. Considering the risk of these missions, it is fortunate that the Dutch did not lose more of the flying boats, although time would quickly change this.

Although Dutch flying boats had encountered Japanese aircraft on a number of occasions throughout December, their primary role was still to avoid combat and concentrate on reconnaissance. The MLD was able to substantially reduce the number of air engagements thanks to Marechaussee units stationed in outlying provinces of the NEI. A typical report that the commander of GVT.6 received from a police detachment in the Natoena Islands revealed that the Japanese adhered to a rigid patrol schedule over the South China Sea:

"1000 southbound over Sedanau ... 1300 northbound over Sedanau ... then southbound again at 1500 ... and northbound once again at 1700"[34]

Using these reports, the MLD was initially able to minimize its air combat encounters with the Japanese. But although highly effective in the early part of the war, the system quickly broke down as the Japanese moved south and began occupying Dutch territory previously occupied by the Marechaussee and MLD units. With no radar or spotter network to rely on, the MLD began to suffer heavy losses from Japanese airpower. On December 31, Admiral Helfrich sent the Dutch government-in-exile in London the following telegraph to end the year:

> "Japanese air action is clearly concentrating on MLD support points and air fields. The conduct of our fliers is excellent. Seven X-boats lost.[35] I have suspended attacks on shore targets by flying boats due to increased Japanese air defenses...."[36]

Still, Helfrich knew he could not hold out for long without substantial help from the British and Americans. But reinforcements in the strength he needed were not forthcoming, and he would be forced to go on the offensive again with his flying boats fewer than three weeks later. And without fighter escort of any kind, they again lost heavily to the advancing Japanese forces.

However, at least one of Helfrich's wishes came true when 205 Squadron received a flight of badly needed reinforcements. On December 31, four PBYs arrived from Gibraltar, nearly doubling the squadron's number of operational aircraft. Three of the flying boats— FV-N, FV-P and FV-Q — went to the naval air station at Seletar, while FV-O was deployed to the seaplane base at Kogalla. Two weeks later, the Royal Navy seaplane tender *Tung Song* departed the port of Sabang and joined them at Singapore. However, FV-Q was lost almost immediately when it failed to return from a raid on Singora on the coast of Malaysia.

5

January, Part I:
The Japanese Move South

January 1942 began with a flurry of movement by the MLD to new operational bases. In less than a month, the Japanese had driven the MLD back from virtually every one of its northern prewar bases. Despite determined Dutch attempts to strike back, this sledgehammer assault put them firmly on the defensive for the remainder of the campaign. During January, the MLD and other Allied forces would be driven even farther south.

The New Year saw GVT.6 on the move to Tajan on the Kapoeas River on Borneo. Here, the squadron relieved GVT.1 and took over reconnaissance duties over the South China Sea in a triangular area bounded by Natoena-Tambelan-Sarawak. Hiding its planes under the low-hanging branches of thick trees on the river banks, the squadron flew a number of missions against the airfield at Kuching and harassed Japanese craft traversing the rivers and east coast of Borneo.

In Malaya on January 1, FV-U (formerly Y-53) was one of two Royal Air Force Catalinas from 205 Squadron that were ordered to carry out an evening raid on the captured airfield at Gong Kedah in northern Malaya. Although the two seaplanes inflicted little damage to the Japanese facilities, heavy AA fire destroyed FV-U's starboard engine and badly damaged the other. Still, the pilot managed to bring his PBY back to Seletar in one piece.

About this time, the repeated raids by Japanese "Mavis" flying boats on the MLD base at Sorong prompted a Dutch response. Without air cover or effective AA defenses, these attacks had forced the Dutch to all but abandon the base shortly after the attacks began. Although aircraft were unable to use the base on a regular basis, a small ground force remained with a stockpile of supplies to service any Allied plane that might arrive at the port. In an effort to relieve pressure on Sorong, and to perhaps make it secure enough to resume flight operations on some level, the Dutch requested assistance from their Australian allies.

In response, 24 Squadron (RAAF) sent three Hudson bombers from Laha Airfield on Ambon to fly a CAP over the harbor on January 1. It was hoped that these speedy aircraft would be able to intercept the Japanese raiders and encourage them to not return. Blessed with incredible structural strength that gave them superior maneuverability for a twin-engine aircraft and good defensive armament, the Hudsons were certainly more than an even opponent for the "Mavis." But after circling the base for two hours, the Hudsons saw nothing and turned for home. It was at that point that one of them suddenly spun into the sea and crashed; one badly burned survivor was eventually pulled out of the water.

On the 2nd, GVT.4 moved to Telok-Bajor near Tarakan to relieve GVT.7, which had operated from the base since December 7. Upon arrival, the squadron took over reconnaissance duties over the Celebes Sea. The next day, GVT.7 headed home to Morokrem-bangan for repair and overhaul of its planes and much-needed rest for the aircrews and ground personnel. To initiate the new arrivals, the Japanese also chose January 3 to launch their first air raid on the island in preparation for its invasion one week later.

With the Japanese threatening to pour across the East Indies, the Dutch frantically sought reinforcements from the United States. In an effort to enlist more aid, Lieutenant-Governor Hubertus J. van Mook was dispatched to Washington, DC. Doctor van Mook left Java aboard a KNILM plane on January 4 and flew to Sydney, Australia. From there, he departed for the United States on January 8 aboard the PBY Y-70, which had recently arrived from Pearl Harbor. Piloted by Lieutenant A.D. de Bruyn, Y-70 flew van Mook to California via the Southern Pacific air route and Pearl Harbor. He continued on to Washington for a series of quick visits with government officials before returning to the East Indies aboard Y-70 in late January.

About this time, the Dutch transferred five PBYs to PatWing 10.[1] The unit had suffered heavy losses since evacuating the Philippines, and the USN turned to the MLD for reinforcements, as the Dutch could not man all the PBYs they had on hand. Three of these aircraft—Y-39, Y-41 and Y-42—came directly from the MLD flight-training school at Morokrembangan, which was in the process of being shut down as the Dutch moved their training operations from Java to Australia.

A fourth PBY, Y-43, was brand new and came from the MLD reserve pool.[2] But since most of the records detailing this transfer were destroyed when Java fell, the identity of the fifth Catalina remains unclear, although the author believes it could have been Y-50 despite that aircraft being listed in certain Dutch records as being lost in MLD service in February 1942.[3] Nonetheless, after several days of maintenance, the first Dutch PBYs entered service with PatWing 10 in late January.

At the same time, the Dorniers of GVT.4 flew a number of reconnaissance missions over Davao. Based on the strength of their reports, nine B-17s from the 19th Bomb Group at Malang airbase on Java flew north to Borneo's Samarinda Airfield on January 3. The next morning, Major Cecil E. Combs led eight of the bombers on a dawn strike against Davao Harbor. Although five Zeros attempted to intercept, they could not reach the bombers' altitude before they dropped their ordnance. The bomber crews claimed to have sunk a destroyer and with three hits to a battleship and multiple strikes on a number of smaller vessels.[4]

However, the only damage inflicted was to the heavy cruiser *Myoko*, which suffered a direct hit on her #2 turret, killing 35 crewmen and wounding 29 more. As a result, the cruiser was forced back to Sasebo naval base in Japan for extensive repairs. She did not return to service until February 26.[5] No other ships were hit, although a number of others suffered light to moderate splinter damage, including the heavy cruiser *Nachi*.[6] The seaplane tender *Chitose* also suffered splinter damage to four seaplanes on her deck, despite being some 550 yards away.[7]

Japanese submarines were now becoming increasingly active in the Java Sea. On January 3, *I-58* sank the 7,395-ton Dutch transport *Langkoeas* north of Bawean Island.[8] Although her crew abandoned ship in good order, the Japanese submarine captain then embarked on a massacre of the survivors. *I-58* first rammed a lifeboat; she then opened fire on the remaining lifeboats and killed all but 3 of the freighter's crew of 94, who were eventually rescued.

Just 90 miles off the north coast of Java, the area around Bawean was a major shipping lane. The presence of a rogue submarine in these waters necessitated an increased MLD presence until it was eliminated. As a result, every available Dutch navy plane at both Morokrembangan and Tandjoeng Priok, including the Fokker T.IVa's of GVT.11 and GVT.12, was immediately put on patrol duty in the vicinity of the sea lanes between Soerabaja and Batavia.

That evening, one of the patrol planes sighted a blur under the water near the Westwater Channel, the primary entrance to Soerabaja. The pilot immediately attacked with depth charges, bringing a large oil slick to the surface. Confident he had crippled a Japanese submarine, the pilot remained over the oil slick while a number of other planes dropped additional depth charges in the surrounding area until dark.[9]

At first light, another plane attacked with depth charges, bringing more oil to the surface. The seaplane then landed and collected a sample of the floating oil and flew it to Tandjoeng Priok. There, chemical analysis revealed that its mixture was likely Dutch and had probably originated from the 2,596-ton KPM steamer *Van der Wijck*, which had capsized in that area in 1936. Based on this information, MLD high command concluded that the first pilot had seen the wreck's submerged silhouette in the shallow water and mistaken it for a submarine. Repeated attacks then ruptured the wreck's bunkers, letting oil reach the surface.

On January 7, eight Japanese flying boats attacked Dutch installations on Ambon, including MVK Halong. They dropped nearly two dozen bombs and carried out a number of strafing attacks that killed three and wounded four others. Seven more aircraft targeted the naval air station the following day, although there was little damage done and no casualties. At the time, it was believed that the Japanese were testing the island's defenses in preparation for their planned invasion.

In the early morning hours of January 9, *I-58* sank the 2,380-ton *Camphuys* in the northern Java Sea. The Dutch cattle ship was bound for Singapore from Banjoewangi, Borneo, with a cargo of 1,700 live pigs in crates on the top deck and 35 cattle in the lower decks. The helmsman evaded the submarine's first torpedo, which prompted the Japanese commander to surface.

Camphuys's master then tried to outrun *I-58*, but the submarine opened fire with its deck gun and quickly scored a series of hits, including two under the waterline, that killed five crewmen and started a raging fire on the bow. Unarmed and unable to outrun his attacker, the Dutch captain ordered full stop and sent his crew over the side in the remaining lifeboats. The Japanese gun crew continued to shell the ship as the crew went into the water, killing two more crewmen. The submarine then disappeared, leaving the ship to burn and slowly sink.[10]

An ML Martin bomber from an airfield on Borneo located the survivors late that morning. Several hours later, X-32 of GVT.7 landed near the three lifeboats and picked up 54 survivors, including 7 badly wounded crewmen, and flew them to Morokrembangan. An American destroyer rescued the remaining 60 survivors early the following morning. On board, they found the survivors of the 1,003-ton KPM steamer *Benkoelen*, which had been forced aground in sinking condition by the submarine *I-65* on the previous afternoon.[11]

That same evening, *I-57* heavily damaged the 3,077-ton Dutch naval fleet tanker *Djirak* (*TAN-3*) off Sepajang in the Kangean Islands.[12] The tanker was sailing alone when the submarine battle surfaced at 1800 and opened fire with her 5.5-inch deck gun. With a top speed of only 10 knots, *Djirak* had no chance of outrunning *I-57*, which could easily make 20 knots on the surface, and the unarmed tanker was hit repeatedly as her 40 crewmen went into the lifeboats.

These men put ashore on Sepandjang Island, where a PatWing 10 PBY on routine patrol sighted them two days later. In response to its signal, GVT.7 dispatched X-32 from Morokrembangan to rescue the tanker's 38 survivors. Although not sunk, *Djirak* was left abandoned and drifting in a sinking condition. It is unclear when she sank, although two days later, Y-41 sighted her shattered hulk with several hundred fuel drums floating in the water nearby.[13]

On the 12th yet another Japanese submarine struck. This time it was *I-56*, which sighted the 2,065-ton KPM steamer *Patras* in the Lombok Strait. The submarine fired one torpedo that the merchant ship managed to avoid; this brought *I-56* to the surface, where her crew manned the deck gun and opened fire. Captain J.J.A. van der Starre then attempted to run, but *Patras* had a top speed of only 13 knots while *I-56* could make nearly 18 knots on the surface. As a result, she quickly closed the range and began registering hits on the zigzagging steamer.

Suddenly, the Japanese quit firing and the submarine executed an emergency dive. The reason for her sudden departure was the surprise appearance of X-23 on the horizon. Although the Dornier was on a training flight and carried no depth charges or bombs, her presence alone was fortunately enough to drive off *I-56*, which went to look for easier prey. To ensure that the submarine did not return, X-23 patiently circled overhead for a brief period before a shortage of fuel forced its return to Morokrembangan. The reprieve brought about by the X-boat allowed *Patras* to put out her fires and safely continue her voyage.

Later that same day, a Dornier of GVT.6 sighted two empty lifeboats from an unknown ship 25 miles off Tandjoeng Datoe on the northwest coast of Borneo. But despite making an extensive search of the area, the plane found no other signs of flotsam or survivors and eventually continued on its patrol. It is unknown what ship the lifeboats might have belonged to.

At 1110 on January 17, a force of Ki-21 "Sally" medium bombers from the 60th Sentai hit British Far East Forces headquarters in Singapore. As the bombers pounded their primary target, two Ki-43 "Oscar" fighters from the escorting 64th Sentai took the opportunity to strafe Seletar. The 205 Squadron Catalinas FV-Y (Y-52) and FV-P were destroyed at their moorings, while FV-T and FV-W (Y-54) were badly damaged, the latter suffering severe fire damage. As a result of this attack, the squadron was left with only five operational aircraft.

By early January, the Dutch were concerned about Japanese troops infiltrating across the Malacca Strait to Sumatra from occupied Malaya. They were also concerned about the possibility of a surprise invasion of north and central Sumatra from the Indian Ocean. For these reasons, on the 6th, GVT.8 detached X-17 to operate from Blinjoe, Banka, to fly reconnaissance and escort convoys from the Soenda Strait and Indian Ocean to Singapore. After the sinking of the *Langkoeas*, X-17 was to be especially alert for Japanese submarines that were reported in this area as well. On the 25th, X-17 moved to Lake Toba and flew reconnaissance missions between central Sumatra and the island of Nias off Sumatra's southern coast in the Indian Ocean.

January 8 saw the arrival of the first PBY by way of the new Western ferry route across the Atlantic Ocean via Africa and Rangoon.[14] The fall of Manila and occupation of the southern Philippines had by now cut the established prewar route from the United

States to Java. Despite the extra distance of the new air route, over the next two months, new Catalinas continued to arrive and provide the MLD with reinforcements, although all but a handful would arrive after the fall of Java.[15]

On January 10, the American, British, Dutch and Australian governments agreed to form a joint Allied command. Formed 33 days after the start of the Pacific War, this command was called ABDA, for the four nations it represented. Covering a vast area bound by the northern coast of Australia in the south and the Burmese-Indian border and Chinese coast in the north, ABDA theoretically included the Philippines, but General MacArthur's isolated garrison remained an independent command throughout the short life of ABDA.

Overall command rested with British General Sir Archibald Wavell, who reached Java from India on the 10th to officially activate ABDA. Three subcommands — ABDA-LAND, ABDA-FLOAT and ABDA-AIR — were set up to coordinate the respective land, sea and air aspects of the war around the Malay Barrier. However, friction between the Allies concerning ABDA's top command positions was evident from the start, particularly among the Dutch, upon whose territory most of the fighting was now taking place.

With the exception of Major-General Hein ter Poorten, KNIL, who received command of ABDA-LAND, the Dutch were shut out of ABDA's top command positions. ABDA-AIR was assigned to Major-General Lewis H. Brereton, USAAF, who served as command-in-chief until Air Vice Marshal Sir Richard Peirse, RAF arrived. ABDA-FLOAT was assigned to Admiral Thomas C. Hart, who had evacuated the USN Asiatic Fleet from the Philippines to Java in late December. Although Admiral Helfrich retained tactical command of local Dutch naval forces in the NEI, he was excluded from any strategic direction within ABDA.

Helfrich's only regular source of information concerning the strategic direction of ABDA was a Dutch naval officer acting in the liaison role. This lack of information was a constant irritation for Helfrich. Although Admiral Hart regularly met with Helfrich to

Y-70 at the PAA seaplane facility in Dinner Key, Miami, prior to departing for Java via the Atlantic Air Route in January 1942 (photograph courtesy of Institute for Maritime History).

update him, this was a formality and not an invitation for strategic input on the operation of ABDA. As Helfrich soon learned, ABDA was primarily an American and British command, which often put national interests ahead of Allied objectives.

To what degree Helfrich cooperated with General ter Poorten is unknown.[16] However, the general met daily with Tjarda van Starkenborgh Stachouwer, the governor-general of the Netherlands East Indies, who under the Dutch Constitution was commander-in-chief of all Dutch forces in the Far East. The governor-general of course then circulated all information to his commanders. Exactly how much ter Poorten really knew can be debated, as the Americans thought the British spoke for the Dutch due to their dominant position in the Far East.

However, the British did not trust the Dutch and told both them and their own Australian allies very little about the strategic direction of ABDA. By keeping the Dutch and Australians in the dark, Prime Minister Winston Churchill sought to manipulate Allied war planning and conceive a Pacific strategy that would preserve as much of the British Empire as possible. However, the Americans discounted British efforts and dominated Pacific War planning.[17] For their part, the Australians were somewhat disillusioned by prewar British promises of aid that went unfilled and placed their faith in the Americans and their more visible means of support.

As it turned out, ABDA was powerless to prevent the Japanese from driving down the length of the East Indies. The primary problems were insufficient strength, poor allocation of resources on more than one occasion and, at least in part, the British, who rarely chose to be team players when the situation did not suit their national interests.

The Dutch and Australians put far more faith into ABDA than did the Americans or British. The Dutch needed Allied support to hold the East Indies, while Australia firmly believed at the time that the East Indies likely represented the last shield between its mainland and Japanese invasion. With this in mind, the Australian government made a firm commitment to building up the Dutch defenses, although their military situation was little better.

However, the British and Americans were interested in holding the East Indies merely as a tool to help retain their own territory. Once Malaya fell and the Philippines were written off, both quickly lost interest in defending Dutch territory. Australia was chosen as the springboard for a counteroffensive against the Japanese. The Dutch, with no military or political leverage, were left to twist in the wind as their East Indies Empire crumbled around them.

Nonetheless, the Dutch did manage a small victory within ABDA. When ABDA-AIR was formed, all long-range reconnaissance planes (minus the British, who continued to operated independently of ABDA) were combined into a joint subcommand called REC-GROUP. Each country's planes remained under national command but carried out strategic ABDA directives according to how each commanding officer thought it best to execute an assigned mission.

The reconnaissance group was initially put under the command of Captain F.D. Wagner, commander of Patrol Wing 10. However, intense political pressure on President Franklin Roosevelt by the Dutch soon brought about a change in command. On January 18, Captain G.G. Bozuwa of the MLD formally took over command of REC-GROUP, although Wagner stayed on as his chief of staff. Their staff consisted of five KM, two RAN, two USN and one RAF officers. REC-GROUP first operated from the city of Lembang on western Java until the end of January, when it relocated to the Bandoeng Technical High School.

Not all of these missions involved reconnaissance flights. With the number of land-based bombers too small to force the point, the Dutch and American seaplanes were forced back into a bomber role, just weeks after Admiral Helfrich had made the decision to withdraw the MLD from these types of action due to heavy losses. By the end of the East Indies campaign, the MLD represented the bulk of ABDA's long-range bomber force.

January 9 brought the first MLD air raid of the year. It was the last mission off Tarakan, as a Japanese invasion force was fast approaching the island. With 12 100-pound bombs aboard, X-13 took off to attack Jolo on the night of January 9–10. Although one bomb fell in the town, three burned or destroyed several buildings on the airfield. The remainder cratered the south end of the airfield. On the way out, two fighters scrambled and followed X-13 out to sea for some distance before the flying boat's pilot managed to shake them off.

En route to Tarakan, X-13 received a signal to proceed to Telok-Bajor, a small auxiliary seaplane base located on the Beraoe River, approximately 65 miles south of Tarakan. A Japanese invasion convoy was nearing the island, and the rest of GVT.4 had already been evacuated earlier that morning.

TARAKAN

Although on the outskirts of the Dutch East Indies Empire and only 25 square miles in diameter, Tarakan was of critical importance to the Japanese. Their primary target was the island's 700 oil wells, refineries and airstrip. The wells could pump 5,000 barrels of crude oil a day, the quality of which, it was said, was so pure that it could be pumped directly into ships without refining. Although the swampy runway hardly warranted the name and was often closed by bad weather and poor runoff facilities, the Japanese needed it to provide air cover for their planned invasion of Balikpapan, some 200 miles to the south.

Under the command of Rear-Admiral Sueto Hirose, the Tarakan invasion convoy left Davao on the night of January 7–8 carrying the 56th Infantry Regiment and 2nd Kure Special Naval Landing Force aboard 16 transports. Ships of the 2nd Base Force, 11th and 30th Minesweeper Divisions, 31st Submarine Chaser Division and the patrol boats *P-36*, *P-37*, *P-38* and *P-39* escorted them. The 4th Destroyer Flotilla provided additional close escort with the light cruiser *Naka* and the 2nd, 9th and 24th Destroyer Divisions. The 23rd Air Flotilla at Jolo and seaplanes from the seaplane tenders *Sanyo Maru* and *Sanuki Maru* provided air cover and A/S protection.

As Admiral Hirose neared Tarakan on January 10, the Japanese formally declared war on the Netherlands. Despite the Dutch declaration of war against Japan on December 7 and the open hostilities that the two nations had engaged in for the past month, Japan had failed to declare war on the Netherlands or any of its territories. It is also interesting to note that their formal declaration of war coincided with their first attempt to capture a major piece of Dutch territory.

The Tarakan force reached the island early on the morning of January 10. At 0730, the island's lightship reported that it was under air attack, and Japanese aircraft bombed and strafed the vessel until it sank at 0900; the lightship's three-man crew of naval reservists then abandoned ship and was later pulled out of the water by approaching Japanese ships. The commander of GVT.4 now received orders from KM HQ on Java to find the convoy and report on its size and course.

X-14 and X-21 were ordered into the air at 1130 and succeeded in making contact with the convoy some 90 minutes later. To remain undetected and avoid the convoy's Combat Air Patrol, the squadron commander aboard X-21 initially flew north at wave-top level along the swampy Borneo shoreline until sighting the masts of the Japanese ships in the distance. He then popped up just high enough to see the convoy before ducking back down after 3 to 5 seconds. Repeating this tactic, X-21 began transmitting reconnaissance reports on the convoy around 1400.

However within 10 minutes of the first transmission, several Japanese fighters appeared over the convoy. To avoid detection, the X-21 dove low and flew a straight line at full speed away from the convoy for several minutes. The tactic worked, and the Dornier was not sighted. The pilot then returned a short time later and continued his low-level reconnaissance without being seen. Based on his reports, the KNIL dispatched a number of Martin bombers from Samarinda II, a secret airfield in the interior of Borneo. Attacking in the face of heavy AA fire, the KNIL pilots claimed two unconfirmed hits and three Japanese fighters shot down but could not stop the convoy.

Meanwhile, X-13 had been ordered at 1300 to fly south down the Borneo coast in the Makassar Strait to locate and warn off the motorship *van Masdijn*.[18] En route from Samarinda, Borneo, she carried 50 KNIL soldiers who were to reinforce Tarakan's garrison. However, with no radio her captain had no idea that the Japanese were about to blockade the island.

But before the Japanese could seal the blockade, the Dutch submarine *K-X* slipped away, despite having to fight off bomb and strafing attacks from two of *Sanyo Maru's* "Petes" while traversing the island's minefield on the surface. The KM patrol boat *P-1* and the civilian motor launch *Aida* joined her. However, the minelayer *Prins van Oranje* was less fortunate; she was sunk by the destroyer *Yamakaze* and the patrol boat *P-38* northeast of the island. Her loss effectively completed the blockade, and any attempt to land reinforcements on Tarakan had become hopeless.

The flying boat sighted *van Masdijn* near Bilang-Bajor Island around 1500 and landed alongside to pass along her orders. However, a Japanese flying boat appeared overhead almost immediately, forcing X-13 to take off; as the X-boat clawed for altitude, the Japanese plane attacked and scored a direct bomb hit on the *van Masdijn*, killing 10 men, including her captain. A crewman took control of the badly damaged ship and ran her aground on a nearby reef. X-13 gave what help it could in the air and then landed to pick up survivors. Unable to evacuate all the survivors in a single trip, the seaplane picked up only the seriously wounded and those men who could not swim and flew them to Balikpapan.

X-14 and X-21 were still over the convoy when they received the following signal from the naval commander on Tarakan: "In the Event AA Fire Is So Strong That It Precludes a Successful Attack GVT.4 Is to Continue on to Balikpapan." Based on this message, the Dorniers withdrew without attacking at 1730. Shortly after landing, they were ordered to rescue the remaining survivors from the *Masdijn*. Splashing down in the Makassar Strait just after midnight on the 11th, they rescued 45 survivors off the wreck and transported them to Balikpapan.

By January 13 the Japanese had forced KNIL Lieutenant-Colonel S. de Waal and the battered remnants of his 7th Infantry Battalion to surrender. But before doing so, the KNIL demolished the island's oil wells and refineries and caused significant damage to the airfield. At the same time, KM ground personnel also destroyed the naval air station's buildings and workshops.

However, engineers from the 2nd Base Force had the runway operational again by January 16, although it consistently remained in poor shape throughout the remainder of the East Indies campaign. Still, its reopening allowed aircraft of the 23rd Air Flotilla to be immediately moved onto the airfield in order support the invasion of Balikpapan, which lay some 315 miles south of Tarakan. The flotilla's headquarters officially moved onto the base on January 25.

On the night of January 13–14, X-13 and X-21 evacuated 30 civilians and 15 BPM[19] personnel from Telok-Bajor to Balikpapan. The squadron then operated from Balikpapan until January 22, when it was ordered back to Soerabaja. On the night of the 15th–16th, X-14 landed at Boelongan on Borneo's east coast to rescue escapees from Tarakan. This group included 25 KNIL soldiers who had escaped via small boat. The Dornier also brought out the crew of a Dutch Martin bomber that had crash-landed on Tarakan's airfield after being engaged by two "Petes" off the *Sanyo Maru*. Despite the danger of air attack, the evacuees were flown to Balikpapan without incident.

THE MINAHASSA PENINSULA

As the Tarakan force moved toward Tarakan, six transports and the 1st Base Force under Rear Admiral Kyuji Kubo departed Davao on January 9. His convoy carried the sailors of the 1st Sasebo Special Naval Landing Force, which had orders to take Menado, Kema and Bangka Roads on the island of Celebes. Their objectives were the airfield near Menado and seaplane base on Lake Tondano on Celebes' Minahassa Peninsula. The 334 paratroopers of the Yokosuka Naval Air Landing Force would support them. Rear-Admiral Raizo Tanaka's 2nd Destroyer Flotilla, with the 15th, 16th and 1st/8th Destroyer Divisions, provided escort for the convoy. The 11th Carrier Squadron with *Mizuho* and *Chitose* provided air cover; "Mavis" seaplanes of the 21st Air Flotilla, now operating at will from Davao, supported them.

As the convoy moved south on January 10, one of the MLD planes sighted three Japanese destroyers bombarding Sangi, a small island midway between Mindanao and Menado. The information was relayed to PatWing 10, which ordered its planes at Ambon to attack the ships immediately.

Just 200 miles south of Davao, Sangi was well within range of Japanese fighters, and the American aircrews were not optimistic about their chances of successfully completing the mission. Nonetheless, three PBYs went out at 1400 to attack the Japanese destroyers. However, 50 miles south of Sangi they sighted the convoy, which was reported as 10 transports escorted by 6 cruisers and 18 destroyers. Forgetting about the destroyers off Sangi, the three PBYs all made bomb runs across the convoy in the face of heavy AA fire. Bombing from 17,000 feet, all nine 500-pound bombs missed, and the Catalinas returned to Ambon.

GVT.17 (Y-58, Y-59 and Y-60) was ordered to make a strike on the invasion fleet to contest the landings. Although Y-59 was unable to locate the convoy and returned home without dropping her bombs, the remaining two PBYs attacked in the face of heavy flak and fighter interception without fighter escort of their own. Y-58 was last seen falling toward the ocean some 20 miles off the coast shortly after her bomb run; it never returned to base and apparently fell victim to a "Pete" from *Mizuho*. At the same time, a flight of "Petes" simultaneously swarmed over Y-60 shortly after it completed its bomb run. Y-60 suffered heavy damage with two dead and two seriously wounded but managed to return to Halong.

Despite losing one plane, four PatWing 10 PBYs following GVT.17 scored no hits either. Eleven RAAF Hudsons from Laha airfield on Ambon followed. Not even the faster, more maneuverable bombers were able to avoid the floatplanes, although they did claim four hits and four fighters shot down with two losses of their own. Unfortunately, none of these can be confirmed. In a later raid the Hudsons shot down one "Pete" and damaged two more so badly that they were forced to crash-land on the water, where they sank. Still, the only damage to the Japanese invasion fleet off Menado was limited to a near miss on the 7,620-ton transport *Amagisan Maru*.

The Japanese landed a strong invasion force at Menado on the morning of January 9. There were still a few MLD ground personnel at Lake Tondano following the Japanese air raid of December 26. The first indication these men had of the landings on Celebes came when a large Japanese flying boat landed in the middle of the lake at 0900 and began unloading troops. Although a KNIL detachment in the area was equipped with a rapid-fire 37mm cannon, the seaplane took care to remain well out of its range. Japanese paratroopers also began dropping near the base on the 11th, spurring the MLD ground personnel to destroy Kalkas and withdraw into the rugged interior of Celebes. After an arduous trip by automobile that lasted several exhausting days, they reached Makassar on the island's southern tip.

Despite heavy resistance from KNIL troops, the Japanese were able to take control of both Kema and Menado by January 11. However, the KNIL troops held out long enough for their engineers to complete preplanned demolitions that badly damaged the airfield facilities and runway. As a result, the Japanese were unable to make use of Kalawiran Airfield until January 24. Still, the capture of the Minahassa Peninsula not only gave them a firm foothold in the East Indies, but it also extended their sphere of air superiority. At the same time, the Japanese had effectively isolated American forces in the Philippines from resupply, except by submarine and long-range aircraft, which now had to circumvent occupied territory.

In mid-January the first of the reformed GVTs went back into the line. GVT.5(NEW) had spent the period between December 28 and January 12 training and reequipping with PBY Catalinas. The squadron went back into action on the 12th and operated from Tjilatjap until being pulled back to Morokrembangan on February 5. During this deployment, GVT.5(NEW) operated in the A/S role for convoys in the Indian Ocean, escorting a total of 34 ships.

Four days later, on January 16, GVT.18 with its three Catalinas, flew into Tjilatjap to join GVT.5(NEW).[20] There, GVT.18 took over reconnaissance patrols in the area amid Java, Sumatra and Borneo. It remained at the port until March 1, when its planes were detailed to fly Admiral Helfrich and his staff out of Java.

GVT.2(NEW) was now reactivated and moved back into the line. After being destroyed at Lake Tondano on December 26, the squadron moved to Morokrembangan, and its personnel had reequipped with and trained on new Catalinas between December 30 and January 13. The planes assigned to GVT.2(NEW) were Y-62, Y-63 and Y-64.

On January 19, the squadron moved to Emmahaven, the port of Padang on the southern coast of Sumatra, where it provided A/S support for convoys in the Indian Ocean.[21] From January 22 to 28, the squadron flew off Lake Toba in central Sumatra until that base was also discovered. The seaplanes then moved south to Oosthaven on the 28th and to Tandjoeng Pandan on Biliton Island two days later. The squadron returned to Tandjoeng Priok when Biliton came under air attack.

The newly reformed GVT.3(NEW) also became operational on January 16. Flying out of Morokrembangan, the squadron extensively trained on PBYs. In particular, heavy emphasis was placed upon air gunnery, night flying and bombing. The aircrews undoubtedly realized that this was an omen as training continued for the next several weeks.

By mid-January GVT.8, GVT.16 and the newly formed GVT.18 were operating from Tandjoeng Priok. Between the 19th and the 21st, all three squadrons provided A/S escort for the MS.2 convoy, which consisted of the 44,786-ton British transport *Aquitania* carrying 3,456 troops bound for Singapore. *Aquatania* entered Ratai Bay on southern Sumatra on January 20, where she transferred her troops to seven smaller ships of a convoy later designated as MS.2A to keep the valuable transport out of range of Japanese bombers. Later that day, GVT.8 released X-16 for duty on Lake Toba, where it flew reconnaissance missions over the east coast of Sumatra.

6

January, Part II: The Dutch Go on the Defensive

BALIKPAPAN

January 18 began one of the oddest chapters in the East Indies campaign. It also clearly showed the contempt the Japanese had for the Dutch and their ABDA allies. Upon capturing Tarakan, the Japanese found the island's oil wells and refineries already demolished. Their next objective was the oil-rich port of Balikpapan, and the Japanese did not want a repeat of the demolitions, which would severely limit Tarakan's production capabilities for months. So, they sent the KNIL commander at Balikpapan, Lieutenant-Colonel C. van den Hoogenband, a message threatening brutal reprisal and mass executions against the town's populace and garrison if the pump facilities and oil refineries were not turned over to the invasion force intact.[1]

To carry the message, the Japanese picked two men from the captured Dutch KNIL prisoners—Captain A.H. Colijn and Captain G.L. Reinderhoff. Colijn, an army reservist, was also manager for BPM, while Reinderhoff was chief-of-staff for Tarakan's garrison commander.[2] With three Japanese interpreters and two Indonesian state police officers, the men were put aboard the *Parsifal*, a captured 20-ton BPM motor launch, and sent south toward Balikpapan.[3]

At 1630 on January 19, the launch was south of Mangkalihat in the north entrance of the Makassar Strait when X-13 and X-14 (the latter flown by Lieutenant-Commander S.H. Rosier of GVT.4) from Balikpapan sighted it. The two Dorniers circled the boat several times, obviously looking over it and the small Japanese flag flying from the stern. Then, they saw two Europeans appear and wave a Dutch flag. But the sea was too rough for a landing, so the flying boats went home after making a report.[4]

Down on the motor launch, the occupants were more than a little distressed. Certain the Dorniers were about to attack, Reinderhoff frantically looked through the cabin until he found a Dutch flag. He tore down the "Rising Sun" and frantically waved the Dutch flag and prayed. Just when all aboard thought the Dorniers would attack, they disappeared into the darkness of the night. All aboard spent the rest of the night drinking sake to celebrate being alive.

At 0700 the following morning, X-21 from GVT.4 made contact with *Parsifal* while on its morning reconnaissance flight. Again, Lieutenant-Commander Rosier was aboard. Water conditions were calm, so after thoroughly checking out the launch, X-21 landed some 500 yards off and slowly taxied in as the crew covered the launch with the machine guns and 20mm cannon. Reinderhoff was ill, so Colijn rowed them both over to X-21 with great difficulty and explained the situation.

After the two Dutchmen were taken aboard, it was all they could do to keep the crew from destroying the launch with cannon fire.[5] Finally the Japanese and the Indonesian policemen were left to their own devices, and X-21 flew the men to Balikpapan, where they delivered their message.

Colonel van den Hoogenband immediately put the two men and 25 other evacuees aboard a plane to Java and issued orders to destroy the oil wells and refineries as soon as the Japanese invasion fleet appeared.[6] With preparations in place, he contacted KNIL HQ on Java and arranged to have the army and BPM demolitions personnel evacuated so that the Japanese could not retaliate against them.

BPM moved quickly to evacuate a number of its personnel by sending in a Grumman G.21 "Goose," which flew four company officials—including two women—to Bandjermasin. The MLD evacuation began the evening of the 21st when four Dorniers left Morokrembangan for the four-and-a-half-hour flight to Balikpapan. But just 30 minutes out of Soerabaja, they encountered severe weather over the Java Sea and Makassar Strait. Despite poor visibility, the X-boats could see flames from Balikpapan's burning oil wells and refineries a full hour from the port.

Disaster struck when they reached Balikpapan, where the flying boats were to land on the Songei River and begin loading. But the weather grew worse while water conditions and visibility remained extremely poor. As a result, one plane ran low on fuel, gave up trying to land and returned to Morokrembangan empty. X-14 of GVT.4 then attempted to land but exploded in a ball of flame as it splashed down on the water. Apparently the pilot—2nd Lieutenant R.H.J. de Vries—had hit a large wave or a floating obstacle hidden in the dark water. Although Aircraft Machinist Mate J. de Lege survived, de Vries and three other crewmen were killed.[7]

Watching one plane turn away and another explode on the water had to be disturbing for the remaining two crews. But to their credit, they did not leave and managed to land in the rough water without serious damage. They took on 58 of the 120 militarized BPM demolition personnel at Balikpapan, along with all remaining MLD ground personnel, and flew them to Soerabaja.[8] Afterwards, the surviving planes of GVT.4 remained at Morokrembangan and flew reconnaissance and air/sea rescue missions in the Java Sea until January 27.

Back on Java, there was a great deal of concern at MLD HQ regarding the secret paperwork and naval codes carried aboard X-14. The plane had crashed in shallow water, and no one was sure of its condition. During the hasty evacuation, there had been no time to ensure that the classified paperwork had been destroyed. If the Japanese discovered the plane and any paperwork intact, the entire code network of the MLD and KM would be comprised. However, it appears the Japanese failed to search the sunken hull of X-14 or the paperwork in question had been destroyed, for the codes were never compromised.

As the Dutch destroyed Balikpapan, a Japanese invasion force departed Tarakan the night of January 20–21. They originally planned to leave January 16, but the Celebes operation delayed the invasion for a week by tying up air units that were to cover the convoy. Even then, air cover was spotty; according to the famed Japanese ace Saburo Sakai, the Tainan Air Wing was not able to put more than three Zeros over the convoy at one time due to bad weather, maintenance problems and aircraft shortages.[9] And since the airfield at Tarakan proved unsuitable for mass flight operations, most of the aircraft allocated to cover the invasion were forced to remain at Jolo and fly long-range missions against southern Borneo.

Nonetheless, the small number of aircraft operating from Tarakan still managed to inflict losses on the MLD. On January 21, the Dutch lost Y-51 of GVT.16 to Japanese fighters while the PBY was on a long-range reconnaissance patrol out of Tandjoeng Priok. Led by a C5M "Babs," four Tainan Air Wing Zeros caught the seaplane on the Barito River near Bandjermasin and burned it. The crew later escaped aboard a second PBY sent to pick them up, although it too had to fight off three Japanese fighters. Her gunners claimed two fighters shot down, but the Japanese reported no losses. Y-51 was a total loss and was replaced by Y-56 several days later.

This fighter sweep, and others like it from Tarakan, was carried out in conjunction with a concentrated air campaign initiated by the 21st Air Flotilla from its new base at Menado. To support the invasions of Balikpapan and Kendari, the flotilla sent a number of air strikes against Kendari and Ambon to reduce ABDA airpower. At the same time, the unit intensified reconnaissance patrols over Western New Guinea to help ensure that the Allies were not attempting a build-up of forces in that part of the archipelago. The IJN's 2nd Carrier Division with the heavy carriers *Hiryu* and *Soryu* further supported the operations with air strikes on Ambon.

The Balikpapan invasion force consisted of elements of the IJA's 56th Infantry Regiment and 146th Infantry Regiment, which had just completed the conquest of Tarakan. Close escort for the convoy's 16 transports consisted of the patrol boats *P-36*, *P-37* and *P-38*, remnants of the 11th and 30th Minesweeper Divisions[10] and the 31st Submarine Chaser Division. The 4th Destroyer Flotilla provided a covering force with the light cruiser *Naka*, which led the 2nd Destroyer Division, 1st/9th Destroyer Division and 1st/24th Destroyer Division. As at Tarakan, *Sanyo Maru* and *Sanuki Maru* provided A/S protection and air cover.

The seaplane tenders trailed the convoy by 24 hours, and their aircraft had orders not to operate too near the convoy or anywhere in the vicinity of Balikpapan prior to the invasion. This was done to avoid encountering Zeros from the Tainan Air Wing, which was flying intensive strike missions in the area and had orders to shoot down anything it encountered on the day of the invasion. While one can assume that the Tainan Air Wing pilots would have been able to distinguish their biplane counterparts, history shows that is not always the case for combatants of any nation. In any event, the Japanese elected to give the Zero pilots free reign.

ABDA reconnaissance planes quickly picked up the convoy on January 21 as it moved down the Makassar Strait; initial reports put its strength at 15 warships and 38 transports. Two days later, Dutch planes reported three groups of Japanese ships nearing Balikpapan. One of these aircraft, X-20 of GVT.7, was heavily damaged on January 20 while landing in poor visibility at Makassar. It flew to Morokrembangan for repairs, and X-35 came out of reserve to replace her.

With these reports, KM HQ stopped or rerouted shipping to Borneo ports. The Dutch destroyer *Van Ghent* was en route to Bandjermasin and Balikpapan with a small interisland merchant ship loaded with rice and other stores when the Japanese landed at the latter port. They proceeded on to Bandjermasin, but were then forced back to Soerabaja on the 22nd without re-supplying Balikpapan. Meanwhile, *K-XVIII* scuttled the Balikpapan lightship *Orion* with her deck gun to hamper the landings and prevent her capture by the Japanese.

Preceded by a small group of nationalist Indonesian Marechaussee, who served as pathfinders, the Japanese went ashore at Balikpapan in the early-morning hours of January 24. As one unit secured the airfield at Manggar, the Japanese' main force moved on Balikpapan city. The port's main defenses consisted of 1,200 KNIL regulars. Although the 6th Infantry Battalion held prepared positions, Colonel van den Hoogenband chose to withdraw into the interior of Borneo without a serious fight in order to initiate guerrilla warfare. As a result, Balikpapan was completely in the hands of the Japanese by the evening of the 25th. Aircraft of the 23rd Air Flotilla moved onto the airfield on January 28.

Meanwhile, X-29 — which had just returned from Morokrembangan — rescued 32 survivors from the 2,493-ton Russian merchant ship SS *Perekop*. Although Japan and the Soviet Union had signed a nonaggression pact the previous year, a "Nell" from the Mihoro Air Wing sank the steamer and killed eight crewmen east of Natoena Island while on an anti-shipping patrol. X-29 rescued her remaining crew, including four wounded, and flew it to Pontianak for medical attention.

Later on the night of the 24th–25th, X-19 of GVT.4 crashed in the rice paddies near Fort Menari at Soerabaja's Westwater entrance. The plane was returning from a night flight to Greater Masalembo Island, a tiny island in the North Java Sea. Due to bad weather, the Dornier had failed in an attempt to rescue 10 crewmen of an American LB-30 that had crashed on January 17 following a raid on Menado.[11] In the dark, the exhausted pilot put the Dornier down in a rice paddy he thought was the channel to Morokrembangan. The plane broke up on impact, killing both pilots.[12] GVT.4 disbanded two days later, and its one remaining Dornier, X-24, went into the reserve pool.

By now, exhaustion was common among all MLD flight crews. Many, such as the pilot of X-19, were flying 15 to 18 hours a day for 10 or more days at a time. Although the High Command attempted to rotate squadrons to Java for rest, the Japanese advance severely hampered these efforts. In addition, many of the airmen had to help service their planes or plan upcoming missions. Frequent moves to new bases, punctuated by air raids, made life for MLD airmen even more difficult.

KENDARI

As the Balikpapan force left Tarakan on January 21, a convoy of six transports simultaneously sailed from Menado for the port of Kendari on the southeast coast of Celebes. It carried the 1st Sasebo Special Naval Landing Force, which had secured Menado and Kema two weeks earlier. Escorted by the auxiliary vessels of Rear-Admiral Kubo's 1st Base Force, the light cruiser *Nagara*, the 15th and 16th Destroyer Divisions and the seaplane carriers *Chitose* and *Mizuho*, the convoy moved through the Peleng Strait and appeared off Staring Bay at 0200 on January 24.

All Allied shipping had cleared the bay except for the PatWing 10 tender *Childs*. She had arrived during the night of January 22–23 with 30,000 gallons of aviation fuel for the Kendari II airstrip, which B-17s from Java used as a staging base for attacks on the Southern Philippines. As other ships cleared the harbor, *Childs'* crew worked feverishly to unload its volatile cargo. The crew became particularly motivated after an enemy observation plane flew over the harbor.

The operation was completed just before dawn, and *Childs* got underway. As she entered the South Channel, lookouts sighted four Japanese destroyers on an intercept course. At 0532 one of them challenged *Childs* with the signal "A8Y ... A8Y ... A8Y." Signalman Rod Nordfelt did not know what it meant, so for lack of a better response, he returned the signal, which briefly confused the Japanese.[13] But at 0535 the destroyer challenged again.

Fortunately, a rain squall blew over *Childs*, hiding her from the approaching destroyers. Lieutenant-Commander J.L. Pratt took advantage of the brief cover by changing course and running down the narrow channel at full speed in near zero visibility. So extreme was the need for speed that boiler room engineers locked down the safety valves in order to get more steam pressure.

As she cleared the south channel, lookouts reported landing craft entering the North Channel. Their attention was quickly diverted by the four destroyers that now pursued. However, they apparently thought *Childs* was a harmless merchant vessel incapable of hindering the landings, for they quickly turned away to protect the anchorage.

Thirty-five minutes later, three fighters undoubtedly called in by the destroyers came in low for a better look. They quickly discovered *Childs* was not defenseless when heavy machine gun fire drove them off. Five minutes later they returned, but AA fire drove them off for good with the leader trailing smoke.

At 1415, a single-engine cruiser floatplane appeared and challenged the seaplane tender with the signal "A8Y." *Childs'* signalman again responded with an identical signal, but the pilot saw through his deception and immediately dropped two bombs at 1422. Both missed, and AA fire quickly drove off the plane. Pratt was now certain a cruiser was near and immediately turned southeast at full speed and made Soerabaja two days later without problems.

With fewer than 400 troops supported by four armored cars and a handful of AA guns, the local KNIL commander could put up little resistance.[14] His task was made even more difficult by the fact that many of his Indonesian troops had already deserted in the face of heavy air attacks that preceded the actual invasion. As a result, the Japanese were able to take possession of Kendari II by the evening of the 24th with only two men wounded. Although Dutch army and air force personnel managed to destroy most of the air field's installations and fuel supplies, 1st Base Force engineers had the runway operational within 24 hours. Meanwhile, *Chitose* and *Mizuho* provided air cover until the 21st Air Flotilla arrived on January 25.

With the loss of Kendari, MLD operations in the northern East Indies could now only be carried out at great peril. And not only did the Japanese now control most of the air over the East Indies, but their bombers also could now hit Morokrembangan, Soerabaja and other airfields on Java at will. Beginning in the first week of February, this would have a profound impact on the MLD's operations.

BANDJERMASIN

Despite the dramatically increased Japanese air presence over Borneo and Celebes following the loss of Balikpapan and Kendari, MLD and USN planes continued to fly regular reconnaissance missions up the Makassar Strait to Balikpapan, Kendari and points along the Minahassa Peninsula. Soon after the fall of Balikpapan, one of these aircraft reported the presence of a large convoy assembling in the port. Initial reconnaissance reports put its strength at 20 transports with an escort of three light cruisers and 10 destroyers. The ABDA High Command correctly assumed that this concentration was an invasion force destined for either Makassar on southwest Celebes or Bandjermasin on the east coast of Borneo.

Initially, this convoy was to move south and seize the airfield at Bandjermasin. However, after strong ABDA naval and air counterattacks at Balikpapan, the Japanese felt overexposed and believed that they did not have adequate naval resources to effectively cover the operation. As a result, they changed their plans and went with a two-pronged attack using fewer naval resources, with the primary focus being on land movement. In the meantime, the transports withdrew to Palau to refuel.

On January 27 units of the 146th Infantry Regiment sailed from Balikpapan aboard a small force of barges. They had orders to skirt the Borneo coast and then advance overland on Bandjermasin, taking a number of smaller port cities in the process in order to secure their flanks. Three days later, a battalion from the 146th Infantry Regiment also set out from Balikpapan and moved overland toward Bandjermasin. The two columns linked up near Ulin Airfield on February 10. The town and airfield were both in Japanese hands by that evening, but the Dutch forces had badly damaged the airfield before being withdrawn to Java by air. As a result, the runway remained out of commission until February 25.

AMBON

With Kendari II in their hands, the Japanese felt secure in moving against Ambon, which both they and the Dutch regarded as a key outpost in the Allied defense of the Eastern East Indies. While the KM regarded Ambon as little more than a staging base for its submarines, for the MLD it was the headquarters for their operations in that part of the archipelago. At the same time, MVK Halong served as a major secondary base for Dutch and American seaplanes scouting Japanese movements. For the Japanese, capturing Ambon would eliminate a major Allied air base, add to their sphere of air superiority and further secure their flank from Allied counterattack during the invasion of Java. At the same time, it would ensure the isolation of Dutch forces in New Guinea from supplies, reinforcements or evacuation.

A number of PatWing 10 PBY and J2F utility aircraft had been based at Halong since early January. However, life at the partially completed base was not easy. While Dutch personnel occupied the complex's completed barracks, the American crews and RAAF personnel from nearby Laha Airfield were assigned to Halong's unfinished barracks and mess halls.

These barracks had no beds and consisted of concrete slabs and walls without windows or running water. The sudden influx of allied personnel had also overwhelmed the island's primitive supply chain, thus ensuring a near constant shortage of food, which was generally bad to begin with. And finally, although the Australians and Americans got on well, tension between Dutch and PatWing 10 personnel constantly simmered just far enough below the surface to negatively influence low-level allied cooperation at a time when it was critically needed.[15]

Despite primitive living quarters for the aircrews at Halong, the harbor itself was excellent for Allied seaplanes. Ambon's inner harbor was almost completely enclosed by hills reaching some 800 feet in altitude. The harbor's narrow entrance was securely blocked with a log boom that was protected by an extensive barrage of 70 mines both inside and outside the harbor.

The Japanese had pounded Ambon from the air since the first week of January in preparation for its upcoming invasion. Their first air raid on the island came on January

7 and concentrated on MVK Halong and Laha Airfield, from which three Dutch Buffalo fighters and a squadron of Hudson bombers from 13 Squadron (RAAF) operated.[16] Together with a handful of Dutch AA batteries, the Buffalos represented the island's entire air defense.[17] Twelve USAAF P-40s were also slated to operate off the island with the bombers, but they never arrived.

In the face of such feeble defenses, the Japanese were able to operate over the island almost at will. In their first raid, the Japanese completely surprised the base and caught the Dutch fighters on the ground. Their bombs damaged one Buffalo and obliterated two of the Australian Hudsons while also damaging the airfield facilities. The bombers also targeted the GM vessel *Valk*, which tended to the aircraft of GVT.17 in Halong harbor. Although *Valk* was undamaged in this raid, the KM high command on Java ordered her captain to leave the area soon afterwards.

On January 14, the Japanese dramatically increased the weight of their attacks on Sorong. They wanted to ensure that no Dutch planes would interfere with the invasion of Ambon. Sorong, which had been under regular attack from enemy flying boats operating from Palau and Davao since mid-December, was soon completely isolated and untenable. Within days, Captain Bozuwa ordered the ordnance and fuel stocks destroyed and the base permanently abandoned.

A second raid on Ambon followed on January 15 when 27 "Betty" bombers from the Kanoya Air Wing again raided Ambon. In a repeat of the initial air attack, nine escorting fighters from the 3rd Fighter Wing quickly disposed of the two remaining Dutch fighters, allowing the bombers to work unmolested from the air. Again concentrating on the airfield and naval air station, they destroyed another 13 Squadron Hudson, although seven others were undamaged. Bombs also severely damaged the naval air station before the raiders turned for home.

Meanwhile, three fighters provided cover while six Zeros came down to strafe the air station, where they found two PatWing 10 PBYs landing in the harbor. Completely unaware that Japanese aircraft were in the area, 22-P-7 was hit almost immediately, and the starboard wing exploded in flames as shells penetrated its fuel tank.[18] However, the pilot managed to put his PBY down without further damage, and the fire was extinguished. 22-P-8 was also forced down in flames shortly afterward and beached, where the PBY became a burned-out wreck. The fighters then turned their attention to 22-P-10, which was quickly destroyed at its mooring.

After the Zeros departed, Dutch ground crews pulled 22-P-7 into Halong's only surviving hangar for repairs. They found that although all the fabric on the starboard wing had been burned away and the hull was pocked with shrapnel hits, the plane seemed structurally sound. However, because of the island's weak air defenses, all remaining USN aircraft were ordered to withdraw later that day, and the damaged PBY was abandoned in the hangar when the remaining PatWing 10 personnel and aircraft flew out early the following morning.

Their departure was timely, as four 3rd Air Wing Zeros guided by a C5M "Babs" scout plane returned to Halong the following day. Although pickings were scarce with the withdrawal of PatWing 10, they still claimed to have destroyed a twin-engine flying boat. However, since there were no American planes left on the base and no Dutch aircraft were lost that day, the claim was likely a repeat claim on 22-P-7, which survived this attack as well.

Following this attack, GVT.17 also evacuated Ambon for Morokrembangan on the

16th. A lack of AA defenses and no fighter presence made it impossible for the squadron to continue operations from the base. The squadron had also been stationed at Halong since before the start of war, and its crews needed rest after six weeks of uninterrupted operations.[19] In addition, with the loss of Y-58 and the heavy damage suffered by Y-60 over Kema, GVT.17 was down to only one effective aircraft. Y-67 replaced Y-58 from the reserve pool upon their return to Java.

On the 24th, 18 "Nells" from the 23rd Naval Air Flotilla again hit Ambon, all but demolishing what was left of Halong. The lone remaining hangar, most repair shops, fuel dumps and barracks were destroyed. The still unrepaired 22-P-7 was finally destroyed for good when the hangar was leveled. At the same time, Zeros burned two PatWing 10 PBYs (22-P-5 and 22-P-10) on the water. Later that day, more than 50 aircraft from the 2nd Carrier Squadron (*Hiryu* and *Soryu*) added to the destruction.

A fourth American PBY operating from Ambon that day survived because it was on patrol. 22-P-4 evacuated Ambon for good the following day, carrying 36 evacuees that included the two destroyed PBYs' aircrews and a number of MLD ground personnel. As they departed, Japanese carrier planes again pounded Halong. Two more PatWing 10 PBYs flew in from Java on the 27th to evacuate 25 more Dutch personnel and civilians, including Captain Hekking and his staff.

The MLD ground personnel who had remained behind now worked to rig the sea-plane ramp and few remaining repair shops, ordnance dumps and fuel stocks for demolition and ensure that they were successfully destroyed before the island fell. Just before the Japanese landed, a small reserve stock of aviation fuel that had been saved for emergency flight operations was contaminated with turpentine, and the fuses of all remaining ordnance were thrown into the sea. Their last act was to burn the KM's archives and other records.

At the same time, KM shore personnel destroyed the submarine base and fuel oil stocks and burned the port's warehouses. All of these men were supposed to have been evacuated once the demolitions were completed. But due to a breakdown somewhere in the KM's overloaded communications network, their evacuation was botched, and the Japanese captured most of them. However, three of the MLD men were evacuated at the last minute aboard an Australian Short Sunderland flying boat that flew in to help bring out RAAF personnel.

Even after the Dutch and Americans had evacuated Halong, the Hudsons of 13 Squadron continued to operate from Laha Airfield. This was because the Australians saw Ambon as a critical link in the defense of the NEI; if the NEI fell, Australia would be open to attack from the Japanese. For this reason, the Hudsons remained at Ambon and continued to fly reconnaissance and strike missions in the face of ferocious air attacks. But by January 28, the raids were too severe for even the Australians, and 13 Squadron withdrew its aircraft as well.

The Ambon invasion force sailed in two groups. The first five transports sailed from Davao on January 27 with elements of the 56th Infantry Regiment. The destroyers *Arashio* and *Michisio* of the 8th Destroyer Division and the sub chasers *Ch.1* and *Ch.2* escorted them. The following day six transports carrying the Kure Special Naval Landing Force left Menado escorted by the 2nd Destroyer Flotilla, and the two convoys joined on January 29. They received air cover A/S support from *Chitose* and *Mizuho*, which were screened by the 1st/15th Destroyer Division, 21st Minesweeper Division and two patrol boats. Two heavy cruisers and two destroyers covered the operation from the Celebes Sea.

The landing itself started early on the morning of January 31. Naval ground troops began moving ashore before dawn and were quickly followed by army troops. Despite fierce resistance from the combined Dutch/Australian garrison, Ambon fell on February 4, depriving the MLD of its most important forward base. The loss of Halong was critical, as allied reconnaissance aircraft damaged while operating in the northern NEI would now have to fly all the way to Java.

CONTINUED RESISTANCE

Despite the pending loss of key seaplane facilities at Ambon and Sorong, the MLD continued to strike back as best it could. On the 16th X-29 of GVT.6 strafed the runway at Kuching. Returning to base, the pilot reported three merchant ships of about 2,000 tons each in the harbor. Two days later, X-28 and X-29 attacked the merchant ships but hit nothing. In the process, X-29 suffered damage that forced its return to Morokrembangan for repairs; she rejoined the squadron several days later.

They returned with X-31 on the 19th, concentrating on the airfield and two large and two small merchant ships in the harbor. However, a heavy rainstorm limited visibility and forced the aircrews to bomb and strafe from high altitude. As a result, the planes achieved poor results despite encountering only light AA fire.

GVT.6 returned to Kuching later that afternoon, and all three seaplanes circled the airfield for an hour attacking targets of opportunity. Despite heavy return fire from Japanese AA,[20] the Dorniers laid 18 bombs on the airfield but inflicted only light damage, although one reportedly destroyed a fighter as it was taking off to intercept the Dutch planes. Another bomb hit what appeared to be an ammunition dump, causing a huge blast as the squadron turned for home.

The squadron returned to Kuching on the 22nd. However, despite circling the city for several hours, the planes encountered bad weather and couldn't drop more than eight 100-pound bombs. In this attack X-29 hit the quays and left them in flames. With this, GVT.6 called off its assault on Kuching. Spies for the Netherlands Interior Service[21] later reported that the three-day campaign had badly cratered the runway and burned several planes and that a single 500-pound bomb dropped on the airfield had killed some 400 Japanese on the runway.

Still, by late January, the main force of the MLD had been driven back to Java. Only a few squadrons of Dutch planes still flew in the outer reaches of the East Indies. It was only a matter of time before they too were pushed back to Morokrembangan as the Japanese began their final push to break Dutch resistance. The tenders also followed their seaplanes back to Soerabaja after being constantly targeted by Japanese bombers. The last tender to "come in out of the cold" was *Poolster*, which arrived at the ME from Pontianak on January 13.

The IJN now attempted to clear all remaining ABDA airpower from the Eastern East Indies. The first indication of their presence was a reconnaissance plane over Koepang on January 25. The next morning, the 3rd Air Wing sent six A6M2s guided by a C5M "Babs" to hit Timor. Arriving over Koepang Harbor, three of the fighters stumbled across a KNILM Ga.21 "Goose" amphibian that had just taken off. Completely surprised by the Zeros, the unarmed "Goose" almost immediately dove into a small ravine, killing all aboard, including the pilot, wireless operator, flight mechanic and two passengers.[22] The fighters then proceeded to work over the dockyard installations.

Although not a military aircraft, the Grumman G.21a "Goose" was extensively employed through-out the NEI by civilian, corporate and religious organizations (photograph courtesy of San Diego Aerospace Museum).

The remaining "Zekes" proceeded to Penfoi Airfield, where they found a number of Allied planes dispersed in uncamouflaged aircraft pens. In the absence of AA fire, they first burned a loaded civilian Dragon Rapide on the runway, killing its female pilot and five passengers. They then proceeded to strafe and burn a second civilian aircraft and a stranded American P-40E Kittyhawk belonging to the 17th Pursuit Squadron. With all Allied aircraft destroyed, the Japanese turned their attention to the hangars, barracks and radio station.[23]

Two fighters then wandered out over the Soemba Strait, where they randomly encountered a DC-2 attached to 36 Squadron (RAAF). The transport was en route to Penfoei from Soerabaja when the Japanese attacked. In a brief, one-sided fight, the Douglas was also soon forced into the sea, where it sank. The four crewmen then spent 30 hours floating in shark-infested waters before washing ashore on Soemba Island, where local Indonesians summoned Dutch authorities to care for them.[24]

Meanwhile, Y-59 of GVT.17, which had been pulled back to Morokrembangan after the fall of Menado, was heavily damaged on the 24th when two Japanese fighters caught her over the Java Sea while escorting the damaged Dutch submarine *K-XVIII* to the ME. The damage was so extensive that the Catalina had to immediately return to the naval air station for comprehensive repairs.

K-XVIII had been stationed off Balikpapan to interdict Japanese landings. Although she failed in an attack on *Naka*, she succeeded in sinking the 6,988-ton transport *Tsuruga Maru*. However, a counter–depth charge attack by the subchaser *Ch. 12* screen caused severe damage to her electric engines. As a result, she could not travel while submerged and had to make the entire distance from Balikpapan to the ME on the surface. For most of her trip, MLD seaplanes were the only aircraft with sufficient range to provide air cover. After Y-59 was damaged, three USAAF B-17s and later P-40s from Java escorted the submarine.

On the 26th, X-29 of GVT.6 retaliated by attacking a small Japanese schooner on

Borneo's Sarawak coast between Tandjoeng Api and Kuching. The Dornier was on routine patrol when the crew sighted a schooner of about 300-tons laden with troops and dove to attack. In a bitter fight, the X-boat suffered heavy damage from small-arms fire but left the ship in flames and broke for home. In return, Machinist Mate T. Veldman was killed and another crewman wounded in this action. X-29 flew to Morokrembangan for extensive repairs on the 28th.

This invasion force was sighted at 2000 on the night of the 27th by a Dutch coast watcher on the west coast of Borneo. Although he signaled KM HQ that a Japanese force of about 20 ships was rounding Tandjoeng Datoe on a southerly course, Admiral Helfrich was annoyed that the watcher had included no ship descriptions.[25] GVT.6 was ordered to fly a night reconnaissance mission but could not locate the convoy. The planes went out again at first light and discovered the Japanese force in the Sambas River, just south of Pemangkat on Borneo's southwest coast. However, the "fleet" contained no large ships, but rather consisted of 10 small native craft and six motorboats ferrying some 500 troops.

The MLD planes attacked with 100-pound bombs and strafing with little effect. Based on GVT.6 reports, the Dutch light cruiser *Java* was dispatched from convoy duty in the Soenda Strait to intercept. *Tromp*, screened by the destroyers *Piet Hein* and *Banckert*, was also ordered to stand off and engage the Japanese main force if it was sighted. But because *Java* had to wait until the covering force got into position, she reached Pamangkat several hours too late and missed the Japanese force; the four vessels then withdrew to avoid air attack. The Japanese had landed at 0700 on January 28 and quickly moved to occupy the port city of Sambas and its MLD base. They then moved south and occupied Mampawang, Pontianak and the ML airfield at Sinkawang.

In response to the MLD raids on its convoy at Pemangkat and Sinkawang, five G3M "Nells" from the Mihoro Air Wing struck the GVT.6 auxiliary base at Tajan. With most of its supplies destroyed in this attack, the squadron withdrew to Ketapang on the southwest coast of Borneo. In the process, 120 drums of aviation fuel, 50 cases of oil and a large supply of bombs were destroyed, as they could not be taken out. The aircraft dock and buoys were also scuttled to prevent their capture. The squadron flew reconnaissance missions along the Borneo coast from Ketapang until the 30th. When Japanese troops approached the base, X-28 and X-31 withdrew to Morokrembangan, where they joined X-29.

As the Dutch struggled to maintain a foothold in the NEI, the British seaplanes of 205 Squadron were being forced out of Malaya by intense Japanese air raids. Having lost six PBYs since the first week of December, the squadron evacuated its last five operational aircraft from Seletar on January 29. Setting up operations at Tanjoeng Priok, FV-N, FV-R, FV-U/Y-53, FV-V and FV-W/Y-54 came under the command of Captain Bozuwa's REC-GROUP and were detailed to fly reconnaissance missions over the Java Sea and South China Sea.

Shortly after their departure, the tender *Tung Song* was ordered from Seletar to the port of Oosthaven on Southern Sumatra. There, she set up a temporary base to help extend the range of the squadron's Catalinas. In her absence the American seaplane tender *Holland* provided support for 205 Squadron at Tandjoeng Priok.

On January 31 the MLD high command received reports of a Japanese convoy in the area of Boeton Island, some 50 to 75 miles south of Kendari. In response, GVT.3(NEW) was ordered to mount a night attack from Morokrembangan. Although the squadron arrived at Boeton in good order, it was unable to locate the Japanese and spent a good deal of time searching for the elusive convoy. It eventually sighted a lone Japanese ship near Kendari, which it attacked with unknown results. The squadron had little time to spend over the target as all of the PBYs were running low on fuel and were forced to turn for home. This mission closed out the month of January.[26]

By the end of January, the Dutch retained a tenuous foothold at only Bandjermasin on Borneo's east coast and Makassar on the southern tip of Celebes. From their newly acquired bases at Balikpapan, Pontianak, Sinkawang (a former KNIL airfield in the interior of Borneo) and Kendari, the Japanese could now hit virtually every target on Java and Southern Sumatra. The only harbor of significance that lay outside their reach was Tjilatjap on the south coast of Java. At the same time, Kendari II and a captured secondary airstrip on the island of Ceram allowed regular attacks on Timor, which also lay on the Japanese list of targets. Its capture would cut the Allied supply line to Java and further isolate Allied forces on the island.

7

February, Part I:
The Air Assault on Java

The month of February saw the biggest loss of MLD planes during the East Indies campaign. The majority of these losses can be credited to Japanese bomber raids and fighter sweeps across Java. Morokrembangan was a prime target for repeated air strikes as the Japanese moved to reduce ABDA air power.

The Japanese also sent their submarines south again as they moved farther into Dutch territory. From February 1 to 3, X-17 from GVT.8 rescued nearly 100 survivors from the KPM merchant ship SS *Van Overstraten*, which had been sunk by the Japanese submarine *I-64* some 550 miles west of Sabang, Sumatra, on January 22. The ship's 103 survivors had spent 10 days drifting in the Indian Ocean before 93 were picked up by the MLD plane and flown to Sinabang, a small port on the western coast of Sumatra. The remaining 10 survivors reached Sinabang in sloops.

The first air action of the month came on February 1 when Y-63 of GVT.2(NEW) and Y-57 (still temporarily attached to GVT.2[NEW]) sighted a Japanese convoy off the Anambas Islands while on a long-range reconnaissance patrol. While shadowing it, they were intercepted by a "Pete" from the seaplane tender *Sagara Maru* flown by Naval Air Pilot H. Ichikawa.[1] Showing absolutely no hesitation, Ichikawa brazenly attacked the two flying boats.

A sharp air battle raged for the next 25 minutes, pitting the nimble "Pete" against the lumbering PBYs. At this point in the NEI campaign, many MLD seaplanes, including Y-57, were undermanned due to a severe personnel shortage. As a result, Y-57's commander had to man a weapon himself, leaving Sergeant W. van der Tweel to fly the aircraft. They were further hampered by weapons jams in the nose position, where the gunner had to twice clear his guns.[2]

Although the Japanese pilot made three very aggressive passes, the Dutch gunners could not score any critical hits on the floatplane, although they claimed to have knocked pieces off of it. Finally, several long machine gun bursts sent it into a steep dive, and crewmen on both seaplanes claimed to have seen the "Pete" crash into the sea.[3] However, the floatplane made it back to the *Sagara Maru*, although its condition upon arrival remains unknown.

In return, the Japanese pilot and his rear gunner expended all their ammunition, hitting Y-57 more than 50 times throughout the fuselage and hull. The damage punctured its fuel tanks and caused heavy oil leaks and heavy flooding upon landing at Blinjoe on Banka Island's Klabat Bay. As the temporary base had no facilities, Y-57 was forced back to Tandjoeng Priok for repairs.

Meanwhile the Japanese continued their operations on Celebes. They had already taken Menado on January 11 and Kendari on January 24. Makassar was to follow on February 8. Although the Dutch did not have an exact date, they knew a landing was about to take place and sent the Catalinas of GVT.3(NEW) to evacuate MLD personnel from the port city on February 2.

THE DESTRUCTION OF GVT.7

By the end of January, GVT.7 was operating from a string of remote support bases between Bali and Roti Island in the Lesser Soenda Islands in the Sawoe Sea. The Sawoe Sea and air space over Timor was now extremely dangerous for MLD planes due to Japanese fighters. The Japanese were still actively adhering to their plan of systematically eliminating all MLD air bases that could be found.

This oppressive Japanese air presence over the archipelago soon led to another disaster similar to that which had befallen GVT.2 and GVT.5 at Lake Tondano in late December. This time the squadron's only survivor was X-33, which was badly damaged on January 30 while landing at the port of Dilly on Timor. Although not fatal, the resulting leaks in the hull were serious enough to force the seaplane's return to Morokrembangan for extensive repairs.

X-13 was ordered to replace X-33 at Rotti Island on January 30, but its timing was unlucky. Shortly before its arrival, the remaining Dorniers of GVT.7 (X-32 and X-35) were discovered on the water by an enemy reconnaissance plane. Alerted to the presence of the Dutch seaplanes, the Japanese immediately sent a strike force on February 7. They found X-35 pulled up on the beach for repairs, while X-32 was moored close to shore; X-13 had just landed. The bombers completely surprised the Dutch and burned all three flying boats without loss. Two MLD radio operators were killed in the attack.

With that raid, MLD operations in the Sawoe Sea came to an abrupt end. The survivors of GVT.7 were transported by ship to Koepang, where they joined GVT.6, which had been en route to relieve them. From there, X-3 and X-23 flew the personnel of both units back to Morokrembangan. There, GVT.7 reformed with the reserve Dorniers X-1, X-20, X-24 and X-36.[4] Afterwards, because of air raids that now rolled across Java, GVT.7(NEW) operated off Java from a secret base on Lake Grati (near Modjokerto) for the rest of February.

February 2 saw the first Japanese air attacks on Allied airfields across East Java, although they did not hit West Java and Soerabaja until the following day. On the 3rd, 72 bombers and 44 fighters attacked the port at 1007. Bombing from 20,000 feet, they concentrated primarily on the naval base but did destroy a hangar and a number of planes at Morokrembangan.

Twelve Dutch Curtis CW-21B "Demon" fighters intercepted a Japanese formation over Soerabaja but were effectively kept away from the bombers. In a freewheeling series of dogfights, the Dutch shot down three 3rd Air Wing Zeros but lost seven Demons in exchange. At the same time, seven Curtis 75A-7 "Hawk" fighters from Perak slipped into a second bomber formation before their fighter escort could respond. The Dutch claimed one probable kill and several others damaged before escorting Zeros shot down five of the Hawks without loss. Six American P-40s of the 17th Pursuit Squadron also scrambled and shot down one bomber and one Tainan Air Wing Zero for the loss of a single P-40.

The next victim was a Ryan floatplane. At the controls were a Dutch student pilot and Ernest Lee, one of the 12 American civilian flight instructors in the East Indies to help train MLD pilots. The trainer was on final approach in Soerabaja's harbor with the student at the controls when exploding bombs tore across its path, causing him to lose control. Lee tried to wrestle the floatplane back into the air, but the STM plunged into the water and sank immediately. Although both pilots survived, Dutch soldiers on shore thought they were Japanese and opened fire. Fortunately they missed and the pilots were able to swim ashore.

Whereas the bombers ignored Morokrembangan, the fighters did not. Zeros of the 3rd Air Wing skimmed over the American gunboat USS *Isabelle* to strafe at masthead height, ignoring AA fire from her .30 machine guns. X-31 of GVT.6 was the first lost, strafed on the water until it burned. A short time later, two Zeros caught Y-40 over East Java;[5] as one pilot chopped her out of the air, his wingman shot down a B-17C from the 19th Bomb Group 10 miles south of Singosari.

Other fighters also attacked Morokrembangan, inflicting heavy losses on MLD reserve planes and front-line aircraft that were under repair. Front-line aircraft losses included X-6, X-30 and the still non-operational X-37.[6] A number of training and auxiliary seaplanes were also lost, including two Do. 15 "Whales" attached to the flight-training school.[7] D-41 was heavily damaged on the water and would be written off after the attack, while Zeros shot down D-43 near Soerabaja while on a training flight. They also caught Y-61 from GVT.3 over the Madoera Strait and shot it down as well, although it appears that this aircraft was possibly able to return to Morokrembangan in a severely damaged condition.

Two MLD Fokker T-IVs (T-20 and T-22) and a second Ryan trainer were lost on the water. The Japanese fighters also caught three Fokker C-XI floatplanes at the base.[8] Although all three of the single-engine floatplanes were badly shot up, it appears that none of them was completely destroyed. However, without spare parts, it is unlikely that they were ever repaired. As a result of this damage, all would later have to be destroyed by MLD ground personnel to prevent their capture when the base was evacuated in early March.

Counting Earnest Lee's STM, 15 MLD planes were shot down, destroyed, burned or damaged beyond repair. Together with fighters lost in the air and losses on the ground, ABDA losses totaled between 30 and 40 aircraft that day.[9] In return, the Japanese lost one bomber and four fighters. One of three C5M "Babs" light reconnaissance planes that had provided navigational guidance for the fighters was also lost attacking a PatWing 10 PBY as it landed near Madoera.

In addition to massive aircraft losses, damage on the ground was severe. Both Perak Airfield and the ME had been badly damaged, as were the airfields at Singosari and Madioen. Substantial damage had also been caused to Soerabaja's inner city when a flight of Japanese bombers dropped its ordnance in the area in an attempt to destroy the Dutch High Command. Total Allied casualties for the February 3 raid numbered 31 killed and 85 injured.[10]

As the Japanese hammered Morokrembangan on the 3rd, P-43 and P-44 from PatWing 10 sighted the Japanese barge fleet that had departed Balikpapan on January 27 as it slowly moved down the Makassar Strait toward Bandjermasin. However, ADBA could do little about it amid the chaos of the Japanese air strikes, and the force eventually put ashore some 50 miles southeast of Bandjermasin several days later. Nonetheless, to monitor its progress in the meantime, PatWing 10's commander sent P-43 and P-45 back up the strait the following day.

Top: "Beehive" style air raid shelters had to be built above ground at Morokrembangan due to the area's high water table (photograph from *Soerabaja 1900–1950* [2004], courtesy of Asia Maior Publishers). *Bottom:* Perak air field (with Morokrembangan in the background) was a frequent target of Japanese aircraft during the intense air raids of February and March 1942 (photograph from *Soerabaja 1900–1950* [2004], courtesy of Asia Maior Publishers).

Although P-45's crew sighted no naval movement, it encountered a large formation of approximately 40 bombers with a strong fighter escort south of Balikpapan. While the main formation continued on to Soerabaja, three of the Zeros broke away and proceeded to maul the PBY. In a running dogfight, the PBY dodged in and out of the clouds until the fighters finally gave up and rejoined their formation. Nursing his badly damaged plane home, the pilot landed at Morokrembangan later that day with a dead engine and the hull looking like a sieve.[11]

The second attack on Java came on February 5, when 27 Zeros and a C5M of the Tainan Air Wing struck Morokrembangan at 0933. Four Demons and two Hawks intercepted with seven USAAF P-40s. As in the first raid, they were unable to turn the raiders away and again suffered heavily. Bounced out of the sun and hopelessly outnumbered, the Dutch lost two of the Demons almost before they knew what hit them. Tainan Air Wing fighters then encountered eight B-17s that had just taken off for a mission to bomb Balikpapan and shot them up badly as well. In the meantime, another C5M guided in 11 Zeros of the 3rd Air Wing, arriving over Soerabaja 30 minutes later; almost immediately, two pilots claimed both Hawks over Soerabaja and Madoera, respectively.

Unopposed in the air, the bombers remained over Morokrembangan for 62 minutes, dropping 38 500-pound bombs. A number of repair shops were gutted, and one hangar was obliterated when a bomb penetrated the roof and detonated four 500-pound bombs slung under the wings of the American PBY 22-P-1. Bombs also heavily damaged barracks, fuel depots and water mains. As the bombers turned for home, Japanese fighters now turned their attention to the air station.

The PBYs of PatWing 10 had already been sent to a remote secondary base. However, for unknown reasons, P-43 (former MLD Y-43) remained on the water at Morokrembangan and was lost to strafing Zeros. They also burned Y-50, X-22 and X-33 as they lay on the water.[12] For good measure, they also destroyed D-45 and D-46, two Do. 15 "Whales" attached to the flight training school.

The fifth PBY lost that day was Y-72, which ran into a flight of four Japanese fighters near Waroe, just south of Soerabaja, while on what was likely a training flight with the MLD's flight training school. Although one wing and an engine were badly shot up, the PBY's pilot managed to put the Catalina down near the city, and it was transported back to Morokrembangan by truck several days later. As two of the Zeros shot up Y-72, two more remained above the fight and protectively circled the squadron's C5M "Babs" that had guided them in.

It was during this attack on Morokrembangan that an MLD NCO named Gerard van Schooten won the Bronze Cross, one of Holland's highest military honors. Despite the risk of drawing attention from the fighters, which strafed anything that moved, van Schooten took a motorboat out into the harbor and rescued a number of men who had escaped from their burning aircraft. After delivering them to shore, he then took fire extinguishers and other equipment out to help save a number of less heavily damaged planes. Three weeks later, he would be awarded a second Bronze Cross for gallantry in action.

The MLD also lost another of the Naval Flying School's Ryan floatplanes. At the controls was none other than Earnest Lee, the instructor who had barely escaped with his life in the initial raid two days earlier. Intercepted by a Zero at 7,000 feet some 20 miles north of Soerabaja, Lee dove to just above the sea as the Japanese pilot followed him down. Jinking wildly, he caused the Zero to make three passes before hitting the STM.

Bullets and cannon shells shredded the fuselage, floats and windscreen, but neither Lee nor his student was hit.

A second Zero now joined his wingman, scoring a number of hits on the trainer's wings while the first Zero circled. Then, apparently low on fuel or ammunition, each fighter made a final pass before turning away. Miraculously, the floatplane was still in the air after the 25-minute engagement. Perhaps even more amazing, both Lee and his student pilot escaped unharmed. Lee then put the badly damaged floatplane down in a rice paddy, where it immediately sank.

GVT.5(NEW), which had just become operational again that day after reforming with PBYs following the disastrous Japanese air strike against Lake Tondano, escaped damage and flew into Tjilatjap the next morning. However, the Japanese did heavily damage the reserve Catalina Y-71 as it sat in a hangar. Ground crews made it flyable with emergency repairs, and it was sent to Tjilatjap on the 7th to replace Y-67. Shortly after the squadron's arrival, the latter had been damaged in a collision with Y-65 and was returned to Morokrembangan for repairs.

That same day the Japanese launched a third raid against Morokrembangan in retaliation for the recent MLD attacks on their invasion operation at Tandjoeng Datoek. Nine Zeros from the Tainan Air Wing shot up the base early in the morning, claiming two seaplanes destroyed on the water. These were likely older reserve or auxiliary aircraft, as no front-line MLD or PatWing 10 aircraft was lost at Morokrembangan that day. Also, since both the MLD and PatWing 10 had been quick to abandon Morokrembangan as a primary base after the first two raids, it is likely that the aircraft were actually inoperable wrecks left from the attacks of February 3 and 5.

More air strikes against both the ME and Morokrembangan followed on the 8th, 9th (two attacks), 10th, 11th, 18th, 19th, 20th, 21st and 25th. Dutch fighter strength had been broken in the first two raids, so there was virtually no air cover. Only six ML Demons remained, and these were quickly withdrawn to reinforce ABDA air defenses in West Java. For the remainder of the campaign, American P-40s of the 17th Pursuit Squadron, together with a handful of Dutch and British AA guns, provided East Java's only protection against air attacks.

Within days of these devastating raids, Morokrembangan was all but abandoned. All operational MLD planes at the air station were dispersed to isolated scatter bases and small lakes throughout the interior of Java. Although ground crews remained to service the few Allied seaplanes that dared inhabit the base, the near constant presence of Japanese aircraft overhead prevented Morokrembangan from playing an important role for the remaining month of the East Indies campaign.

Meanwhile, although the MLD had been forced out of Dutch New Guinea, the Japanese still periodically caught civilian aircraft at isolated outposts. This was the case on February 8, when two Zeros with a 3rd Air Wing detachment based at Ambon took off to strafe the ports of Dobo and Kapalauan Aru. At Dobo, Naval Air Pilot 1st Class Yoshihiko Takenaka and Naval Air Pilot 3rd Class Nobutoshi Furukawa attacked and burned a Grumman G.21 "Goose" belonging to the Netherlands New Guinea Petroleum Company. The seaplane had already been heavily damaged in a previous attack, and the Zeros now finished it off for good.[13]

About the same time, Lieutenant Toshitata Kawazoe and Naval Air Pilot 3rd Class Tadahiro Sakai, also with the 3rd Air Wing at Ambon, took off for a strike mission against the port of Saumlaki. En route to their destination, they also attacked the same Grumman immediately after Takenaka and Furukawa departed, although the two groups were unaware of each other's presence over the port. Not realizing their error, these two pilots claimed the same aircraft destroyed.[14]

Meanwhile, the MLD continued to strike back as best it could. GVT.2(NEW) had been patrolling the west coast of Borneo since January 30 when it managed a small measure of revenge on February 6. Y-62 and Y-64 were on a reconnaissance flight out of their base at Tandjoeng Pandan when they sighted a Japanese merchant ship of about 6,000 tons in the North Api Strait. Dropping eight 500-pound bombs, they claimed a direct hit on its after-funnel and a near miss that left her on fire and listing. The identity of this ship is unknown, but the 6,788-ton *Kurama Maru* was lost to unknown causes in the general area, although her loss is listed as February 9.[15]

While on patrol the following day, the third plane of GVT.2(NEW), Y-63, sighted a small boat full of men waving frantically to attract the crew's attention. Upon landing, Y-63 found them to be MLD ground personnel from Pontianak. When the Japanese reached them, they had moved overland to Ketapang, where they secured a small prau and decided to take their chances on the open sea.

The MLD's joy of rescuing a group of its own was soon tempered by another loss. This time it was the Catalina Y-38, which was still attached to the MLD flight training school. Its pilot had to make an emergency landing in the Westwater Channel at Soerabaja following a training flight. Although he put the Catalina down without trouble, it was lost soon afterwards. While under tow the PBY collided with the tug and suffered such heavy damage that it sank.

While other MLD planes engaged the Japanese over the increasingly unfriendly skies of Java, GVT.18's Y-48 carried General Wavell from Tandjoeng Priok to Singapore for a series of meetings. As the general boarded the plane for his return flight later that night, he fell down a 10-foot seawall at Seletar and injured his back. As a result, he was in a great pain during the flight back to Tandjoeng Priok; nonetheless, Wavell refused to remain in the hospital and returned to his headquarters.

MAKASSAR

The Makassar invasion force comprised the same infantry units that had captured Kendari. It sailed from Staring Bay on February 6 carrying the 1st Sasebo Special Naval Landing Force aboard six transports. The auxiliary vessels of Rear-Admiral Kubo's 1st Base Force, the light cruiser *Nagara* with the 8th, 15th and 21st Destroyer Divisions provided close escort. En route, the 1st/24th and 9th Destroyer Divisions and the minesweepers W.15, W.16, W.17 and W.18 from Balikpapan reinforced them. Vice Admiral Takeo Takagi provided distant cover for the operation with his 5th Cruiser Squadron and two destroyers.

The 11th Carrier Squadron (*Chitose* and *Mizuho*) provided air cover with support from the aircraft depot ship *Sanyo Maru*. However, in an ironic twist, *Chitose* herself was lost for the remainder of the East Indies campaign on February 10 when attacked by three USAAF LB-30s south of Celebes.[16] Badly damaged as a result of this attack, she was forced to return to Japan for repairs. *Chitose* did not return to action until March 31, 1942, when she took part in a series of Japanese operations designed to occupy the north coast of Dutch New Guinea.

Moving ashore at Makassar, the Japanese encountered resistance from some 900 widely scattered KNIL regulars, recent conscripts and Home Guard auxiliary troops. The heavily outnumbered Dutch forces in Makassar held out only long enough for the airfield to be destroyed. In this action, the Japanese lost only five dead and another five wounded. Under cover of a rearguard, the Dutch then withdrew into the interior of Celebes to the Tjamba Position, an eight-and-a-half-mile defensive front in extremely rough terrain that had been prepared before the war.

In a hard-fought engagement at the Tello Bridge near the town of Maros, the Dutch rearguard ambushed a column of Japanese troops riding bicycles. The KNIL force claimed to have killed some 300 of them with intense mortar and machine gun fire before being forced to surrender in subsequent counterattacks. The Japanese almost immediately massacred the surviving Dutch troops. Meanwhile, the Tjamba position held out until March 27, when the KNIL commander surrendered his remaining troops and some 600 European civilians. In a surprising show of respect by the Japanese, the KNIL officers were allowed to keep their swords.

With their occupation of Makassar, the Japanese now controlled all of Celebes, with the exception of small pockets of Dutch guerrillas who continued to hold out. They were now in a position to launch their planned invasion of Timor in an effort to cut the flow of air reinforcements to Java from Australia.

THE LOSS OF X-29

On February 11 X-29 of GVT.6 went down following a failed evacuation flight to Bandjermasin. From January 14, the MLD had evacuated a steady flow of civilians and KNIL troops from the port. However, these flights abruptly ended when X-29 was detailed to make an evacuation flight to the city. Although repaired at Morokrembangan after its encounter with the Japanese schooner on January 26, X-29 was not considered completely airworthy and was not fully trusted by its crew. Nonetheless, the flight went well until the pilot set down on the river at Bandjermasin. As he did, a hail of gunfire erupted from the shore.[17]

Ramming the throttle forward, the pilot managed to drag the Dornier off the water and disappear into the coming darkness with heavy damage. The flight home was without incident, but as X-29 crossed over Madoera and descended into Morokrembangan, two engines abruptly quit. The pilot tried to make an emergency landing in the Westwater, but the plane cartwheeled into the water and exploded. Three crewmen were killed immediately, while the plane's commander and another crewman survived. Although the survivors were picked up by a launch from Soerabaja at dawn, the badly wounded pilot died the following day.[18]

By this point in the campaign, MLD offensive actions had all but evaporated, and its aircraft were limited to reconnaissance missions. Still, air action remained brisk as the Japanese quickly moved south. On the 12th, X-17 of GVT.8 went out on a reconnaissance flight over the South China Sea. Near Shallow Water Island (south of Billiton Island), it was bounced by two Japanese floatplanes and forced into a running dogfight before they turned back. These were "Petes" from either *Kamikawa Maru* or *Sagara Maru*, which provided air cover for a large invasion force that was bearing down on southern Sumatra and Banka and Billiton islands.

Between February 15 and 20 X-17 and X-18 of GVT.8 flew a series of supply missions to support Allied troops still fighting in central Borneo. They flew to Sitang on the

Kapoes River loaded with ammunition, portable radios, medical supplies and food for British Indian troops who had withdrawn from British Borneo in December. On return trips they evacuated 45 European women and children, dependents of KNIL personnel. It is interesting to note that Dutch policy apparently did not include the evacuation of families of their Indonesian troops.[19]

On the other side of the archipelago, GVT.3(NEW) loaned several flight crews and aircraft to GVT.2(NEW) at Tandjoeng Priok between February 13 and 19 as the latter was short of personnel. From there, they flew reconnaissance patrols over the South China Sea and Java Sea in conjunction with 205 Squadron PBYs, which were now conducting limited flight operations from Oosthaven on the southern tip of Sumatra following their withdrawal from NAS Seletar at the end of January.

SOUTHERN SUMATRA FALLS

The Japanese had been making regular reconnaissance flights over Banka Island and the city of Palembang on southern Sumatra since the first week of February. They had also increased the frequency and intensity of their air attacks on Palembang's main airfield and Allied convoys reaching and departing that city. Convoys leaving and entering the East Indies through the northern Soenda Strait were also targeted on a regular basis.

This activity was clearly in support of an invasion convoy that reconnaissance aircraft from Palembang had reported to be concentrating near the Anambas and Natoena Islands. Air reports on February 6 put its strength at one cruiser, four destroyers and four transports.[20] At the same time, a Japanese airborne division was reportedly poised for action at Camranh Bay.[21] With Malaya in the bag and British forces in Singapore on the verge of surrender, the Japanese were ready to begin the isolation of western Java with the occupation of Banka and southern Sumatra.

In response to this build-up, General Wavell urgently requested that General Hein ter Poorten, the KNIL commander-in-chief, reinforce Palembang, Banka and Billiton, two small islands off the coast of Sumatra. Billiton's primary importance lay in the large number of tin mines on the island, while Banka contained an excellent harbor that could be used for further naval operations against Java. General ter Poorten addressed Wavell's concerns by sending the 9th Infantry Battalion to the two islands aboard two transports escorted by *Java*. The operation was carried out on February 5 under cover of a strong covering force of British and Australian warships. Although attacked by Japanese bombers, none from the latter force suffered any damage.

On February 9 an advance force sailed from Camrahn Bay carrying elements of the 38th Infantry Division, who had orders to seize Banka Island. The light cruiser *Sendai*, 20th Destroyer Division (with the destroyer *Fubuki* attached), two sub chasers and the 21st Minesweeper Division escorted its eight transports. They were followed the next day by a covering force of *Ryujo*, the 7th Cruiser Squadron (with the heavy cruiser *Chokai* attached) and the 19th Destroyer Division.

The invasion of Palembang was to be spearheaded by 360 paratroopers of the IJA's Airborne Raiding Regiment, which would seize the city's oilfields and refineries. They would be reinforced by a main body composed of the 229th and 230th Infantry, which left Camrahn Bay on February 11 aboard 13 transports. The light cruiser *Kashii*, frigate *Shimushu*, sub chaser *Ch.9* and four destroyers from the 11th and 12th Destroyer Divisions escorted them. Both convoys were preceded by submarines of the 4th Submarine

Division, which had orders to operate against ships evacuating Singapore and any ABDA warships attempting to interdict the Sumatra and Banka operations from Tandjoeng Priok.

The British Catalina FV-Y/Y-52 sighted the Banka convoy on February 12 and reported 12 transports escorted by nine destroyers 20 to 25 miles off the coast of Sumatra. Although the pilot attacked out of low clouds, he immediately encountered heavy AA fire from the escorts but claimed a number of near misses before turning away. ABDA Headquarters correctly assumed that this convoy carried troops for the invasion of either Banka or Palembang. In response, the RAF immediately began preparations for the eventual withdrawal of *Tung Song* to Tandjoeng Priok, and 205 Squadron operations at Oosthaven soon came to an end.

Y-55 of GVT.16 again picked up the convoy at 0735 on the morning of February 13. Her wireless operator reported two cruisers, two destroyers and two transports approximately 60 miles south of Anambas Island on a south-southwest course. Thirty minutes later, the PBY reported another convoy composed of one cruiser, three destroyers and eight transports moving south 20 miles east of the first group. Other reconnaissance planes reported three cruisers, five destroyers and one transport on a westerly course some 60 miles north of Banka at 1530; and at 1630, two destroyers and fourteen transports 100 miles north of Billiton moving south-southwest.[22]

On February 13 the Japanese took Banka. Muntok, the island's primary harbor, then became the primary staging point for invasion convoys moving on southern Sumatra and western Java. To provide the anchorage with air cover, *Kamikawa Maru* and *Sagara Maru* were ordered to detach six "Petes" from their combined complement of sixteen aircraft. They would operate from a temporary seaplane base in Muntok Harbor.[23] ABDA HQ almost immediately received word of their arrival, although they were reported as flying boats. A force of RAF Hurricanes was dispatched from Palembang, but failed to find the seaplanes and returned home empty-handed.[24]

It was now clear that the Japanese intended to seize Palembang. To stop them, Admiral Doorman sortied with his Combined Striking Force at 1600 on the 14th. Bad luck soon struck that night as the Dutch destroyer *Van Ghent* ran aground in the Stolze Strait and was lost; her crew was taken off by *Banckert* and returned to Soerabaja. *De Ruyter* launched a floatplane at dawn that reported the presence of seven cruisers and three destroyers 45 miles north of Banka. However, all were moving northwest at high speed and Doorman was unable to intercept.

In return, the CSF was sighted by a floatplane from *Chokai*, which promptly reported its position. Beginning at 1150 that morning, the Allied ships were subjected to a series of intense air attacks that lasted throughout the day, and the British cruiser *Exeter* had its Walrus seaplane put out of action as it sat on the ship's catapult. Without air cover, Doorman was forced to withdraw his ships out of range of the Japanese bombers. Although none of the ships was hit, several had suffered near misses and all were low on fuel from high-speed maneuvering.

With Doorman's withdrawal, the road to Palembang lay wide open for Admiral Ozawa's invasion force. The invasion kicked off on the morning of the 14th as the Airborne Raiding Regiment gained a foothold on the city's airfield and among many of the oil wells, pumps and refineries. Although the KNIL garrison launched a series of strong counterattacks, it proved unable to dislodge the Japanese forces.

Admiral Ozawa's invasion convoy anchored off the mouth of the Moesi River at 0830 on February 15. All ABDA could do was send out reconnaissance planes to track his movements. One of these planes, Y-62 of GVT.2(NEW), encountered a flight of A5M "Claude" fighters from *Ryujo* as it shadowed the convoy at 0700. The PBY slipped away before they could attack and reported a *Kaga*-class heavy carrier and six destroyers in the vicinity of the Anambas Islands. It also reported being intercepted by German-made Messerschmidt ME-109 fighters, which the Japanese never flew. Clearly MLD recognition skills left much to be desired.

Meanwhile, the Japanese main force quickly moved to relieve the paratroopers, who were still gamely holding out. Despite extremely heavy air attacks from RAF and RAAF units, their ground troops pushed up the Moesi River in barges in an effort to reach the paratroopers.[25] When they reached Palembang on midnight of the 16th, General Wavell ordered southern Sumatra abandoned.

"CONVOY HIT BY BOMBERS"

At this point, ABDA High Command determined that Billiton was untenable and attempted to evacuate the infantry company deployed to the island just two weeks earlier. On February 17, the Dutch destroyer *Van Nes* and KPM passenger ship *Sloet van de Beele* were ordered to execute the operation. Admiral Helfrich had opposed the troop transfer to Billiton from the beginning. He thought the island was too small and isolated to be effectively defended and was now extremely annoyed with having to expend valuable Navy resources to withdraw the troops.[26]

Nonetheless, the evacuation initially went well. The transport embarked the KNIL troops and a large number of European civilians without problems, and both ships then raised anchor and sailed for Java. However, shortly after their departure, a Japanese seaplane from the heavy cruiser *Mogami* sighted them and signaled, "Large Merchant Ship and Destroyer Sailing Southward of the Gaspar Straits." In response, 15 G3M "Nells" of the Genzan Bomber Wing and 10 B5N "Kate" level bombers from *Ryujo* were immediately dispatched and quickly found *Van Nes* and *Sloet van de Beele* sailing alone without air cover.

As the Japanese bombers appeared overhead, the Dutch cruiser *Tromp* and Y-45 picked up a signal from *Van Nes* reading "Convoy Hit by Bombers." Soon after, the PBY received another signal reporting that the destroyer had been "Slightly Damaged." A third signal reported that *Sloet van de Beele* had been lost and that the destroyer was under heavy air attack. There were no more radio transmissions as *Van Nes* was sunk under a hail of bombs at 1615.

On the 17th, X-17 and X-18 sighted a Japanese destroyer in the Banka Strait off Tandjoeng Lelari. Although both Dorniers made a number of bomb runs on the ship, the squadron commander, Lieutenant-Commander W. van Prooijen, was confused by the actions of the ship and refused to let them drop any bombs. He initially believed that the destroyer might be Allied because it held a steady course and speed, even when the seaplanes threatened to attack.

However, when Van Prooijen went down for a closer look, a barrage of AA fire lightly damaged X-17. At that point, still unsure of the ship's nationality, he withdrew without attacking. One possibility for the destroyer's erratic behavior was the fact that the Banka Strait offered such little maneuvering room. Her captain might have concluded that the risk of damage from the two seaplanes was smaller than trying to evade their bombs in such a confined area.

By the morning of February 19, KM HQ in Soerabaja had not received a transmission from *Van Nes* since the previous afternoon. Harboring no illusions as to her fate, Dutch naval authorities issued a position report and ordered all available Allied air and naval units to initiate search-and-rescue efforts. Within hours, X-28 of GVT.6 sighted the first group of survivors while on a reconnaissance patrol out of Morokrembangan. Setting down on the water, it rescued 21 men from *Sloet van de Beele* and flew them to the ME.

The Dutch auxiliary minesweeper *Djombang* rescued another 38 survivors from the transport several hours later and returned them to Tandjoeng Priok. In the meantime, the KM commander at Tandjoeng Priok asked the Royal Navy for assistance. In response, the Australian sloop *Yarra* departed the harbor on February 20. A lifeboat filled with survivors had been sighted in the same general area previously swept by *Djombang* and the Australian ship turned toward it.

However, X-16 of GVT.8 sighted the sloop and rescued its survivors while the Australian ship was still 25 miles off. The Dornier crew also sighted a second lifeboat and several individual rafts later that day. Despite his plane being damaged and long past its scheduled 200-hour overhaul, the pilot again demonstrated the rugged construction of the Do. 24 by rescuing two officers and 35 crewmen from *Van Nes* and another 37 men and one nurse from *Sloet van de Beele* in three flights. X-18 rescued 34 more survivors from the transport later that day.

But as impressive as X-16 might have been considering its condition, the grand prize went to 2nd Lieutenant H. Dorré (KMR) flying GVT.18's Y-45 on February 21. The PBY left MVK Priok that morning and sighted a lifeboat approximately 100 miles off the coast of Java. Upon landing, the seaplane's flight crew found it to contain 27 survivors from *Sloet van de Beele*, whom they promptly returned to Tandjoeng Priok. During the return flight, the survivors told of being in contact for a short time with a sloop loaded with 80 survivors.

Upon landing, Dorré immediately made plans to go back out in search of the lifeboat. X-18 was supposed to accompany him but was still refueling when air raid klaxons sounded the approach of Japanese planes, so Y-45 hastily took off alone. Although the PBY searched for hours in the same area where the first boat had been found, the crew sighted nothing. As evening came on, Dorré was low on fuel and about to turn for home when a crewman sighted a speck on the water in the falling dusk — the missing lifeboat!

Upon landing, Dorré found 79 men commanded by Billiton Island's head civilian official. He reported that they had been in the boat for four days without food or water, other than a few cans of condensed milk. Dorré conferred with a crewman and they concluded that the condition of the men was too poor to leave any in the boat, and that it was also too dangerous to await the arrival of X-18. As a result, he decided to take all 79 men aboard, although they would put the PBY a full two tons over its maximum flight weight.

Despite nearly ramming the stationary lifeboat in the process, Dorré managed to eventually lift Y-45 off the water in what surely ranks as one of the longest take-offs on record for a PBY. As he cleared the water, X-18 belatedly arrived overhead and could only watch as the Catalina turned for home. Upon their arrival at Tandjoeng Priok, Dorré and his crew received a hero's welcome. But more important to the crewmen, they received a 24-hour pass.

Meanwhile, X-18's trip was not wasted, as its crew almost immediately sighted a large circle of survivors floating in the water a short distance away. Upon landing, the X-boat rescued another 52 crewmen from *Van Nes* and returned them to Tandjoeng Priok as well. Under the command of the destroyer's first officer, Lieutenant-Commander B.C. Fock, these men had spent 92 grueling hours in the water without food or water.

Based on X-18's position report, the Royal Navy ordered 205 Squadron to dispatch one of its PBYs from Tandjoeng Priok. This operation resulted in the rescue of another 11 survivors from *Sloet van de Beele*. However, the physical condition of these men was so poor that all died shortly after their return to Java. This proved to be the last mission flown by the squadron from Tandjoeng Priok and the last of its operational PBYs soon departed for Tjilatjap.

As the MLD's rescue operation wound down, controversy erupted over the KM's handling of the rescue effort. It was believed that many more lives could have been saved had KM HQ initiated a rescue effort sooner. Many believed that even a few hours would have saved hundreds more lives before the currents dispersed them. At least one group of survivors reportedly landed on a small island in the Java Sea and starved to death when they were unable to attract the attention of passing planes.

The number of survivors pulled out of the water totaled 358, although a number of others died of injuries afterward. It is unknown how many passengers and crew were aboard *Sloet van de Beele*, although the number 1,058 has been given.[27] In addition to 400 KNIL troops, she reportedly took on large numbers of European civilians as the entire island was being evacuated. However, only 272 of her passengers and crew were rescued. From *Van Nes*, a total of 86 survivors were pulled from the ocean with another 68 being lost in the attack or succumbing at sea.[28]

Most of the MLD planes that rescued survivors of *Van Nes* and *Sloet van de Beele* were returning from minelaying missions over Sumatra. The Allied retreat from Palembang started a frenzied minelaying operation between February 22 and 24 by the planes of GVT.16 (Y-51, Y-56, Y-57); GVT.18 (Y-45, Y-47) and X-17 of GVT.8 in the mouth of the Moesi River and in the Banka Strait. Flying out of Tandjoeng Priok, the Dutch seaplanes laid magnetic mines[29] in nonstop air operations to deny the Japanese free access to these vital arteries.

On the evening of February 23, Y-47 was lost on one of these minelaying flights. While landing at Tandjoeng Priok, the Catalina crashed into the water and exploded in flames, killing five of its seven crewmen. Exactly what caused the PBY to crash is unknown, although heavy fog combined with pilot exhaustion was strongly suspected as most MLD pilots and aircrew were spending 16 to 18 hours a day in the air for days at a time without a break. A persistent fog that constantly hung over the base was also thought to be a contributing factor.[30]

By this time in the campaign, exhaustion among Dutch flight crews was common. In mid-February, MLD Chief Medical Officer Lieutenant-Commander P.C. Broekhoff reported to the KM chief-of-staff that the flight crews were suffering from severe physical and mental exhaustion brought on by long hours of flying and constant withdrawals. He regarded the situation as being critical and strongly urged more rest for the crews. In response, the chief-of-staff promised to try to provide longer rest periods if operations permitted.[31]

Broekhoff would later write that the MLD squadron commanders had become convinced that extended night operations without proper rest were useless. This was because where a seaman aboard a surface ship might stand watch for maximum of one hour, air crews were doing the same thing for up to 12 hours at a time. The interrupted monotony of nothing but ocean and seascape made them unable to effectively perform their tasks. Medics aboard the aircraft were also seeing an increase in visual problems among crewmen. But while annoying and sometimes frightening, the symptoms usually disappeared with rest.[32]

But despite the chief-of-staff's best intention, there was simply no way to rotate the squadrons out of the line for longer periods of rest. The manpower shortage faced by all branches of the KM also applied to the MLD, which, as the reader has already seen, was obliged to relinquish control of no fewer than eight of its new PBYs to the British and Americans as it had no crews to man them. And although flight times became somewhat shorter as the Dutch were pushed back toward Java, there was little or no respite as this allowed the Japanese to intensify their air campaign and put even greater pressure on the surviving flight crews.[33]

On February 18, another of the single-engine Fokker reconnaissance planes went missing during an air raid on Soerabaja. The famed Japanese fighter ace Saburo Sakai, flying with the elite Tainan Air Wing, caught W-12 (flying off the cruiser *De Ruyter*) over Maospati, Java, while the floatplane was on patrol along the north coast of Java. Sakai broke formation just long enough to shoot down the hapless plane in flames, giving the ace his 12th kill of the war.[34]

Although the pilot of W-12 had a parachute, his observer did not. So when the pilot bailed out, he went over the side with his crewman hanging on to his belt. Unfortunately, the force of the parachute opening caused the observer to lose his grip and fall to his death. The pilot safely reached the ground.

On the 19th, JAAF units struck Western Java for the first time using their newly captured airfields on southern Sumatra. Escorted by 19 Ki-43 "Oscars" from the 59th and 64th Fighter Groups, five Ki-48 "Lillys" of the 84th Bomber Group attacked Semplak Airfield at 0930. Eight ML B-339s intercepted over the airdrome, but the "Oscars" easily kept the badly outnumbered Dutch fighters away from the bombers. Although a totally different design, the "Oscar" was nearly equal in performance to IJN's "Zero" in virtually every respect, except range and armament, where the Army fighter was substantially inferior. Despite their claims of two fighters shot down, the Buffaloes were completely outclassed; unable to compete in the brief, one-sided dogfight, they had four planes shot down and a fifth was forced to crash-land.[35]

Unhindered in the air, the "Lillys" took their time and destroyed nine Allied planes and one of the airfield's pristine wooden hangars. Among the losses were a Grumman G.21 "Goose" and two Sikorsky S-43 flying boats operated by KNILM. An elderly tri-motor Fokker F.XIII belonging to the airline was also destroyed, as was one of the ML's Ryan STM primary trainers. Four RAAF Hudson bombers were also lost; to top off the raid, fragments from one of the bombers totaled a Sikorsky seaplane when it blew up.[36]

EVACUATION OF THE
FLIGHT TRAINING SCHOOL

The 19th was a busy day for the MLD, which shut down its flight training school and evacuated its planes and personnel to Australia so that training could continue out of range of Japanese air strikes. The aircraft evacuated included Y-49, which had been attached to GVT.3(NEW) and five of the older reserve Dorniers (X-5, X-7, X-8, X-9 and X-10). They never returned to Java and Y-49 later flew with surviving MLD forces following the fall of Java in early March.

The Dorniers were among the oldest in the MLD's Do. 24 fleet, having been delivered to the East Indies between 1938 and 1939. Well beyond their operational prime before the outbreak of war, they had been assigned to the flight training school. In addition, years of constant flight had worn them out to the extent that they were now extremely difficult to maintain in the face of heavy air attack. When the Dutch later moved all flight training operations to the United Sates in April 1942, the five X-boats were sold to the RAAF for continued use in training and supply roles. Finally, with no more spare parts available, the last plane was eventually scrapped in 1943.

The subject of transferring Dutch flight training to Australia had first been raised during the initial ABDA Conference on January 10. There the ML's chief-of-staff, Colonel E.T. Kengen, took up the matter with his RAAF counterpart, Air Vice Marshal Sir Charles Burnet. Following a brief flurry of telegraphs between the East Indies and Australian governments, the ML dispatched Major M. van Haselen and 2nd Lieutenant H.L.A. van der Kroef to Australia on February 1 to make the necessary preparations. According to the agreement, Australia would provide airfields, training aircraft and any additional instructors that were needed.

On February 10, the KM liaison officer in Australia, Commander G.B. Salm, signaled Admiral Helfrich and ter Poorten that the Australian government had consented to the request. Based on this agreement, both the MLD and ML initiated steps to shut down all flight training operations on Java as soon as possible. Eight days later, the 14,000-ton KPM ship MS *Boissevain* departed Tandjoeng Priok carrying 300 ML cadets and VVC and sport club trainees from the airfields at Kalidjati and Tasikmalaja, respectively. She carried no aircraft.

Boissevain was followed the next day by the 9,000-ton motorship *Tjinegara* of the Java-China-Japan Line. The latter transported 232 cadets and 34 Ryan STM primary trainers from the MLD flight school.[37] Most of the flight-school instructors were flown out aboard Y-49 and the Dorniers.

The MS *Abbekerk* and MS *Zaandam* followed them, departing from Tjilatjap on February 27 and March 1, respectively, with more than 300 MLD and ML cadets. These included a large number of observer and bombardier trainees from the ML, in addition to the remaining MLD cadets being trained as radio operators and air gunners. Despite a severe shortage of supplies aboard *Abbekerk* and the constant threat of Japanese submarines that now operated in force south of Java, both ships safely made Australia without problem.

Upon arrival in Melbourne, the cadets were assigned to different locations depending on the level and stage of their training. Those aboard *Boissevain* and *Tjinegara* were assigned to the airfield at Malalla. Those flight trainees with basic training only were ordered to the Parafield Airfield. Remaining MLD personnel were assigned to Naval Air Station HMAS Rathmines on the east coast of Australia, where they completed their operational training on the Dorniers and PBYs. Those ML cadets with no previous flight training were held at Melbourne.

Although free from the Japanese air raids sweeping across Java, the MLD and ML quickly ran into other obstacles that hindered their ability to conduct flight training. These included a crippling shortage of aviation fuel caused in part by the expansion of the RAAF and the rapid arrival of large numbers of American planes, which put space on Australia's limited number of airfields at a premium.[38]

At the same time, the poor condition of the RAAF's training aircraft, coupled with the absence of additional aircraft on order from the United States, further slowed the process. Finally, with the East Indies on the verge of collapse, no one — Australian, Dutch or American — was sure of Australia's ability to defend itself against Japanese invasion. With these factors in mind, the Dutch made further plans to move their flight training operations to another location at the earliest possible convenience.[39]

The next logical choice was to move the operation to India, where the MLD could draw on the facilities and logistical support of the Royal Navy. However, training facilities for the ML would be severely limited, and the Dutch wished to consolidate their remaining resources. Curaçao in the Netherlands West Indies was then considered. But the island, although sheltered from attack, faced a fuel shortage and possessed limited facilities that could accommodate the sudden influx of nearly 600 flight trainees.[40]

Thus, the decision was made to move flight training to the United States. Although halfway around the world, the United States offered ample fuel stocks, safe training grounds and perhaps above all, convenient access to additional aircraft that were needed to ramp up flight training. The Dutch government-in-exile formally requested the cooperation of the United States on March 17, 1942, which Army Chief-of-Staff General George C. Marshall promptly provided. Armed with this guarantee, the entire Dutch contingent boarded the 20,000-ton steamer *Mariposa* at Melbourne and departed for San Francisco on April 20.

As the MLD began the first phase of its evacuation from Java, 205 Squadron also began to quietly set the stage for its own evacuation of Java. On February 16, the FV-V, FV-R and FV-W/Y-54 were ordered to Tjilatjap; they were followed by FV-N on the 17th. FV-U/Y-53 was also supposed to fly in on the 18th but was unserviceable after damaging a float while landing at Tandjoeng Priok in late January. FV-R was ordered to proceed to Columbo on the 18th. The squadron had been on Java for only three weeks and was already making plans to evacuate the island.

By late afternoon of February 21, the Catalinas of 205 Squadron were already operating from Tjilatjap. One of these, FV-V was returning from an anti-submarine patrol when its pilot flew low over the American heavy cruiser USS *Houston*, which had just entered the harbor. Unfortunately, Dutch AA gunners mistook the PBY for a Japanese seaplane attacking the cruiser and opened fire. The blasts blew a hole in the plane's port wing and the pilot was forced to jettison his depth charges at low altitude in order to attempt an emergency landing. However, the subsequent explosions further damaged the PBY so badly that it was written off upon landing.

Despite regular A/S patrols by GVT.5(NEW) and 205 Squadron aircraft operating out of Tjilatjap, Japanese submarines continued to inflict losses on Dutch merchant ships in the Indian Ocean. On February 18 and 19, MLD aircraft reported attacking two Japanese submarines. Y-71 spotted what was thought to be a submerged submarine and dropped depth charges but could not observe the results. Although Japanese submarines were operating south of Tjilatjap, their claims cannot be verified, and it is possible that over-anxious flight crew attacked whales, which was not an uncommon occurrence for flying boats of all countries on A/S flights.

On February 22, Y-71 of GVT.5(NEW) escorted the KPM merchant ship MS *Pijnacker Hordijk* into the Indian Ocean. The initial leg of the mission went well with no enemy contact. However, as night fell, the seaplanes were forced to turn for home, leaving *Pijnacker Hordijk* on her own; 90 minutes after their departure, the *I-58* sank her. In response to her SOS, the merchant ship *Rengat* rescued 50 of her crew and later transferred them to the GM auxiliary vessel *Zuiderkruis*.

8

February, Part II: The Dutch Crumble

THE LOSS OF BALI AND TIMOR

As Admiral Doorman returned from the Banka Strait on February 14, an MLD reconnaissance plane sighted seven transports escorted by three cruisers and seven destroyers assembled off Kendari. Three days later, another MLD plane reported that three transports escorted by two cruisers and two destroyers had left Kendari and were now some 50 miles south of Ambon. At this point, ABDA was unsure of their destination but believed that it was an invasion force bound for either Bali or Timor. But until the convoy's true destination was ascertained, neither ABDA-FLOAT nor Admiral Doorman was willing to put to sea.

At 0910 on the 18th, four cruisers and two unidentified ships were sighted 140 miles south of Makassar. Air reconnaissance picked them up again at 1500 that afternoon 60 miles northeast of Bali. By now, they held a course for Bali, and the Allies began making plans to contest their pending invasion. However, Admiral Doorman was having difficulty concentrating his ships after the action in the Banka Strait and was unable to act in a timely fashion.

Although reported multiple times, the sightings were actually one convoy that had left Makassar on February 17 with two transports escorted by the 8th Destroyer Division. Aboard the transports was the 3rd Infantry Battalion (less one company) and supporting units from the 48th Infantry Division's 1st Formosa Regiment. Trailing behind in distant cover were the light cruiser *Nagara* and the 23rd Destroyer Division. The covering force remained in the Banda Sea while the invasion convoy entered the Bandoeng Strait and landed its troops early on February 19.[1]

Despite heavy air attacks all throughout the 19th and a strong Allied naval counterattack on the night of February 19–20, the Japanese had control of Bali and its airfield by that morning. The local Balinese Defense Corp quickly deserted, leaving the few Dutch regulars on the island little option but to withdraw across the two-mile-wide Bali Strait to eastern Java. The invasion of Bali had originally not been in Japanese plans, but Kendari's airfield was often closed by bad weather, preventing them from hitting Soerabaja on a regular basis. Thus, Bali was needed to maintain their aerial assault on Java's defenses.

On the same day the Bali convoy left Makassar, the seaplane tender *Mizuho* sailed from Kendari with a lone submarine chaser as escort to reconnoiter the area around Timor and establish an air presence. Later that day, nine transports sailed from Ambon carrying the 228th Infantry Regiment and 3rd Yokosuka Special Air Landing Force, which

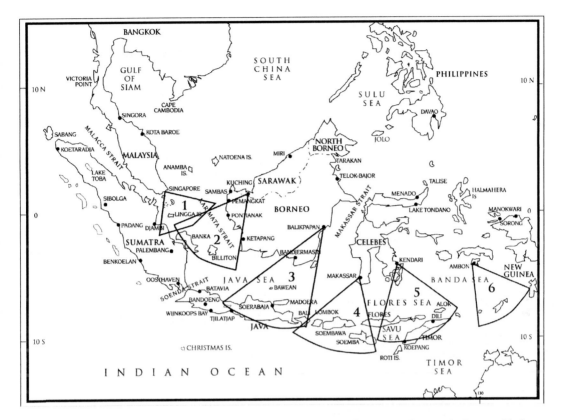

Japanese Air Superiority February 25, 1942. Legend: (1) Sphere of Japanese air superiority provided by JNAF units operating from Singapore. (2) Sphere of Japanese air superiority provided by IJN units operating from Kuching. (3) Sphere of Japanese air superiority provided by IJN units operating from Balikpapan and Bandjermasin. (4) Sphere of Japanese air superiority provided by JNAF units operating from Makassar. (5) Sphere of Japanese air superiority provided by IJN units operating from Kendari. (6) Sphere of Japanese air superiority provided by IJN units operating from Ambon.

had orders to seize the island with the goal of cutting air reinforcement from Australia to Java. Their close escort consisted of the cruiser Jintsu with the 15th and 16th Destroyer Divisions and *Umikaze* from the 24th Destroyer Division.

On the 18th five more transports also departed Ambon for Timor. They had a close escort of the 1st/24th Destroyer Division, two minesweepers, three fast transports and three sub chasers. Rear Admiral Takagi's 5th Cruiser Squadron and two destroyers screened the operation from the Timor Sea. The Japanese went ashore at Koepang and Dili on February 20 and effectively had the island under their control by the 24th. A combined Australian/Dutch guerrilla force held out in the interior until mid-1943 but had no impact on the pending invasion of Java.

The Japanese preceded their invasion of Timor with a heavy air raid on the northern Australian port of Darwin on February 19. The attack was carried out by Vice-Admiral Choichi Nagumo's 1st Carrier Fleet, which consisted of the 1st Carrier Squadron (*Akagi* and *Kaga*) and the 2nd Carrier Squadron (*Hiryu* and *Soryu*). Although the 3rd Carrier Squadron (*Shokaku* and *Zuikaku*) had returned to Japan in late January, Nagumo's force was still essentially the same one that had attacked Pearl Harbor on December 7.

The force had departed Palau on February 15 with orders to attack Darwin. The raid would serve two functions. The first was to support the invasion of Timor that was due to begin on the 20th. The second was to interdict the flow of supplies to Java from Darwin, which had by now developed into ABDA's main supply base outside the East Indies.

Akagi and *Kaga* had just returned to Palau from Truk, while *Hiryu* and *Soryu* were fresh off supporting the invasion operation at Ambon. They were screened by the 1st/3rd Battleship Squadron, 8th Cruiser Squadron and light cruiser *Abukuma* with her 1st Destroyer Flotilla (with the destroyer *Akigumo* attached).

Nagumo put into Kendari on the 17th and made a high-speed run across the Banda Sea the following night. By dawn of the 19th, his strike force was in position in the Timor Sea to attack Darwin. The four carriers launched 188 planes—36 fighters, 71 dive-bombers and 81 level bombers—that formed the first wave of the attack. Fifty-four JAAF Ki-21 "Sally" bombers from Ambon and Kendari would form a second wave that would concentrate on the port's facilities and airfield.

Eight ships were sunk in the attack, and three were saved only through beaching; 10 others were damaged. On the ground the Japanese destroyed virtually every Allied plane at Darwin. The USAAF lost 11 P-40s from the 33rd Pursuit Squadron, one LB-30 and three USAAF Beechcraft biplanes, while the RAAF lost six Hudsons with another and a Wirraway damaged.

En route to Darwin, nine Zeros also shot down the PatWing 10 PBY 22-P-9, which made a crash landing in the ocean near Melville Island. When the Japanese arrived over the harbor, they found the PatWing 10 Catalinas P-4, P-8 and P-41 (the former MLD Y-41) lying quietly at anchor undergoing maintenance. Almost before their crews knew what had hit them, three Zeros from *Hiryu* set all of the PBYs ablaze. The tender *Preston* lay nearby and also came under attack but was able to clear the harbor despite being badly damaged by a dive-bomber.

Combined with the Darwin raid, the loss of Bali and Timor effectively closed the eastern half of the Netherlands East Indies to the MLD and PatWing 10. Although both units continued to periodically fly operations in the area, they were now extremely vulnerable to Japanese fighters that seemed to roam every corner of the area. At the same time, the Japanese now had a suitable air base just two miles off the eastern shore of Java, which allowed them to further intensify their air strikes on Morokrembangan, although very few Allied seaplanes were still operating from there.

On February 25 X-21 went missing while on a reconnaissance and minelaying mission over Bali and the Lombok Strait. Despite repeated radio calls throughout the day, it did not answer and never returned. Only after the war was it learned that a Zero of the Tainan Air Wing had scrambled from Bali's Den Passar Airfield and shot down the X-boat with no survivors.[2] X-21 was the fourth plane lost in two days, and the toll was to go still higher.

Losses for the MLD began to mount at an alarming rate. With the Japanese now on the doorstep of Java, the remaining Dorniers and Catalinas had few places left to hide, and barely a day passed without MLD planes seeing action of some kind. To make matters worse, their own AA guns also frequently fired on them. In an effort to remedy the problem, all Dutch planes painted over their traditional orange triangle national markings and replaced them with a red, white and blue square to avoid confusion with the red circle indicative of Japanese aircraft.

"Plane #42 Did Not Return to Base and Is Presumed Lost"[3]

On February 24, P-42 (MLD Y-42) went missing on a reconnaissance patrol over Makassar. The plane initially arrived over the harbor just before dawn, where the crew reported three transports and a submarine before turning for home. However, 45 minutes later the PBY was ordered to turn around and bomb the transports, despite the fact that it would put the plane over its target in daylight.

Japanese fighters intercepted the seaplane long before it ever reached the harbor. Just after dawn, she signaled *"Am Being Attacked Fighters."*[4] But by dodging in and out of the clouds, P-42 was able to avoid them and make a bomb run in which her pilot claimed one hit and one near miss before diving back into the clouds to continue the northward swing of his patrol. Unfortunately though, this would very shortly lead to the PBY's demise.

Approximately two hours later the Catalina was again intercepted by Japanese fighters; P-42's radioman sent an urgent message in the clear: *"Am Being Attacked by Aircraft. North Many Planes and Fleet."*[5] The PBY had stumbled across the Japanese invasion convoy bound for Eastern Java and was now about to pay a steep price for doing so. Unable to evade the enemy this time, the PBY disappeared without a trace or another radio signal, leading Captain Wagner to post the above melancholy report in PatWing 10's war diary.

By the last week of February, seaplane fighters from *Sanyo Maru* and *Sanuki Maru* were operating at will over both the South China and Java seas. Their operational area covered a huge swath of territory, stretching from the Anambas Islands to Soerabaja. As land bases become available in southern Sumatra and Borneo, they were reinforced by Japanese Army and Navy land fighters, which further restricted the ability of the Allied flying boats to effectively operate.

This fact was driven home yet again on the 24th when X-17 and X-18 of GVT.8 bombed a concentration of Japanese warships and transports assembled off Muntok Island. Despite bombing through heavy cloud cover and taking heavy flak, they claimed one hit on a transport. On the way out, three Zeros of the 22nd Air Flotilla — which had reached the island's airfield the previous day — intercepted the Dorniers near North Wachten Island in the Thousand Islands chain.

X-17 went down in flames almost immediately with no survivors.[6] The seaplane's overturned hull was later photographed by Y-64. The fighters then hammered X-18 until it too broke into flames and made a forced-landing on the sea and sank. Although the entire crew survived, it was forced into the water without lifeboats. Fortunately, the Japanese left them alone, and they were able to swim ashore near the lighthouse on North Wachten Island. They were rescued by the auxiliary minesweeper Hr.Ms. *Djombang* and returned to the ME the following day.

The Japanese further reinforced their point with an aggressive air attack on Y-48 of GVT.18 later that day. The PBY was on convoy escort duty off the coast of Sumatra when attacked by Japanese aircraft and badly damaged. Although 1st Lieutenant KMR P.D.M.A. Biljard managed to bring his crippled aircraft back to Tandjoeng Priok, the plane was so badly damaged that it would never fly again.[7]

Following the loss of Banka and southern Sumatra, the Dutch were determined to limit Japanese naval traffic moving through the area. On the night of February 24–25, Lieutenant-Commander G.F. Rijnders received orders to take the Catalina Y-69 out on a minelaying mission to the Banka Strait. Carrying two unwieldy magnetic mines on improvised racks under each wing, the PBY proved extremely difficult to fly; the mission was not made any easier when the Y-boat ran into high winds and heavy rainstorms shortly after taking off from Tandjoeng Priok.

However, the flight crew very quickly forgot about the high winds because the mines it carried were prevented from arming only by a large ball of cotton that was intended to dissolve in seawater. As they plowed through the driving rain, the plane's crew prayed that the cotton would not prematurely dissolve and detonate the mines.[8] Fortunately, they did not, and Y-69 dropped all of its mines in the Banka Strait and returned home without incident. The Dutch later claimed that these mines damaged two Japanese ships, but this is unconfirmed.

Meanwhile, JAAF planes from southern Sumatra continued to attack targets throughout western Java. On the 25th, 26 "Oscar" and "Nate" fighters escorted 15 Ki-48 "Lily" bombers on a raid to Tandjoeng Priok. They caught Y-62 of GVT.2(NEW) on the water at the seaplane base and splintered it badly, although ground crews were able to quickly repair the damage. The Japanese claimed five other planes damaged that day, but none was from the MLD.

THE LOSS OF Y-63

The Japanese continued to solidify their air supremacy over the Western Java Sea as they made plans for the invasion of Java. Y-63 of GVT.2(NEW) was the next MLD plane lost as the Japanese tightened their grip. It left Tandjoeng Priok at 2100 hours on the 26th for a night reconnaissance patrol over Banka Island and the Banka Strait. The orders were to search out an invasion force thought to be approaching Java.

By 2300 Y-63 was south of Banka, where it reported a large number of enemy warships and transports. Turning north, the PBY continued up the strait. At 0300 on the 27th, Y-63 was over Muntok harbor, where its radio operator reported flying over a large concentration of Japanese ships at an altitude of 1,000 feet at a range of two miles. This was the last contact, although two naval radio stations on Java tried to raise the plane for several hours afterwards.[9] It would not be until after the war ended that the KM and MLD would learn of the plane's fate from its pilot following his release from a Japanese prison camp.

By daybreak, Y-63 was over the southern entrance of the Banka Strait. The pilot, 1st Lieutenant W.P.A. Ditmar, had two choices—1) return to base without orders to avoid Japanese fighters or 2) stay in the area and undoubtedly meet the enemy. He chose the latter and decided to remain in the area until 0630. Seeing nothing, the plane remained on its patrol route until 0640, when the PBY turned south for Tandjoeng Priok.

Ditmar tried to avoid enemy fighters by flying under the clouds at 1,300 feet. However, a patrol of six "Nates" from the JAAF's 12th Flying Battalion suddenly appeared out of the clouds in two tight formations of three planes each and bounced the PBY. Raking the seaplane, the fighters roared past. As they came around for a second pass, the radio operator gunner recovered and put a long burst into one of the "Nates," which immediately trailed black smoke and dove into the sea. Both waist gunners and the plane's NCO pilot claimed to have seen the plane crash.

At the same time, the starboard waist gunner hit a second fighter several times. It disappeared into a rain cloud and was not seen again. However, the four remaining "Nates" now attacked with a vengeance. Y-63 tried to hide in a nearby rain cloud, but it was too small and did not last long. The Japanese soon found the PBY, which was flying low to the water in a desperate bid to escape.

Attacking from behind, the fighters then proceeded to saw the flying boat out of the air. The copilot was hit in the head and fell onto the controls, sending the plane diving toward the water.[10] Ditmar managed with difficulty to regain control, only to find the starboard aileron completely gone and the fuel tanks shredded, forcing a crash-landing on the water in Force 3 conditions without power. Touching down, the PBY bounced high into the air before slamming into the water.

Y-63 sank in about seven minutes, giving the crew barely enough time to pile into a badly holed rubber raft with the wounded pilot. Luckily, the Japanese were not in a vindictive mood and did not strafe the men in the water as they circled the sinking PBY. After 22 hours in the punctured dinghy (which the wounded pilot plugged with his fingers to keep it inflated), the crewmen landed on North Gebroeders Island, where the exhausted men slept on the beach.

The next morning a Japanese reconnaissance plane flew over but failed to see them. The men now attempted to find food and plug the raft, but both efforts failed. They then tried to shoot a large gorilla but missed. They finally resorted to eating snails. Meanwhile, others searching the island found an abandoned motorboat with some water aboard. Although the propeller was damaged, they got it into the water at high tide and sailed for Sumatra on the 1st.

That night, a heavy rainstorm blew in, soaking the exhausted men, who still had no food or water. With the current against them and only paddles from the rubber raft to move them along, the launch made little progress. They finally reached the coast of Sumatra on the 3rd, where they met two praus that towed them ashore. For 100 guilders they rented a prau to replace the launch that was close to sinking.

On March 3 they reached Ketapang on the southwest coast of Sumatra. Here, they rented another prau to take them down the coast to Soekoer for 50 guilders. From here they would cross the Soenda Strait to Java. The men received a warm welcome from the villagers and were able to rent a prau paddled by four Javanese for 50 guilders.

During a stop at a small island in the Soenda Strait, the Javanese paddlers tried to steal the prau. However, after a short scuffle with the MLD crewmen, the Indonesians disappeared into the jungle. The group then crossed the strait and landed at Anjer, Java, on March 6. There, to their dismay, a local official informed them that the Japanese had landed a week earlier and now controlled most of Java, including the entire western half.

Still hoping to escape, the men left the wounded pilot with the official for medical attention and continued to Batavia. The remaining six crewmen split into two three-man groups and headed for Tjilatjap by separate routes. The first group was surrounded by Indonesians shortly after leaving Anjer and murdered. A short time later, the second group was robbed by local villagers and betrayed to the Japanese, who took them into custody.[11] Sergeant-Pilot van Dijk was cared for in the hospital until being sent to Serang Prison. He would later be killed in 1944 when the transport he was aboard was torpedoed and sunk by an American submarine.

Y-65 AND Y-71 OVER USS *LANGLEY*

The Japanese were now closing in on Java as their air power engulfed the island. This made the need for fighter planes critical, so the USN agreed to dispatch the seaplane tender *Langley* to Java with 32 P-40E fighters. The last leg of *Langley*'s voyage to Tjilatjap was dangerous and open to Japanese air attack from the newly captured Den Passar airfield on Bali, a small yet strategically vital island just two miles off the eastern shore of Java. It was planned that *Langley* would reach Tjilatjap by noon on February 28. Based on this timetable, she would be in the most danger during the morning hours of February 27.

To provide her with A/S protection, the commander of GVT.5(NEW) was ordered to maintain air cover over the tender on the morning of February 26. Beginning at 1300 that afternoon, Y-65 and Y-71 alternately flew A/S patrols during the daylight hours. The first day went well with no Japanese planes or submarines sighted. However, trouble loomed the next day when a long-range reconnaissance plane from Bali spotted *Langley* and her escort, the American destroyers *Whipple* and *Edsall*, while they were still some 100 miles south of Tjilatjap. The ships had hoped to travel this last stretch under the cover of darkness, but a series of conflicting orders concerning the tender's naval escort kept her at sea in a series of critical course reversals.

Initially, her orders called for *Langley* to be escorted into Tjilatjap by the two destroyers. However, when Y-65 and Y-71 appeared overhead, they signaled new orders that they and the Dutch minelayer *Willem van der Zaan* were to provide escort.[12] But when *Langley* rendezvoused with the minelayer, her captain, Commander Robert P. McConnell, discovered that *Willem van der Zaan* could make only 10 knots due to a leaking boiler pipe. This was three knots less than *Langley*'s top speed, and McConnell was unwilling to remain with the limping minelayer.

If forced to stay with the minelayer, McConnell reasoned that *Langley* would lose the cover of darkness, which represented her only protection against air attack. With this in mind, he left *Willem van der Zaan* without orders and proceeded ahead with the intention of joining the destroyers. However, several hours later, he received orders confirming that the minelayer was indeed his escort and that *Langley* was to rejoin her immediately.

Orders changed again as *Willem van der Zaan* came into sight; *Langley* was now to join *Whipple* and *Edsall*. Hours behind schedule, this critical series of delays pushed her time of arrival back from the early morning of February 27 to 1700 hours. In the end, Japanese bombers caught all three American ships in broad daylight on the morning of February 27 while still 75 miles south of Tjilatjap.[13] At 1150 *Whipple* signaled many aircraft approaching from the northeast, and all hands went to battle stations. These were 11th Air Fleet G3M "Nells" from Southern Celebes that had been dispatched on the strength of their reconnaissance plane's report earlier that morning.

As the first wave of Japanese bombers appeared overhead, Y-65 and Y-71 were on the scene providing A/S support. Although alone and unescorted, the Catalinas continued to circle the tender and her escort for the first 35 minutes of the attack. As the bombers punished *Langley*, their wireless operators sent out a stream of updates as the pilots stood by to provide whatever help they could.

Despite the bombers having an escort of 15 Zeros, the Japanese initially left the PBYs alone as they focused on the tender. While three fighters flew cover, the remainder strafed *Langley*'s decks. As the seaplane tender's condition worsened, the Dutch decided that it was time to return to Tjilatjap. But shortly after turning for home, Y-65 and Y-71 were intercepted by six Zeros at 1246 as their bombers left the tender and prepared for the long flight back to Celebes. Although Y-71 was lightly damaged, Y-65 suffered the brunt of the attack. In an unequal fight lasting 34 minutes, the fighters shot out Y-65's starboard engine and blew away an aileron.

In return, one of the Dutch gunners shot down the Zero piloted by NAP 1st Class Toyo-o Sakai, which is confirmed by Japanese records.[14] In his log, *Langley*'s captain reported a running air fight between a large flying boat and many fighters in the distance.[15] There was a huge cloud of black smoke, and an object dove to the sea trailing a long streamer of smoke. Whether this was Sakai's fighter or the damaged PBY running for home is unknown.

This action could also have been the Qantas Airlines Empire "C" flying boat "Corio," which was also attacked by the fighter escort about this time. The unarmed seaplane was one of three Qantas seaplanes under contract to the USAAF making regular supply runs between Broome and Java. On the inbound trip, they brought in supplies to Java and took out evacuees on the flip side. Stumbling onto the plane, Zeros swarmed the flying boat and quickly dispatched it with no survivors.

Y-65 was luckier and staggered home to Tjilatjap. The Japanese claimed they shot it down, but it landed in the harbor at 1420 with extremely heavy damage. It never flew again and was eventually destroyed by GVT.5(NEW) personnel when they abandoned the seaplane base on March 3.

Langley was abandoned early on the afternoon of February 27 with *Whipple* and *Edsall* taking off her survivors. But although a total loss, the tender refused to sink despite being helped along by nine four-inch rounds and two torpedoes from *Whipple*. By now, the destroyers were badly overloaded with survivors and in no condition to withstand another air attack, which was expected at any time. As a result, they departed the scene at 1446, leaving *Langley*'s shattered hulk low in the water and heavily ablaze; she eventually sank unobserved later that day.

THE INVASION OF JAVA

With the loss of Bali, Timor and southern Sumatra, Java's fate was sealed, and all that remained was the agony of a Japanese invasion to put the Allied defense of the East Indies out of its lingering misery. To carry out the invasion of Java and effectively bring the campaign to a close, the Japanese drew up a complex, multi-pronged approach that called for simultaneous landings at four separate locations, including three on Western Java and a fourth on its eastern end. The troops involved in these operations would then converge toward the island's center and force a Dutch surrender.

The Western Invasion Force

The invasion of western Java was assigned to the 2nd Infantry Division, which would land at Merak and Bantam Bay, and the 230th Infantry Regiment, which would land farther east near Eretenwetan. These units departed from Camrahn Bay aboard 56 transports on February 18 with a convoy escort consisting of the 3rd Destroyer Flotilla, 5th Destroyer Flotilla and 1st Base Force. The four heavy cruisers of the 7th Cruiser Squadron provided close escort, while the 16th Cruiser Squadron and two destroyers provided distant cover for the convoy. *Ryujo* provided air cover and A/S support for all elements of the Western Invasion Force.

Reconnaissance aircraft sighted Rear-Admiral Kurita's 7th Cruiser Squadron near Anambas Island on February 23. It reported one *Atago*-class heavy cruiser, two *Mogami*-class heavy cruisers and one *Natori*-class light cruiser with a number of transports and oilers. Kurita had withdrawn to this location on the 21st after Vice-Admiral Takahashi, the invasion convoy commander, requested and received permission to delay the Java operation for two days " . . . because of the fact that there were three large cruisers, five medium cruisers and eight destroyers of the English Fleet in the Java Sea."[16]

The IJA High Command concurred with his request, and the convoy turned north at a position 120 miles southeast of Anambas for approximately 24 hours. Although there was no naval engagement or substantial change in the strength of the Allied fleet, Takahashi turned south again on the 23rd.

The Eastern Invasion Force

The invasion of eastern Java was assigned to the 48th Infantry Division and 56th Regimental Group, which would land at Kragan, a small village approximately 100 miles west of Soerabaja. Once ashore, one of its objectives was to capture Soerabaja, the ME and Morokrembangan. The 48th Division left Jolo on February 19 aboard 41 transports and was almost immediately spotted by a PatWing 10 PBY, which reported 80 to 100 ships. Nonetheless, the convoy put into Balikpapan on or about the 21st and collected the 56th Regiment (minus a garrison detachment). From there, it moved south on February 23 escorted by the 4th Destroyer Flotilla.

The following day, the 2nd Destroyer Flotilla and 5th Cruiser Squadron joined the convoy in the Makassar Strait after steaming at high speed from Timor, where they had covered that operation. A PatWing 10 Catalina sighted this force near Bali on February 24 and took AA fire, but Admiral Doorman was in no position to interdict their movements. Although the flotilla's destroyers joined the convoy's screen, the heavy cruisers assumed a distant covering position some 100 miles behind; they would join the convoy only in the event of trouble from an Allied naval force. At the same time, the omnipresent *Mizuho*, *Sanyo Maru* and *Sanuki Maru* provided air cover and A/S support for the eastern convoy.

Japanese Forces South of Java

As their invasion convoys moved toward Java, the Japanese also took care to ensure that the island could and would not be reinforced or evacuated by sea. Following the Darwin raid, Vice-Admiral Nagumo had taken his carrier force back to Staring Bay to refuel and refit. From there, he again put out to sea on February 25 with orders to enter the Indian Ocean through the Ombai Strait (between Alor and Timor Islands). His force would take up cruising positions approximately 200 miles south of Tjilatjap with orders to sink or capture any warships or merchant vessels trying to slip into or out of Java's southern ports.

Nagumo's force included his four heavy fleet carriers (*Akagi*, *Kaga*, *Soryu* and *Hiryu*), six supply ships, the 1st/3rd Battleship Squadron, 8th Cruiser Squadron and light cruiser *Abukuma* with her 1st Destroyer Flotilla. Admiral Nobutake Kondo provided the carrier force with a distant cover using his 2nd/3rd Battleship Squadron and 4th Cruiser Squadron with a screen of three destroyers.

"WHERE IS THE CONVOY?"

By February 26 the Dutch and their allies fully expected an invasion of Java at any time. The day before, Japanese destroyers had landed a small combat team on Bawean Island, just 85 miles north of Soerabaja. The Netherlands Meteorological Service was the first to learn of the landing when it almost immediately lost contact with a weather forecasting team it had stationed on the island.[17] After securing the island, the Japanese proceeded to set up a radio and weather observation post of their own to help coordinate the upcoming invasion of Java.

About the same time, Dutch codebreakers informed the Dutch High Command to expect an invasion any day. In response to these indicators, the planes of GVT.17—flying from Morokrembangan—were in the air continuously throughout the 26th. One plane searched the Java Sea west of Bawean, while a second flew east of Bawean to the southern entrance of the Makassar Strait.

At 1300 that afternoon ABDA-FLOAT received a garbled message from a then unidentified MLD plane reporting the presence of 30 transports northeast of Bawean Island. They were moving south at 10 knots with a heading of 245°, putting them on a course for East Java. The plane also sent a second signal just after 1500 reporting the sighting of two cruisers and two destroyers halfway between the Paternoster Islands and Sibbalds Bank 20 minutes earlier.[18]

Although the MLD plane had given a clear position and heading, Helfrich assumed that it had been shot down when nothing more was heard from the flying boat. Because of this, he was greatly concerned about the possible presence of an aircraft carrier providing cover for the convoy. If true, it would be extremely dangerous to send out the Allied fleet to stop the invasion fleet without air cover.

However, the exact opposite was true. Not only was there no carrier present, but in reality, the Japanese invasion convoy bound for East Java had little or no air cover for much of the voyage. Although fighters from Balikpapan had been ordered to provide a CAP for the convoy, weather over the Makassar Strait proved inclement, and their efforts to maintain constant air cover proved spotty at best. So bad was the weather that three Zeros from the Tainan Air Wing were lost, although their pilots were eventually able to return to their unit.

This lack of air cover was driven home at 0800 on the 26th when Y-67 dropped out of the clouds and attacked the destroyer *Amatsukaze* with a single bomb that missed by some 500 yards. Evading return fire from the destroyer, the PBY then disappeared back into the murky sky and was not seen again. Although previously attached to GVT.5 at Tjilatjap, Y-67 was now operating from Morokrembangan following repairs to the damage suffered in its collision with Y-65. While there, its pilot was ordered to fly a reconnaissance patrol over the Java Sea, where he sighted the Japanese fleet and sent the garbled report.

Y-67 continued on to the north, where it signaled the presence of 27 transports, three cruisers and six destroyers northeast of the Arends Islands at 4° 50' South, 114° 20' East.[19] Soon afterwards, the PBY reported being attacked near the Arends Islands by two cruiser floatplanes. As a result of damage suffered in this action, Y-67 was forced to return to Morokrembangan, where it landed late that afternoon. Lieutenant-Commander A. Höfelt then commandeered the PBY and ordered it flown to the auxiliary base at Toeloeng Agoeng as the base was no longer considered safe.

Shortly after Y-67's attack, three USAAF A-24 dive bombers, escorted by eight American P-40s and five ML Buffalos, appeared overhead. They had left Ngoro Airfield on eastern Java at 1600 for a strike mission against the convoy. Once again there was no air cover present, allowing the Allied planes to take their time. Attacking in the face of heavy AA fire, they claimed one direct hit on a transport, but the Japanese later stated that it was nothing more than a near miss.

Meanwhile, Japanese fighter cover continued to break down all throughout the day, and it was only the poor aim of Allied bombardiers that saved the convoy from substantial damage. The final air attack of the day came at 1700, when two B-17s from Java dropped six 500-pound bombs on the destroyer *Hatsukaze* without results. Another flight of B-17s then attacked the destroyer *Yukikaze* the following morning, but it too failed to score any hits.

Despite the presence of a Japanese convoy off Bawean, REC-GROUP could put few aircraft into the air to monitor its movements. The heavy air strikes over the previous three weeks had decimated Dutch and American air strength in East Java so that only a handful of long-range reconnaissance aircraft remained at Morokrembangan. The rest had been evacuated to Australia or dispersed to isolated secondary bases. As a result, PatWing 10 had only three operational PBYs on the base.[20]

At the same time, GVT.17 had only two airworthy aircraft available for service. According to Dutch sources, the American planes did not have working radios, which precluded their being sent on a reconnaissance patrol over the Japanese convoy.[21] The Dutch planes were being held back for night-reconnaissance work to avoid fighter cover. With no American or Dutch naval reconnaissance aircraft immediately available, a USAAF B-17 was sent out over the Java Sea with a Dutch observer aboard.[22]

At 2230 on the night of February 26, the naval radio station at the ME received a signal from KNIL HQ in Bandoeng relaying a phone call received from its 3rd Division, which was deployed some 400 miles away in West Java. At 1830, the divisional staff had received a signal from an American B-17 reporting a Japanese invasion convoy northeast of Bawean at 5° 30' South, 113° East. Although four hours old, this report gave Admiral Doorman a relatively recent fix on the location of the Japanese convoy.

But although everyone knew the Japanese meant to invade Java, no one could say exactly where they intended to land with any certainty. As a result, Doorman was forced to continue searching blindly in the dark for the invasion convoy.[23] Leaving the ME on the afternoon of the 26th, he swept east along the north coast of Java and Madoera in the belief the Japanese might be planning an invasion of East Java to occupy the naval base. He then turned west early on the morning of the 27th and swept along the coast toward Rembang and the Bay of Toeban.

Early on the morning of the 27th, Y-45 of GVT.18 took off from Tandjoeng Priok for a reconnaissance flight over the Java Sea. Flying just under the clouds at about 1,000 feet, the pilot sighted a Japanese fighter patrol near Semerang that he managed to evade. As the Catalina crossed over Toeban at 1100, a force of about 20 ships was sighted. Coming closer, the crew identified *De Ruyter, Java* and a number of ABDA cruisers and destroyers of the CSF.

Passing over the Allied force, Y-45 provided the daily recognition code and continued north. Its orders were to search for enemy submarines operating in the area around Bawean. Although the crew sighted no submarines, the PBY soon made multiple contacts with what was obviously the main Japanese invasion force. Y-45 sent out a flurry of contact reports, all of which were received by KM HQ and relayed to Admiral Door-man's flagship.

At 1340, Y-45's wireless operator reported 20 transports escorted by an unknown number of destroyers approximately 65 miles north-northwest of Bawean Island at 4° 40' South, 112° 15' East; they held a course heading of 180°.[24] At 1345 he reported a Japanese cruiser approximately 135 miles northwest of Bawean with a course of 220°.[25] Five min-utes later he reported 25 transports escorted by two cruisers and six destroyers 20 miles west of Bawean.[26] The warships were moving south at high speed while the transports retired to the north.

As these position reports came through, Doorman was returning to Soerabaja to refuel. After the high-speed sweep along the coast of Java the previous night, many of his ships, particularly the destroyers, were running low on fuel.[27] However, upon receipt of Y-45's report at approximately 1430, Doorman signaled the CSF by spotlight: "*Follow Me. The Enemy Is 90 Miles Away.*"[28] He immediately turned his squadron in the middle of the Westwater Channel minefield and set a course to intercept.

Meanwhile, Y-45 remained over the convoy, playing a cat-and-mouse game with sev-eral floatplanes launched by the cruiser escort. It might have also encountered a num-ber of Tainan Air Wing Zeros flying cover from Balikpapan. One of the Japanese pilots claimed an Allied reconnaissance plane shot down on the afternoon of February 27, but no Allied seaplanes went missing.[29]

After one and a half hours of dodging in and out of the clouds, the MLD plane turned to the west and continued its patrol. At 1600, Y-45's radio operator picked up a signal from *De Ruyter*—"*Cruisers in Action.*" The Battle of the Java Sea had begun. Although the seaplane did not land at Tandjoeng Priok until 1700, it picked up no more radio reports from *De Ruyter* or any other Allied ships of the CSF.

On the night of February 27–28, the ABDA fleet engaged the convoy escort near Bawean. In the first major surface battle of the Pacific War, the CSF lost heavily in both men and ships as the last naval barrier to the invasion of Java dissipated. *De Ruyter, Java,* the Dutch destroyer *Kortenaer* and the British destroyers *Electra* and *Jupiter* were all lost. In return, the Japanese suffered heavy damage to one destroyer and light or moderate damage to several other warships. No transports were lost or damaged, and the landings were delayed by only 24 hours.

As the battle raged, MLD planes continued to fly reconnaissance patrols over the Java Sea. One of these patrols again found the invasion convoy approximately 80 miles north of Bawean. Only lightly escorted by a few destroyers, it had turned away from Java while the escort engaged Doorman's fleet. Meanwhile, to the west, other MLD reconnais-sance planes reported that the western invasion convoy sighted earlier had also turned back near the Thousand Islands. With the destruction of the CSF, it again turned toward western Java.

The last sighting of the eastern invasion force came on the night of the 27th. At 1850 one of the last operational PatWing 10 PBYs on Java left the auxiliary base at Toeloeng Agoeng (near Kediri) for a reconnaissance flight over the convoy that had been reported off Bawean. P-5 flew over the CSF at 1955 during a lull in the action and eventually found the enemy convoy northwest of Bawean at 2222. Ensign Duncan Campbell later told how it took him a full eight minutes to fly over the enormous convoy from tip to tail.[30] After signaling the convoy's position, he remained overhead for the next 70 minutes shadow-ing its slow, ponderous movement toward Java.

As P-5 turned for home, the crew sighted a series of sharp flashes in the distance, followed shortly afterwards by several heavy explosions. It then reported seeing two ships leaving the area at high speed. The crew could not have known that it had just witnessed the fiery end of the Battle of the Java Sea, which culminated in crippling torpedo strikes on *Java* at 2332 and *De Ruyter* at 2334.[31] The ships retiring were *Houston* and *Perth*, the last remaining ships of the CSF.

Although sightings from all reconnaissance flights throughout the day were reported to KM HQ and in turn were routed to Admiral Doorman, there are lingering questions as to whether and when he actually received them. Reasons for this lapse in communications are varied. As detailed earlier, the MLD suffered a severe shortage of shore-based communications personnel, and the volume of daily activities put upon them quickly overwhelmed its facilities.

However, the KM war room at Soerabaja remained fully staffed and equipped throughout the East Indies campaign, and that should have precluded any delays in relaying information to the CSF while at sea. And although the confusion of a multinational command initially created a logjam of information early in the campaign, this cannot be blamed entirely for a Dutch communications infrastructure that apparently was not up to the tasks thrust upon it in the Allies' greatest hour of need.

Still, it is known that *De Ruyter* was in regular contact with Soerabaja throughout the Battle of the Java Sea. On several occasions Doorman requested information on the location and status of the main Japanese convoy. But while reconnaissance reports were available, it appears that virtually all of them arrived hours too late to be of much use to Doorman. An example was the position report of P-5, which reached the ME some 20 minutes after Doorman's flagship had been torpedoed and put out of action.

Reasons for these delays vary. The first is that MLD HQ at Morokrembangan, which received the reconnaissance reports over the KM's aircraft frequency, was slow in relaying them to KM HQ. In this case, confusion could have delayed delivery of these reports to the CSF in the Java Sea. However, given the extremely close prewar training between the MLD and KM, this explanation cannot realistically be accepted, especially when one considers the fact that prewar MLD reconnaissance reports reached the surface fleet in just 10 minutes.

It is also possible that the concussion from *De Ruyter*'s own main guns could have knocked her highly sensitive wireless set off-line. In the early days of the war, this was not unusual for ships of all navies. Concussion also broke the flagship's searchlights, leaving her unable to communicate with the other ships in the CSF, except by small, hand-held lamp.

However, faulty communications cannot be blamed entirely, as there seem to have been regular ship-to-shore communications throughout the battle. At 1857, the Dutch submarine *K-XV* picked up the following wireless signal from Doorman to KM HQ on Java: "*Enemy Retreating to the West. Contact Broken. Where Is the Convoy?*"[32] But shortly after this message was sent, TBS communications between *De Ruyter* and the remaining American and Commonwealth ships—which were poor to begin with—failed completely. It is unknown whether the Dutch ships were still able to communicate with *De Ruyter*.

If they could communicate with the flagship by voice, then KM HQ certainly could too. But if *De Ruyter*'s wireless was off-line, Doorman would not have received the latest position reports sent from Java. It is also believed that he did not receive position reports of a new Dutch minefield laid the previous night.[33] As a result, he spent the night of February 27–28 blindly searching for the convoy before losing *De Ruyter* and *Java* in a cataclysmic finale to the Battle of the Java Sea.

At 2300 hours on the night of February 28, Y-67 was ordered to fly a night reconnaissance mission over the Java Sea to locate the invasion convoy that Admiral Doorman had failed to stop. Y-67 found the convoy southwest of Bawean as it moved south at high speed just after midnight on March 1. It was a beautiful moonlit night without a cloud in the sky, allowing Lieutenant-Commander G.F. Rijnders to easily count 39 transports of all types in two huge columns. To avoid AA fire, he approached away from the moon and was able to remain undetected over the convoy for 30 minutes. His radio operator then notified REC-GROUP at Bandoeng, and Y-67 returned home. Shortly before dawn, this convoy landed troops of the 48th Division and 56th Regiment at Kragan on Java's northern shore.

Later that day the Dorniers of GVT.6 flew a series of final missions over the now deceptively serene Java Sea. Despite combing the area around Bawean for survivors of *De Ruyter*, *Java* and *Kortenaer*, all they found was the Dutch hospital ship *Op ten Noort* being escorted to Bandjermasin by the Japanese destroyer *Amatsukaze*. One Dornier had been ordered out of the ME before dawn to search for survivors but was captured near Bawean. After three hours of searching the area around the hospital ship and dodging enemy ships, the plane returned to base.

With that flight, the MLD's role in the defense of the East Indies ended. All that was left to do now was to execute prearranged plans the KM had for evacuating Java. However, the month of March was to have its share of disasters, although the MLD had turned its attention to evacuation and was no longer undertaking offensive actions.

In an ironic twist of fate, planes ordered by the MLD before the war continued to arrive as the Dutch began to evacuate. On the 28th, the Dutch freighter *Kota Baroe* put into Tjilatjap with six crated Douglas DB-7 light bombers. As the MLD, KM and Allied forces withdrew from the port, a group of 70 naval mechanics struggled to assemble the planes on the wharf while there was still time.

Two of the bombers were assembled at Tjilatjap, while the remaining four were supposed to have been sent still in their crates by train to the ML airfield at Tasikmalaja for assembly. However, it appears that they were never sent and the Japanese captured the planes still on the dock. On the morning of March 5, as the evacuation of Tjilatjap continued, Lieutenant H.V.B. Burgerhout, commanding officer of GVT.5, was ordered to fly one of the newly assembled DB-7s to Tasikmalaja. Despite the simple fact that he had never flown a land plane of this size and type, Lieutenant Burgerhout was the only pilot available.

Taking off from the dock, Burgerhout reached the airfield without difficulty. There, the base commander almost immediately ordered it destroyed, as Japanese troops were about to overrun the field. Crews attempted to disable the other four DB-7s by punching holes in their wings with crowbars and ripping off the carburetors. What happened to the final bomber at Tjilatjap is unknown, although the Japanese captured at least one bomber intact, or enough parts to assemble a complete bomber.

Evacuation operations were also under way at Tandjoeng Priok as a steady stream of naval crews, airmen and ground personnel slipped out of the port before the Japanese took over. As the last MLD planes and personnel departed Tandjoeng Priok on the 28th, a British flight crew and ground personnel worked frantically to repair and fly out 205 Squadron's FV-U/Y-53. The PBY had damaged a float while landing at Tandjoeng Priok on February 18 and was still unserviceable.

However, the port commander would not allow any extra time for repairs, so the men worked feverishly to repair the PBY before KNIL engineers blew up the plane and its hangar to prevent their capture. But when the PBY was hoisted into the fuel-covered water for an engine test, it immediately developed a serious leak during fueling. Before the leak could be repaired, the port commander received orders to begin demolition of the naval air station, slips and all remaining shipping in Tandjoeng Priok. This included FV-U/Y-53, which forced the British personnel to evacuate Java by an alternate route. Japanese troops moved into Batavia and Tandjoeng Priok within hours of Dutch forces pulling out of the city.

9

March: "This Is the End of a Courageous Fight, Admiral"[1]

At 0815 on March 1 Y-66 of GVT.5(NEW) sighted a Japanese naval formation with two battleships and two light cruisers 150 miles south of Tjilatjap. These were the battlecruisers *Hiei* and *Kirishima*, escorted by the heavy cruisers *Tone* and *Chikuma*, from Admiral Nagumo's carrier force, which was now operating at will in the Indian Ocean. Squadron PBYs made contact again at 1600 hours 100 miles south of Tjilatjap; they reported the battleships but apparently did not sight the escorting cruisers. Soon afterward, these ships would participate in a murderous rampage amongst ships evacuating Java; they would also bombard Christmas Island on March 7, heavily damaging the port and sinking a merchant ship.

With their ground forces moving ashore on Java, the Japanese supported the invasion operation with a series of strong air strikes against Dutch installations all across Java. Early on the morning of March 1, nine Tainan Air Wing Zeros hit Morokrembangan, where they caught Y-46 and Y-73 of GVT.3(NEW) on the ground, damaging both beyond repair. This effectively wiped out the squadron.

About this time, PatWing 10 personnel bolted the wing and engine assembly of 22-P-12, a damaged American PBY, to the fuselage of Y-72 and put it back into service as P-46. Several days later this seaplane was evacuated to Australia from Tjilatjap and continued to serve with PatWing 10.[2] The wrecks of the two Dutch Catalinas were destroyed along with the seaplane base, port facilities and ME the following day when the base was evacuated.

By now, the aircraft reserve pool at Morokrembangan was long gone, and many of the MLD squadrons were seriously depleted. Of the four remaining units then based at Tandjoeng Priok — GVT.2(NEW), GVT.8, GVT.16 and GVT.18 — only GVT.16 was fully intact with all three of its PBYs.[3] After the loss of Y-63, GVT.2(NEW) had been reduced to Y-62 and Y-64, both of which were damaged and unserviceable on March 1. Although there was considerable hope for Y-64, the condition of Y-62 was poor after being splinter-damaged on February 22.

GVT.8 had only X-16 remaining after losing X-17 and X-18 over North Gebroeders Island. However, it was presently undergoing a comprehensive 200-hour overhaul and was considered unfit for duty. To make matters, the Dornier was further damaged during an air raid on MVK Priok.

As a steady stream of Allied naval crews, airmen and ground personnel evacuated Tandjoeng Priok, the crew and a group of maintenance men labored to get the Dornier into shape for the long flight to Ceylon. As the plane was pushed out of its hangar, the structure was blown up. A number of Dutch officials then boarded the plane with a New

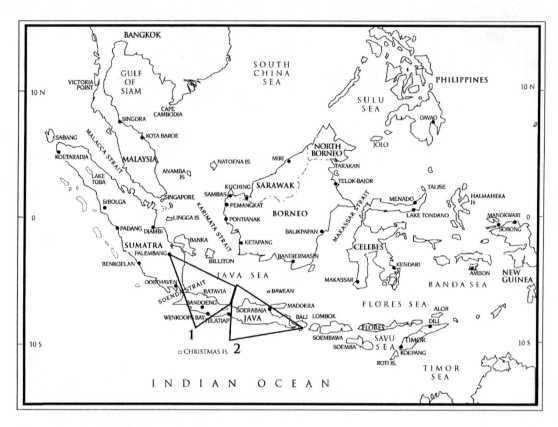

Japanese Air Superiority March 5, 1942. Legend: (1) Sphere of Japanese air superiority provided by JAAF units operating from Palembang. (2) Sphere of Japanese air superiority provided by IJN units operating from Den Passar, Bali.

Zealand bank official and a wounded RAF NCO. The plane then took off— it was the last plane out of Tandjoeng Priok.

Two hours into the flight, X-16 suffered a heavy explosion, and the burning Dornier fell into the sea off the coast of Sumatra. The bank official pushed the NCO out of the plane before it hit the water and exploded. No one else escaped. The official eventually died in the water, but after several hours, the wounded NCO was picked out of the water by a native prau, whose crew handed him over to Dutch officials. He was later transferred to the hospital ship *Wu-Seh* and transported to Bombay, India.[4]

From GVT.18 only Y-45 was operational after seeing the rest of its squadron mates damaged or destroyed in Japan's final push against Java. Y-47 had been lost in the landing accident at Tandjoeng Priok on February 24. Meanwhile, Y-48 was still under repair after being shot up off the coast of Sumatra on February 24.

The aircraft situation was little better at Morokrembangan, where four MLD squadrons had periodically operated from the base prior to the Battle of the Java Sea. Of these, only GVT.17 was at full strength,[5] while GVT.7(NEW) had reformed with the last remaining planes in the reserve pool.[6] Both squadrons were dispersed to auxiliary bases prior to the battle. GVT.6 was also operational with X-3 and X-23, although both planes were badly splinter damaged. GVT.3 also remained stationed at the base, although it existed in name only, as it had no planes.[7]

Meanwhile, GVT.5 continued to operate from Tjilatjap. During its encounter with Japanese Zeros over the *Langley*, Y-65 had been badly damaged and was almost immediately written off upon its return to base. In addition, an air raid would splinter-damage Y-66 beyond repair on March 4. As a result, Y-71 was the only PBY at the port that remained operational by week's end.

By the first week of March, both Morokrembangan and Tandjoeng Priok were virtually untenable due to Japanese air strikes. This led Captain Bozuwa to order the dispersal of all remaining aircraft to auxiliary bases throughout East Java. Although some of these bases were on small lakes, others were little more than nondescript rice paddies and isolated rivers. All were deliberately selected so as to avoid the constant presence of Japanese reconnaissance planes.

Meanwhile, ground crews at Morokrembangan worked to repair Y-62 of GVT.2 and prepare the flying boat for evacuation. Although not fully repaired, it and Y-64 departed Tandjoeng Priok — together with Y-55, Y-56 and Y-57 of GVT.16 — for Lake Bagendit, a small body of water located southeast of Bandoeng. They were followed by Y-45, of GVT.18, which headed for Lake Tjileuntja in western Java.

On the 1st the Dorniers of GVT.6 (X-3, X-23 and X-28) left Morokrembangan for Lengkong, a small, nondescript seaplane base located on the Brantas River near Modjokerto. There they would refuel and fly on to Broome, Australia. The remaining Fokker T.IVs of GVT.11 (T-15, T-16 and T-17) and GVT.12 (T-18, T-19 and T-21) were also ordered into Lengkong. They were followed by GVT.13 and GVT.14 with their four remaining single-engine Fokkers.

GVT.7(NEW) (X-1, X-20, X-24 and X-36) flew to Lake Grati, where they refueled and went on to Lengkong. Upon arrival, they too were ordered to Australia. At the same time Y-70 was attached to GVT.17, and all four planes flew to Rawah Bening irrigation reservoir at Toeloeng Agoeng, a small village south of Kediri. All of the squadrons were ordered to evacuate as many pilots, aircrew and ground personnel as possible from Morokrembangan. Special military trains would move those who could not be taken out by air to Tjilatjap for evacuation by sea.

But despite the best efforts of the MLD, the Japanese still found some of these auxiliary bases. Early on the morning of March 2, nine Zeros from the Tainan Air Wing flying from Bali's Den Passar Airfield attacked a "seaplane base" at Malang.[8] They claimed to have destroyed a single-engine seaplane, two twin-engine flying boats and a large four-engine flying boat.

At this stage of the East Indies campaign, it was almost impossible to identify individual single-engine aircraft lost on Java.[9] However, if the Japanese claims are true, the single-engine aircraft was likely a Ryan STM trainer or one of the Fokker floatplanes from GVT.13 or GVT.14, while the larger plane might have been a KNILM S-42.[10] The identity of the twin-engine flying boats remains unclear, as no MLD Dorniers or Catalinas were lost at Malang that day. Also, all of the older Do. 15 "Whales" and Fokker T.IVs have been accounted for. Just as likely, the Japanese claims could have been duplicate or inaccurate claims. It is possible they could have been wrecked aircraft.

If this was the case, it would appear that the seaplane base attacked by the Tainan Air Wing fighters was actually the secret MLD auxiliary base located on the Brantas River. There was no seaplane base at Malang, and all the auxiliary aircraft attached to GVTs 11, 12, 13 and 14 had been transferred to Lengkong by March 2. Unfortunately there are no records to confirm or deny this hypothesis, although it is the most likely scenario.

EVACUATION

As Japanese troops poured ashore on Java, the Allies began to evacuate the island. On March 1, RAF HQ at Bandoeng ordered 205 Squadron to evacuate its two remaining PBYs from Tjilatjap. FV-W/Y-54 departed for Broome, Australia, that morning and was followed out by FV-H that afternoon. Ground crews departed aboard the tender *Tuong Song*, which also transported personnel from 84 Squadron, 211 Squadron and 151 Maintenance Unit to Fremantle, Australia. This officially closed the book on 205 Squadron in the NEI and Malaya. From December 7, 1941, to March 1, 1942, the unit lost 10 PBYs, and the toll would go even higher.

At the same time, Vice-Admiral W.A. Glassford, commander of USN forces in the NEI, and Rear-Admiral Sir Arthur Palliser, commander of RN forces in the Far East, departed Bandoeng for Tjilatjap. There, they boarded PatWing 10's new hybrid Catalina P-46 and departed Java for Colombo.

Admiral Helfrich followed them that evening. He traveled by car from Bandoeng to Lake Bagendit, where the dispirited admiral and key members of his staff flew out aboard Y-56 early on the morning of March 2. The other two PBYs of GVT.16 (Y-55 and Y-57) and Y-64 of GVT.2(NEW) flew the remainder of his staff out of Tjilatjap.[11] All four aircraft flew to China Bay, Ceylon, where they were to continue the war with what Dutch naval forces remained.

Helfrich flew off Lake Begendit's short waterway with only the uniform on his back and one small valet case. He needed no baggage to carry the miserable feeling of abject failure he had for failing to save the Indies. He left everything behind — his family, home, friends and, perhaps worst of all, thousands of comrades who would not escape. He later wrote how he felt like a miserable recruit in an admiral's uniform as he boarded the plane that day.[12]

Alone in the air, everyone aboard Helfrich's plane kept a tense watch for the Japanese. As the PBY flew up the coast of Sumatra, it circled the Dutch naval fleet tanker *Petronella (TAN 8)*, which, not knowing the identity of the plane, got underway and prepared for air attack. It later flew over the KPM transport *Siberg*, which was en route to Java from Padang, Sumatra, with a battalion of KNIL troops. She was steaming close to shore to avoid detection from the air.

Y-56 then landed at Emmahaven, the port of Padang. There, Helfrich contacted the KNIL garrison commander by phone and informed him that they had sighted Japanese troops moving north from Palembang. Only 42 miles from the port, the Japanese would soon be on his doorstep. After a short stay for rest and refueling, the flight resumed without incident to Colombo, where Helfrich set up his new HQ and reestablished contact with those Dutch naval forces still on Java.

Admiral Helfrich and his staff were not the only ones leaving Java, as a general evacuation of MLD aircraft was now under way. All planes with sufficient range were ordered to make for either Australia or Ceylon. The ports of Broome and China Bay, respectively, were their primary destinations.

Following Helfrich's departure, his chief-of-staff, Captain J.J.A. van Staveren, assumed command of the remaining Dutch naval forces on Java. He was temporarily promoted to the rank of rear admiral and given the responsibility of continuing the naval defense of Java. When that option was no longer viable, he was to implement and oversee pre-planned evacuation plans for the navy and ensure that its installations were destroyed.[13]

March 2 officially ended the KM's offensive air and sea operations in the East Indies. That day the governor-general confirmed Admiral Helfrich's orders to begin the evacuation of all remaining KM and MLD units to Australia and Ceylon. The evacuation was to take place by both sea and air with aircrews given priority, presumably as the MLD still had large numbers of aircraft on order from the United States and planned to take possession of them in Australia or Ceylon.

Any remaining naval personnel at Soerabaja and Tandjoeng Priok who were not flown out were to be transported by rail to Tjilatjap or Wijnkoops Bay on the south coast of Java for evacuation by sea. This is how most MLD ground personnel were taken out. Helfrich's biggest fear was that a rapid Japanese advance would cut off their escape route; his fears intensified when a troop train carrying approximately 2,200 unarmed RAF and RAAF personnel was ambushed and derailed by Japanese troops, supported by mortar fire, inflicting heavy losses on the night of March 6–7.

Due to demands by the KNIL, which was trying to move its troops into position, there were only a limited number of rail cars allocated to the KM. As a result, space was limited for the MLD personnel, who were allowed only a small bag to carry what they could away from the burning hell that was now Java. Despite the psychological blow they suffered having lost the fight so badly, many of these men now faced yet another blow far more crushing.

As the overcrowded trains pulled out of Soerabaja at nightfall on March 1, a mob of tearful family members saw the naval personnel off. Admiral Helfrich strictly forbade the navy to evacuate nonmilitary personnel, including the men's family members. In any event, there was no practical way to evacuate the civilians anyway. As a result, thousands of wives and children were separated from their husbands and fathers at the train station. The troops were evacuated to Australia or Ceylon, while the civilians were left to face three and a half years of brutal Japanese internment.[14]

At Tjilatjap the MLD men joined a mass of military personnel, government officials and civilians— Europeans, Americans, Chinese and Indonesians alike — all trying to evacuate Java. The docks were littered with abandoned military vehicles, supplies and equipment. Much of it had arrived only days earlier. Mixed in was a diverse assortment of abandoned civilian transport, luggage and personal items. In the background, huge plumes of black smoke filled the sky as engineers destroyed the KM's remaining fuel and ammunition stocks.

As the chaos continued, few of the evacuees lucky enough to find a ship away from Java knew that Admiral Nagumo's powerful carrier and battleship task force lay only a few hundred miles south to prevent just such an evacuation. Most of those civilians and government officials who did know still chose to take their chances at sea rather than face certain capture on Java. The military personnel had no choice, for duty compelled them to risk the treacherous voyage.

On March 2, X-3 and X-23 of GVT.6 flew to Broome from Lengkong, followed by GVT.7(NEW) with X-1, X-20, X-24 and X-36 off Lake Grati and GVT.17 (Y-59, Y-60, Y-67, Y-70). They carried the personnel of GVT.11, GVT.12, GVT.13 and GVT.14, which were forced to burn their planes on the Brantas River, as they had insufficient range to reach Australia or Ceylon. Their evacuation by ship, as with the Ryan trainers, was not possible given the rapid Japanese advance and the late date Admiral Helfrich gave for the evacuation to begin.

The commander of GVT.11 (T-15, T-16 and T-17), Lieutenant-Commander J.

Craamer, requested permission to evacuate his Fokker T.IVs to Australia by staging through the Cocos Islands. But since the Cocos were located nearly 1,000 miles south of Java and the Fokkers had a maximum range of only 970 miles, his request was denied.[15] As a result, the aircraft were destroyed along with the single-engine Fokker floatplanes (W-1, W-8, W-11 and W-13) and a civilian Fairchild 24 that had been requisitioned by the MLD.[16]

At 0700 on March 1, Rear-Admiral van Staveren ordered Rear-Admiral P. Koenraad, to destroy the ME and naval air station.[17] The operation at Morokrembangan began at 0530 on the 2nd as the radio station, seaplane ramp, hangars, slips, cranes, docks, fuel and oil stocks and ordnance dumps were rigged for demolition with mines and time-delayed fuses. While ground crews prepared the installations for demolition, others destroyed those unserviceable aircraft that could not be flown out. These included Y-46, Y-73, D-44 (the last remaining Do. 15) and a number of single-engine Fokker seaplanes from the flight training school.

Beginning at 0600, Morokrembangan — the largest, most well-equipped seaplane base in the world — was rocked by a series of heavy explosions. The demolitions were over by 1000, and huge plumes of thick, black smoke filled the sky. At 0600 on the 3rd, the first busload of MLD and KM ground personnel pulled out of Soerabaja. They were bound for Wijnkoops Bay on the southern shore, where they would be evacuated to Colombo by ship.

Although the demolition of Morokrembangan was reported complete at 1100 on March 2, Admiral Koenraad discovered otherwise when he carried out a personal inspection of the ME and naval air station on March 4. The ME was completely demolished, but many of Morokrembangan's hangars still stood, and a number of bombsights and aircraft engines remained untouched. Koenraad immediately called upon KNIL engineers to finish the job. However, it turned out to be a much more difficult job than planned, as desertions, faulty explosives and the sturdy construction of the hangars themselves combined to limit their effectiveness.[18] As a result, many of the facilities at Morokrembangan were captured intact.

Of the Dutch naval personnel on Java, only a battalion (four companies) of Royal Marines remained to continue the fight on the ground. Most of these men were professional soldiers who had been trained for ground combat. The exception was the 3rd Company, which comprised 300 MLD ground personnel who were untrained for combat. Because of their lack of training and the need for their technical services elsewhere, these technicians were soon evacuated.

The company was sent to Andir Airfield, where it was detailed to recondition a number of American P-40Es that had been left to the ML when the USAAF evacuated Java. The mechanics made six Kittyhawks airworthy, and those were immediately thrown into action. Although Java was all but lost, the mechanics were glad to contribute to the fight after having to blow up the MLD facilities. But with the Japanese about to overrun the base, the 3rd Company was then ordered to Wijnkoops Bay for evacuation.

Demolition crews were also working to destroy the seaplane base at Tandjoeng Priok. There, maintenance personnel of GVT.18 were still trying to repair the damage that Y-48 had suffered in an earlier attack. However, ground defenses around the port were threatening to collapse, and it was rumored that the Japanese were about to enter the city by the night of March 2. As a result, MLD ground personnel were forced to blow up the PBY on the 3rd to prevent its capture.

As the Japanese landed on Java, the Dutch destroyed all military installations and equipment, including this floating seaplane dock (photograph from *Soerabaja 1900–1950* [2004], courtesy of Asia Maior Publishers).

At the same time, the seaplane tender *Rigel* was scuttled as a blockship in the northern entrance to the harbor. *Merel, Poolster, Fazant,* a British gunboat and a number of auxiliary minelayers were also sunk by naval gunfire as harbor blockships. From March 1 to March 5, demolition crews ashore blew up hangars, machine shops and virtually any other installation that could possibly be of use to the Japanese. The final phase (perhaps the most damaging for future historians) began at 0600 on March 5 when all of the operational records at MVK Priok were burned in a huge fire, including its squadron reports, secret communiqués and codebooks. The base coding machines were shipped to Bandoeng.

The majority of MVK Priok's naval personnel were evacuated on March 1. Coastwatch positions in the harbor were turned over to KNIL troops as the KM personnel prepared for evacuation by train and motor vehicle. There was no formal order ever given for the navy and civilian demolition crews to abandon Tandjoeng Priok, but it was the logical thing to do once the operation was complete, as they were the only KM personnel left in the city.

A FINAL DISASTER

On March 3, a disaster of epic proportions took place at the port of Broome on the northwest coast of Australia. As the fighting on Java came to a head, this previously isolated port quickly became the primary evacuation point for evacuees from Java. The first planes coming out of Java were Empire flying boats, DC-3s and B-17s, which began arriving on February 25. Within days, they were making nonstop evacuation flights between Java and Broome.

They were soon joined by MLD and ML transport planes, which were also carrying out evacuation flights from airfields and auxiliary seaplane bases all over Java. Although the MLD aircraft had received orders from Admiral Helfrich to take out only essential military personnel needed to help continue the war outside the East Indies, many of the flying boats still departed Java heavily loaded with family members and numerous other nonmilitary passengers. Of all the squadrons that left Java that week, only GVT.6 left without carrying evacuees of any kind.

And of the remaining aircraft, only one left the island with extra passengers who had not been previously approved by the pilot.[19] Although all the squadron commanders condoned the practice of evacuating civilians, it is believed that several senior KM staff officer, such as Rear-Admiral van Staveren, were also aware that MLD flight crews were violating Helfrich's orders and chose not to intervene.[20] As a result, the temporary MLD commander, Captain P.J. Hendrikse, allowed the planes of GVT.7 and GVT.17 to take on up to 35 civilians per aircraft, including his own wife. Although one can understand the desire to save one's family and loved ones when the means and opportunity are available, the practice would have grievous consequences.

Located in the territory of Western Australia, Broome was a small pearling port with a prewar population of about 1,700, although most of its residents had moved away since the start of the Pacific War. Situated on Roebuck Bay, the one-mile-square harbor had a single pier that extended approximately half a mile into the bay at high tide. At low tide, however, a 29-foot tidal range ensured that it ended a full half-mile from the water. Qantas Airlines had three mooring buoys in the harbor and operated a small ferry service for the passengers of arriving seaplanes. The airline also operated a single lighter for refueling its planes.

Broome was poorly equipped to handle the sudden influx of military personnel and civilian evacuees, many of whom could not be adequately fed or housed. And with as many as 57 aircraft carrying 8,000 evacuees arriving in single day, the port facilities were also overwhelmed, leading to refueling times of up to 12 hours. Priority for evacuation was given to the wounded, followed by women and children. They were sent by air farther down the coast to Port Hedland or Perth, but thanks to the large numbers, progress was slow. As a result, many evacuees came down with dengue fever that quickly spread through the town and refugee camps.

On March 2, GVT.17 received orders from Soerabaja via phone to evacuate its four PBYs to Broome that evening. Among the passengers aboard Y-70 were Captain Hendrikse, his wife, seven MLD staff officers and their family members. The total number of civilians carried by the formation numbered 140, most of whom were women and children.[21]

Knowing Broome had limited refueling facilities and that large numbers of Allied planes were already there, the pilot of Y-70, Lieutenant-Commander A.J. de Bruijn, recommended in the air that the formation divert south to the port of Geraldton. However, Captain Hendrikse had his orders, and he was senior officer. He overruled de Bruijn, and the Catalinas went into Broome as planned. They arrived early in the morning of March 3.

Five Dorniers had already preceded them. X-1 and X-20 of GVT.7(NEW) and X-3, X-20 and X-28 of GVT.6 had arrived at the port one and two days earlier, respectively. They spent the night of March 2–3 resting on the mud of Broome harbor waiting for orders and the tide to come back in.

Evacuation operations proceeded smoothly until 1500 on the 2nd, when a four-engine Japanese flying boat appeared. The "Mavis" leisurely circled the harbor at approximately 13,000 feet, photographing the entire harbor. At 0400 on the 3rd, a second seaplane visited Broome. The tower assumed it was a friendly plane from Java and flashed the airfield lights to alert the pilot. The Japanese plane made several low-level passes over the bay and airfield, confirming the presence of Allied planes. It then flew away into the night.

The fighters belonged to the 3rd Air Wing based at Koepang, Timor. Upon receiving the flying boats' reconnaissance reports, the wing commander, Commander Takeo Shibata, ordered an immediate attack on Broome. At 0705, nine Zeros led by a C5M for navigation, lifted off from Koepang and headed for Broome. They were followed by eight more 3rd Air Wing Zeros, also guided by a C5M. This force assumed a course for the port of Wyndham, which lay up the coast from Broome.

This was actually the second raid ordered against Broome. Shibata had ordered a raid on the port the previous morning when he first received word that the Allies were staging through Broome. Although unsure of what the port held, he ordered off a strike force at dawn on March 2. However, with the 3rd Air Wing fewer than 60 miles north of the port, it encountered extremely bad weather and was forced to return to Koepang.

After the appearance of the Japanese flying boats, all of Broome expected some type of attack in the immediate future. Orders were issued for all Allied planes to be away from the port by 1000. So as quickly as the planes could be refueled and loaded, they were sent out. However, only three B-17s, one LB-30 and a flying boat had flown out before the Japanese appeared. They caught seven planes on the airfield and 15 more on the water in Roebuck Bay.

The first flight arrived over Broome at 0930, immediately jettisoning external 320-liter drop tanks that had been required due to the range. Three fighters each were detailed to attack the airfield and harbor, while the remaining three remained up top to provide a CAP. When it became apparent that no Allied fighters were present, these planes also joined the attack. The C5M orbited the port and directed the attack from a safe altitude and was not damaged.

Warrant Officer Osamu Kudo initiated the raid by bouncing an American SOC Seagull floatplane that had taken off for a flight down the coast to Port Hedland. Piloted by Lieutenant Jack Lamade, the SOC was the sole surviving floatplane from the American heavy cruiser *Houston*. In addition to the Australian light cruiser *Perth*, Japanese forces in the Soenda Strait had sunk *Houston* on the night of March 1–2 as they tried to leave the Java Sea. The floatplane had not been aboard when *Houston* went down, having previously been ordered to Broome.

Lamade had just finished refueling and was taking off when Kudo attacked. In an unequal fight lasting just minutes, Kudo forced down the virtually defenseless biplane. Although the plane was badly damaged, Lamade managed to put the shattered SOC down on the water. He and his observer then abandoned the plane without injury.

Kudo now turned his attention to an American B-24 piloted by Lieutenant Edson Kester. The bomber had just taken off from the airfield with 33 servicemen aboard when

Kudo attacked. Kester turned away in a futile bid to escape, but Kudo easily followed and shot down the B-24 in flames six miles off Cable Beach. Thirty-one men aboard died or drowned in the crash. The two survivors—Sergeant Melvin Donaho and Sergeant William Beatty—spent 24 hours in the water before reaching shore. Donaho recovered, but Beatty succumbed to exhaustion shortly afterwards.

When the 3rd Air Wing appeared, the Dorniers still awaited orders while refueling for the flight south to Perth, and the Catalinas had just landed. Most of their passengers remained aboard the crowded planes due to 27-foot waves that made it difficult to ferry them ashore. Even had they gone ashore, there was nowhere to go, as Broome's few accommodations had long since been overwhelmed.

The first seaplane lost was the RAAF "Empire" flying boat *Centaurus*, which lay at the dock with the Qantas "Empire" flying boat *Corinna* loading refugees. Hit by 20mm cannon fire, *Centaurus* exploded into flames almost immediately, and the crew abandoned the plane for the dubious safety of a dinghy. *Corinna* quickly followed. Due to the strict orders of Commander Shibata to concentrate only on military targets, the Zeros did not strafe the crowd of civilians assembled on the dock.[22]

As the Zeros came in low across the water, the Dutch seaplanes returned fire from their moorings, but the fight was no contest. The crew of Y-70 prepared to put the passengers over the side into the plane's inflatable dinghy. But because of seasickness, several of them had much trouble evacuating the plane, which was not helped by the loose dinghy floating away. In the process, fighters strafed Y-70, setting it afire and sinking the plane. The Zeros then burned and sank Y-59, Y-60 and Y-67. X-1, X-3, X-20, X-23 and X-28 soon followed.

At the same time, the second section attacked the airfield, burning or destroying every plane present. At 1030, the Japanese, running low on fuel and ammunition, turned north for the long flight back to Koepang. They had destroyed every plane at Broome.

In barely an hour, the Allies lost 23 planes, including all four Dutch PBYs and all five of the Dorniers. In addition, they destroyed two American PBYs of PatWing 10 and both remaining PBYs of 205 Squadron. On the airfield, fighters destroyed two transports (a Lockheed Lodestar and DC-3) of the ML's air transport service, a RAAF Hudson bomber of 14 Squadron and an American B-24 and two B-17Es of the 435th Bombardment Squadron.

Casualties among the 140 military and civilian personnel aboard the MLD planes included 10 killed, 38 missing and 10 wounded.[23] According to another source, 38 were dead, 16 of which were MLD personnel. These figures include Captain Hendrikse, his wife and two more passengers from Y-70, in addition to 11 dead on Y-59.[24] Although the Japanese did not strafe the survivors in the water, burning fuel killed many. Many of the missing are believed to have been washed out to sea, killed by sharks or trapped in the sunken hulls of the flying boats.

In exchange, the 3rd Air Wing lost a single Zero to ground fire—that of Warrant Officer Kudo. Lieutenant Guus Winckel, a pilot of one of the ML transports, fired a machine gun barehanded from a slit trench throughout the attack. With the barrel resting on his exposed forearm, Winckel fired until he ran out of ammunition. Although severely burned, he hit the Zero flown by Kudo. The fighter trailed smoke and crashed into the sea off Broome, killing Kudo, a highly experienced ace with seven kills.

The 3rd Air Wing also lost the Zero flown by Private 1st Class Yasuo Matsumoto on the return trip to Koepang. After spending more time than planned over Broome, most of the fighters experienced a severe fuel shortage on the return flight, and all were extremely lucky to make it home. Only one — that flown by Matsumoto — was not so lucky; his plane ran out of fuel, and he was forced to ditch in the ocean off Roti Island. He managed to swim ashore and was eventually rescued on March 12.

Ground fire lightly wounded Kudo's wingman, Naval Air Pilot, 1st Class Masaki Okazaki, who made it back to base. Five other Zeros were also hit, but none seriously. Although rifle fire was heavy from the Broome Volunteer Defense Corps, Winckel likely caused most of the damage. For his actions at Broome that day, he was awarded the Bronze Cross, one of Holland's highest military awards.

The second flight of the 3rd Air Wing attacked Wyndham about the same time. However, it found very little at the near-deserted meat-processing port. Arriving back at Koepang an hour ahead of the first wave, it could only report the destruction of a two-engine biplane transport and the burning of a fuel dump. There was no resistance, and none of the Japanese aircraft was damaged. Most of the few remaining residents of Wyndham evacuated the town afterwards.

DIAMONDS[25]

Retiring from Broome, the 3rd Air Wing encountered a KNILM DC-3 60 miles north of the port. The plane and its crew of four had departed Bandoeng, Java, at 0100 loaded with five Dutch pilots, a KNILM airline official, Maria van Tuyn (the wife of a Dutch pilot) and her 18-month-old son. When the pilot (Captain Ivan Smirnoff, a leading ace in the Imperial Russian Air Force in World War I) radioed for landing instructions, he received a cryptic reply: *"The Airstrip Is Okay for the Time Being."*

Minutes later, three Zeros flown by Lieutenant Zenziro Miyano, Sergeant Takashi Kurano and Private Zempei Matsumoto, attacked the DC-3. They crippled the transport in minutes, wounding Smirnoff, one of the pilots, Mrs. van Tuyn and her child. Despite wounds in both arms and a hip, Smirnoff put the burning plane down in the surf off Carnot Beach, some 60 miles north of Broome.

The Zeros then strafed the wreck with machine gun fire, severely wounding the plane's mechanic. Then, with their ammunition expended and fuel extremely low, the Japanese departed. It was most likely this brief action that led to the loss of Private Matsumoto's Zero to a fuel shortage near Roti Island.

The airline official was sent back to salvage the logbooks, mail and a small, unidentified package given to Smirnoff just before the plane took off. Unknown to anyone on the plane, the box, wrapped in brown paper, contained diamonds belonging to N.V. de Concurrent Ltd., a Dutch firm in Bandoeng. Valued at over $20 million (1942 exchange rates), the diamonds had first been evacuated from the Netherlands to Java in 1940 after the German invasion. They were now being transported to Australia to keep them out of Japanese hands.

However, not knowing the value of the box, and more concerned about items of survival, the official made only a halfhearted attempt to retain the box when a large wave knocked him down inside the fuselage as the tide came in. He returned to the beach with a number of items, but the diamonds were not among them. The survivors then made camp under salvaged parachutes in the merciless sun.

That night Mrs. van Tuyn died, followed by the wounded Dutch airman at dawn. Both were buried in shallow graves. Later that morning, a Japanese "Mavis" flying boat appeared overhead after a reconnaissance flight over Broome. The seaplane made a low pass over the wreck and dropped five bombs, most of which failed to explode. It then departed.

Despite repeated attempts, all efforts to seek out help failed. In the meantime, the wounded mechanic and Mrs. Tuyn's infant son died. A rescue mission was finally organized on the 5th when an aborigine notified authorities of a plane wreck some miles south of Broome. A clergyman, an Australian army officer and a second aborigine then spearheaded a rescue party, which succeeded in reaching the survivors' campsite at 0300 on March 7.

As for the diamonds, they remained in the plane unknown and forgotten about by the survivors until Smirnoff reached Melbourne. There, an Australian bank official asked for the box. When told that it had been abandoned in the wreck, Australian police detectives interrogated the White Russian until they were sure he was telling the truth. It was first time anyone had told Smirnoff what the package contained.

About a week after the crash, a local beachcomber named Jack Palmer looted the wreck and found a small leather bag containing the diamonds. Over the next few weeks, he distributed many of the diamonds to a number of friends, including at least one who suggested that they turn them over to the authorities and seek a reward. However, Palmer disagreed with his suggestion and took a number of the diamonds back from him in the heated argument that followed.

However, on April 14, Palmer appeared at an Australian Army recruitment center and turned over some of the missing diamonds when he volunteered to enlist. He told the officer in charge that he had found the diamonds in a bag, but while opening it, the remaining stones had fallen into the surf and were lost. An immediate mission to the wreck site found no sign of the missing diamonds and Palmer was held for trial on the charge of theft.

Meanwhile, small quantities of the missing diamonds began to turn up in Broome, where Palmer had given or traded them to friends, aborigines and shopkeepers. Once word got out that the police were actively looking for the diamonds, it is believed that a number of the aboriginals with stones in their possession threw them away rather than risk being incriminated. Eventually only a small fraction of the missing diamonds were recovered.

In May 1943, Palmer and two accomplices were brought to trial in Perth on the charges of stealing or receiving stolen property. Witnesses, including Smirnoff, flew in from all parts of Australia to testify. However, the evidence was not strong enough to convict the accused. In a celebrated trial that was well documented by the Australian press, a jury of six found the three men not guilty.

As for the remaining diamonds, few were ever found. One story tells of a small package of stones being found in tree in Broome. Another tells of a man who offered to do some repair work in a home in Broome. But when the owners returned, they found the work incomplete and a small hole in the fireplace where it was rumored that a cache of stones had been hidden and retrieved years later. More likely is that Palmer hid most of the stones and retrieved them after the war when interest in the case had blown over.

THE LOSS OF X-36

While Zeros were shooting up Broome, both X-24 and X-36 ran out of fuel and made forced landings. X-24 was able to put down at the small port city of Wallal, where it damaged the port stummel,[26] although the plane remained flyable. At the same time, X-36 set down on 80 Mile Beach, a desolate stretch of coastline along Australia's western shores some 90 miles south of the port. It too was badly damaged and rendered unflyable after running aground on a coral reef.

In response to her signals, *Tung Song*, which was en route to Fremantle from Tjilatjap, was ordered to sweep the area for survivors. However, she saw nothing and proceeded south. A civilian Lockheed 10A owned by MacRobertson Miller Aviation eventually sighted the Dornier. En route from Wyndham to Perth, the plane landed at Broome 30 minutes after the Japanese departed. The pilot loaded 22 evacuees, including a number of wounded, into the Lockheed and took off for Port Hedland. Sighting X-36, the Lockheed's pilot, Captain Jimmy Woods, circled the Dornier and dropped instructions for the crew to remain with the plane. On a return flight to Broome that evening, Woods dropped supplies to the stranded seaplane.

It is likely that the crew had already abandoned X-36 by the time Woods returned. Shortly after landing at Wallal, X-24 intercepted X-36's distress call; refueling the damaged Dornier with gasoline from several civilian vehicles, its pilot took off and was able to rescue X-36's companion flying boat's crew without further damage. Before leaving, the airmen burned the plane to prevent its capture,[27] and X-24 flew everyone to Perth. In the darkness however, Woods probably could not see that the plane had been destroyed.

The Japanese Hit Tjilatjap

On March 4, Tainan Air Wing Zeros escorted 12 G3M "Nells" from Kendari to attack Tjilatjap for the first time. Despite AA fire from the ground, the bombers caused heavy damage to the port facilities and threw the Allied evacuation operation into mass confusion. The fighters remained behind after the bombers left and burned Y-66 of GVT.5(NEW) on the water without loss. They then withdrew.

The following day, aircraft from Admiral Nagumo's carrier force attacked Tjilatjap in effort to disrupt evacuation and resupply operations. In a massive air strike reminiscent of Pearl Harbor and Darwin, 180 B5N "Kate" horizontal bombers, D3A "Val" dive bombers and escorting Zeros from the heavy fleet carriers *Kaga*, *Akagi*, *Hiryu* and *Soryu* destroyed or damaged many buildings and wiped out most of the port and its facilities. They also sank three small interisland steamers—*Rokan* (563 tons), *Tohiti* (982 tons) and *Pasir* (1,187 tons), in addition to the 4,819-ton freighter *Barentz*[28] and the GM vessel *Canopus* (773 tons). Nine other vessels were damaged, including the 1,594-ton freighter *Sipora*.

At this point, the remaining personnel of GVT.5(NEW) had pretty much decided they had just about had enough of Tjilatjap and Java in general. They loaded everyone into Y-71— which was the squadron's last flyable PBY — and flew to the shattered port of Broome.

On March 5 Captain Bozuwa received orders to evacuate Java for Australia, where he would reassume command of all remaining MLD forces from Captain Hendrikse. Commander J.H. van Rinkhuyzen (whom the KM likely wanted to keep out of Japanese hands in order to preserve the location of secret Dutch minefields located throughout the NEI for as long as possible), head of the Dutch Navy's Mine Services in the NEI, and five other officers were to accompany him. They would depart Lake Tjileuntja aboard Y-45 of GVT.18 and the newly repaired Y-62 of GVT.2 for Tjilatjap, where they would refuel before making the flight to Australia.

Y-45, piloted by 2nd Lieutenant A.W. Witholt, departed first at 1600 carrying Bozuwa, Rinkhuyzen and a third officer. Y-62 followed a short time later carrying the remaining officers. Y-45 reached Tjilatjap that evening to find the port jammed with thousands of military personnel and burning fiercely with fires caused by the Japanese carrier air strike earlier in the day.

The presence of Japanese carriers just south of Java apparently unnerved Bozuwa. Shortly after landing, he ordered Witholt to fly his party back to Lake Tjileuntja, where they arrived late that night. The evacuees then returned to Bandoeng, where they planned to complete their escape from Java by another route. As he departed Lake Tjileuntja, Bozuwa told Witholt that it was useless to attempt an escape from Java by air and that he planned to leave the island from Wijnkoops Bay as part of Admiral Helfrich's seaborne evacuation of KM personnel.[29]

Y-62 reached Tjilatjap shortly after Y-45 departed on its return trip. Although it too had been ordered to return to Lake Tjileuntja, its pilot never received the signal, as Bozuwa's order had been transmitted on the REC-GROUP frequency and Y-62 had her radio modulated to the official MLD frequency.[30] As a result of this mix-up, the Catalina remained at Tjilatjap, where it refueled and prepared to depart for Australia with Y-65, whose crew was frantically working to repair its plane after its engagement with Japanese fighters over the *Langley*.

As they worked, 1st Lieutenant G.F. Rijnders and his crew reached Tjilatjap by train. After flying Y-67 over the Java Sea on the night of February 26–27, they had been ordered to proceed to MVK Priok by night train to repossess and fly out Y-53, one of the PBYs that been loaned to the British in December.[31] The plane had damaged a float while landing at Batavia on February 21 and had been abandoned by the British when they evacuated the city. Rijnders got as far as the town of Poerwokerto in East Java, where destroyed bridges stopped the train. From there, he and his men were ordered south to Tjilatjap.

Upon reaching the port, they found the crew of Y-65 working frantically to repair their Catalina. Rijnders and his crew took over P-3, a damaged PBY-4 inherited from PatWing 10. P-3 was one of three PBYs that had flown in from Exmouth Gulf, Australia, on March 2 to evacuate Captain Wagner and his staff but had suffered engine problems. Pressed for time after attempting brief repairs, its crew at the time further disabled the PBY and flew out aboard P-10.

Rijnders, then, found P-3 in extremely poor shape. In its hurried attempt to disable the aircraft, the P-3's American crew had smashed the instrument panels, slashed the tires and cut the rudder cables, among other things. There were also the engine problems that had first grounded the plane. Among these were burned-out starter motors on both engines, which were frozen and refused to turn over.

Nonetheless, Rijnders found a host of willing volunteers to help try to rebuild the PBY, to which he informally assigned the MLD serial number Y-3. The crew and passengers of Y-65, who had given up hope of fixing their own plane, soon joined them. Working nonstop for three days, MLD ground crews recently evacuated from Morokrembangan got Y-3 airworthy.

Carrying eight crewmen and some 50–60 passengers, Y-62 was to make for Broome early on the morning on the 6th. But as the PBYs warmed their engines prior to take-off, the generator wiring to Y-3's starboard engine short-circuited, and it would not start. Unable to lift off on one engine, her crew and passengers could only watch as Y-62 roared off Lake Tjilatjap and disappeared into the night.

To make matters worse, Japanese land bombers again heavily bombed the port later that morning. This raid sank the KPM interisland steamers *Mandar, Dajak* and *Atjeh* and heavily damaged the 696-ton *Poseidon.* Believing these attacks to be a prelude to the invasion of Tjilatjap, port authorities scuttled all remaining ships in port to prevent their capture and block the harbor. By the end of the fighting on Java, 23 sunken ships littered the harbor, totaling approximately 23,000 tons. This ended Tjilatjap's use as a port, leaving a large number of Allied troops trapped on Java with no means of escape.

Fully aware that no ships remained to evacuate them, the crew and passengers of Y-3 set about trying to repair the flying boat. Normally, the plane would have had a separate manual handstarter for both engines, but the starter for the dead engine had disappeared. So, unsure whether it would even work, mechanics transferred the starter from the port engine to the starboard engine. The pilot then started the port engine using the generator, while a crewman hand-started the starboard engine.

Both engines instantly turned over, and the crew made plans to leave immediately. However, the flight would not be easy. Y-62 was to have provided navigation on the flight, as Y-3's damaged compass was off by 10 degrees. The American crew had also taken the navigation charts, so the MLD crew had only a foldout poster from the Australian Railways Company for navigation along the Australian coast. And finally, unable to find any fuel, Rijnders took off with only half a tank of gas for the 1,800-mile flight to Broome.

In the air, he followed a course given to the navigator by Y-62. However, few relaxed given the defective compass and the fact that everyone aboard knew Japanese carriers were operating at will south of Java. The recent engine trouble also weighed heavily on their minds, for if the plane went down, there would be no rescue. Nonetheless, Rijnders hit Broome dead-on the following morning and made a perfect landing. There, Y-3's crewmen rejoined the MLD forces in Australia, and it was turned over to the RAAF.

As Y-3 left Tjilatjap, the Japanese pasted Morokrembangan with yet another air raid. Most of the few planes that remained there were under repair or inoperable. The shattered remains of Y-46 were destroyed, while Y-73 was damaged beyond repair. Naval ground personnel destroyed the plane later that day to prevent its capture. At the same time, they also likely destroyed a number of smaller Fokkers and older Dornier "Whale" seaplanes, which were unserviceable and could not be evacuated from Java. The single-engine aircraft did not have the range to reach Australia or Ceylon, while many of the others had suffered heavy damage in earlier raids and could not be repaired in time or were damaged beyond repair.

And Then There Was One

At this point, Y-45 was the last flyable MLD plane left on Java. Following Witholt's return to Lake Tjileuntja, he was ordered to stand by on March 6 to evacuate 16 naval officers, including Captain P.J.M. Cikot, commander of the KM marine battalion. However, their ETA was uncertain at best, as plans were also being made to evacuate the officers from Bandoeng aboard a DC-5. As it turned out, they were evacuated from Java through Wijnkoops Bay, although the Japanese sank their ship and a number were killed, with the remainder being captured.

When the officers' party failed to arrive, Witholt then decided to leave Java on the morning of March 7.[32] However, bad weather delayed his departure until the following morning,[33] when Y-45 departed Lake Tjileuntja at 1145, carrying his crew, an ML pilot and his wife. The PBY flew to Lake Bagendit, where Witholt hoped to refuel for the long flight to Padang. But upon landing, he learned that the fuel depot had been destroyed several hours earlier. Luckily though, the demolition had been hurriedly completed using pickaxes, and many drums had been punctured in a manner where they still contained a great deal of fuel. By picking through the drums, Witholt and his crew were able to find enough fuel for a seven-hour flight.

Leaving Bagendit, he set course for the small coastal village of Pameungpeuk on the south coast of Java. Here, Witholt hoped to rest up and top off the plane's fuel tanks while he picked up an ML sergeant and corporal whom he had promised to evacuate. Unfortunately, when the PBY arrived overhead, rough sea conditions prevented it from landing, and Witholt was forced to reluctantly continue on to Padang, leaving the soldiers to their fate on Java. Reaching Padang late that night, the PBY was able to refuel as the exhausted crew rested.

The flight continued the next day when the PBY lifted off the water, bound for the Cocos Islands in the Indian Ocean. Witholt also carried out Padang's harbormaster as the NEI had formally surrendered to the Japanese by now and the port had been completely demolished.[34] Although the PBY reached the archipelago without any trouble, disaster befell the plane during the landing. Y-45 struck a submerged reef in the harbor that tore a gash in the flying boat's hull, letting two tons of water flood the Number 3 and 4 compartments. As a result, the Catalina nearly sank in the lagoon before Witholt was able to run the damaged plane onto the beach.

Although the Cocos were British territory, the KM had established a small MLD support base there before the war through an agreement with the Royal Navy. With the help of British residents and 100 coolies, the crew used cement and planks from stored MLD supplies to patch the hole. The crew then waited three days for the cement to dry properly before Witholt would risk putting the PBY in the water. Once assured of the plane's integrity, they then topped off the fuel tanks and flew to Perth, Australia, in a 14-hour flight.[35]

EVACUATION BY SEA

Those MLD personnel not flown out were to be evacuated by ship. But with no escort to protect against powerful Japanese naval units operating south of Java, the prospect of evacuation by sea was an extremely poor one. Of more than 3,000 naval personnel evacuated by ship from Tjilatjap and Wijnkoops Bay on Java's southern coast, fewer than 2,000 reached safety.[36]

Commander B.J.G. Schokking (KMR), the port commander and senior naval officer at Tjilatjap, had orders to evacuate as many KM officers and men to Australia and Colombo through the port as possible. To do the job, he had the transports *Zaandam*, *Generaal Verspyck*, *Tjisaroea*, *Tawali*, *Duymaer van Twist*, *Kota Baroe* and *Sloterdijk*. This number was quickly reduced by *Zaandam* and *Generaal Verspyck*, which Schokking made available to the British when they requested additional shipping to transport their evacuees off Java.

Once the evacuation commenced, the port quickly became crammed with naval personnel of every branch. Most were from Soerabaja, but the group included European and Indonesian personnel alike from every part of Java. There was little organization to the loading, and ships were ordered to depart individually as they filled. Few evacuees knew that the powerful Japanese naval units that had earlier attacked the port still lurked just to the south and would soon take a huge toll on their numbers.

The greatest loss came aboard the transport *Tjisaroea*, which left Tjilatjap with 800 men aboard. As the ship headed for Australia, Japanese warships appeared and ordered her captain to heave to and surrender. Unarmed with no escort or hope of outrunning them, he had no choice but to comply and be escorted to Makassar, where all aboard were made POWs.

Tjisaroea was joined a short time later by the 1,030-ton merchant ship *Duymaer van Twist*. The latter had left Tjilatjap shortly after *Tjisaroea* with 350 MLD and KM personnel aboard. Japanese warships also stopped and boarded her, forcing the transport's surrender. About the same time, they captured the 1,579-ton KPM steamer *Sigli*. A short time later she picked up 50 survivors from the sunken British destroyer *Stronghold* before the arrival of a Japanese cruiser prevented the rescue of any more; those fortunate enough to be pulled from the floats were later transferred to the Japanese cruiser *Maya*.

Of the five transports that originally left Tjilatjap carrying naval personnel, only *Tawali*, *Kota Baroe* and *Sloterdijk* survived the treacherous trip through the Japanese blockade. In the process, they often steamed through the flotsam of Allied ships that had preceded them. Shortly after sailing, *Tawali* sailed through the wreckage of a small convoy that had been annihilated by the Japanese cruisers *Atago*, *Takao* and *Maya* and their destroyer screen just hours earlier. She detoured long enough to rescue 57 survivors from the British depot ship *Anking* before continuing.

MLD personnel from Tandjoeng Priok were slated for evacuation through Wijnkoops Bay aboard the transports *Poelau Bras* and *Siberg* on March 6. This operation proved to be a failure, and nothing more was heard from either ship after they sailed. It was not until after the war that their fates were learned.

Siberg did not even clear the bay and was captured completely intact after her entire crew abandoned ship in a panic on March 6.[37] As with *Duymaer van Twist* and *Tjisaroea*, she had no opportunity to escape and was captured intact. She too was taken into Makassar and her passengers made POWs. The Japanese pressed all the captured ships into service.

The 9,278-ton transport *Poelau Bras* cleared Wijnkoops Bay in good order and set a course for Ceylon. Among her evacuees were the ground personnel of the 3rd Company from Andir and the remaining staff members of the KM's High Command. However, she was sighted soon afterwards by a Japanese reconnaissance plane, and bombers soon appeared overhead, sinking the transport 180 miles south-southwest of Java.

Two lifeboats with 118 survivors reached the coast of Sumatra, where they were interned or made POWs. Among the dead were most of the Marine Battalion's 3rd Company and Rear-Admiral J.J.A. van Staveren. Through no fault of his own, van Staveren's final task of overseeing the evacuation of Dutch naval forces and personnel had failed miserably for the most part.

An Aborted Escape

When Java capitulated and the Netherlands East Indies formally surrendered on March 9 and the smoke cleared, the Japanese found themselves in possession of a large number of captured Allied aircraft. These included the Douglas bombers that the MLD ground crews had frantically tried to assemble on the dock at Tjilatjap. When it became obvious that there was not enough time to finish the job, the unassembled planes were wrecked and left on the dock.

There, the Japanese found them and immediately put a group of Dutch prisoners to work trying to assemble one of the wrecked aircraft using components from the other planes. By May, one of the DB-7s was ready to fly, but the Japanese proved unwilling to fly the bomber off the narrow dock themselves. Perhaps fearing sabotage by the Dutch mechanics, they ordered a KNILM official — Theodore de Bruyn — to find a pilot to fly the plane to Bandoeng.

A KNILM pilot named Karl Rüpplin van Keffikon agreed to make the flight.[38] But he also stated that if an opportunity for escape arose, he would take it. Two Dutch flight mechanics volunteered to accompany Keffikon, and the three men formulated a bold plan. Once in the air, Keffikon would fly the plane inland for 30 minutes to determine if it had enough fuel and range to reach Christmas Island, 300 miles southwest of Java. If it did, he would remove his helmet, the sign for the mechanics to club their lone guard with a large wrench and overpower him. Keffikon would then take the plane to Christmas Island where it would refuel.

But after 30 minutes in the air, Keffikon ascertained that the bomber did not have the range to reach Christmas Island. Because of this, he continued the flight as planned, into Bandoeng. From there, the plane was taken to Japan for evaluation and displayed as a war prize. Its wreck was recovered after the war.

Could Keffikon have made the flight? Provided he had a full tank of gas to begin with, the DB-7 had a range of 525 miles, which normally should have been enough to reach Christmas Island. However, this was Keffikon's first time in a DB-7, and he was no doubt guessing greatly at its range. Also, subtract the distance already flown inland from the plane's endurance, and there was not much room for error. If he was off course even slightly, the flight crew could easily have been lost in the vast emptiness of the Indian Ocean.

In the end, it might have been fortunate that Keffikon and his colleagues did not reach Christmas Island. Japanese troops occupied the island on March 31, capturing its small civilian population and military garrison. Although they held the island for less than a week before withdrawing, the Japanese likely destroyed all fuel, food stocks and other equipment that they could not carry away or did not want. If that was the case, Keffikon and his crewmates could have been indefinitely marooned on the island without food or water.

10

The MLD: A New Hope

With the KM's evacuation of Java and the KNIL's surrender on March 9, the MLD's role in the East Indies campaign officially came to an end. In the bitter air battles over Java and the East Indies, Dutch aircrews had clearly proven they were equal not only to the Japanese, but their American and British counterparts as well. Still, despite tremendous courage, skill and the willingness to sacrifice, superior Japanese numbers, personnel shortages and equipment limitations (including a near complete lack of radar[1]) removed all doubt that the MLD would fall short in the end.

If the actions of the MLD provided any solace for the Dutch, it was purely moral in a losing cause. Despite thousands of sorties and 95 combat encounters in the air and at sea,[2] the East Indies campaign had been a compete failure in virtually every aspect. Not only had the last sizeable Dutch territory been lost (the West Indies were all that remained), the material and human cost had been horrific.[3] This dictated that further Dutch contributions to the Pacific War remain minuscule.[4]

Fewer than half of all KM personnel on Java were successfully evacuated to either Australia or Ceylon. These numbers included 43 percent of the Europeans and 55 percent of the Navy's Indonesian personnel, although as stated earlier, virtually all were forced to leave their family members and loved ones behind on Java to face internment.[5] Among the evacuees were 63 percent of the officers and 55 percent of the NCOs, but just 40 percent of the KM's enlisted personnel. Although these numbers are fairly complete, a postwar commission in Holland ascertained in mid-1945 that 462 Europeans and 2,007 Indonesians remained unaccounted for.[6] Although possible that some of these men deserted rather than abandon their loved ones, it is also likely that most were killed or simply lost in the confusion surrounding the fall of the East Indies.

Of the 69 operational front-line seaplanes operated or received by the MLD from December 1941 to March 1942, 53 were lost in action or destroyed to prevent capture when Java was evacuated, a loss ratio of 77 percent. And of the some 160 aircraft possessed by the MLD before, or acquired immediately after, the start of war, only 15 flying boats and 34 primary trainers survived the campaign and disaster at Broome—a survival rate of just over 30 percent. The survivors included X-5, X-7, X-8, X-9, X-10 and X-24, which were joined by Y-45, Y-49, Y-55, Y-56, Y-57, Y-62, Y-64, Y-69 and Y-71. All were scattered between Australia and Ceylon. All were operating from Rathmines Naval Air Station on the east coast of Australia except Y-55, Y-56, Y-57 and Y-64, which had evacuated Admiral Helfrich and his staff to Ceylon.

Of these, X-5, X-7, X-8, X-9, X-10 and Y-49 had been evacuated from Java in mid-February so that only nine MLD aircraft survived the official evacuation of Java and Broome raid in early March, a loss ratio approaching 95 percent. This is mute testimony as to the complete air domination by the Japanese over the NEI in February and March

147

Table 6: Nationality of KM Personnel Evacuated from Java[7]

Nationality	Lost	Evacuated	Total
European	3,414	2,599	6,013
Indonesian	307	370	677
Total	3,721	2,969	6,690

Table 7: KM Personnel Evacuated from Java[8]

Rank	Lost	Evacuated	Total
Officers	333	561	894
NCOs	396	482	878
Enlisted Personnel	2,968	2,014	4,982
Total	3,697	3,057	6,754

Table 8: Percentile Breakdown of KM Personnel by Branch[9]

Branch	Lost	Evacuated	Total
MLD	50%	50%	100%
Submarine Force	28%	72%	100%
Marines	65%	35%	100%
Surface Fleet	40%	60%	100%
Shore Personnel	75%	25%	100%
Total (Average)	52%	48%	100%

1942. Aside from the trainers, these 15 seaplanes were all the MLD had left with which to continue the war. Although the Netherlands Purchasing Commission in New York had purchased a great deal of new equipment for the MLD prior to the Pacific War, the first new planes had only begun to arrive by March and April 1942.

The Dutch could have evacuated more planes to Australia and Ceylon if they had greater range. From Java, the range to Darwin is 1,295 miles and to Ceylon approximately 2,800 miles, far too great for many of the MLD's smaller planes. Although Dutch airfields remained open in northern Sumatra, the range was great and chance of reaching them through Japanese airspace was small. A number of ML airmen reached Australia and Ceylon after the fall of Java, but they did so in aircraft with greater ranges than any of those destroyed by the MLD.

Upon arrival in Australia, the 232 MLD personnel evacuated aboard *Tjinegara*, including 167 pilot trainees, were almost immediately ordered to the United States. Here, the MLD and ML formed a joint flight training school at Jackson, Mississippi. The 575 cadets were comprised of three groups with varying levels of readiness: 1) those with basic flight training on Ryan and Koolhoven primary trainers; 2) those with intermediate training on Curtis CW-22 Falcons; 3) those pilots with advanced and operational training on single- and twin-engine land- and seaplanes.

The Royal Netherlands Military Flying School initiated flight operations at Jackson on June 6, 1942. A number of subsidiary facilities were also organized throughout the United States, including a number in south, central and west Texas. These included an MLD seaplane facility at Corpus Christi for operational training of pilots and navigator and bombardier training schools at Hondo and Midland. Upon graduation, these aircrews would form the backbone of Dutch air operations in the Pacific for the remainder of the war.[10]

Meanwhile, the MLD suffered a number of difficulties while trying to reorganize and rearm in Ceylon. Most serious was the loss of thousands of highly trained ground crews and maintenance personnel during the KM's failed evacuation of Java. As new planes arrived, the MLD had little trouble finding aircrews, but soon experienced trouble trying to maintain them. Although KLM Airline provided 15 ground crewmen, the Dutch squadron was soon a mixture of Dutch, Indonesian and Commonwealth personnel.[11]

For their part, the British Navy quickly discovered that Y-55, Y-56, Y-57, Y-62 and Y-64 were in no shape for sustained operations. Not only were the seaplanes in poor shape after months of constant flying without adequate maintenance, the crews were psychologically and physically exhausted. The RAF stationed them at Kogalla on the south coast of Ceylon, where it was hoped they could regroup with new aircraft while flying light reconnaissance missions.

Unfortunately, the Dutch PBYs were thrown back into action almost immediately. In early April, a powerful Japanese task force entered the Indian Ocean and launched a series of devastating air attacks on elements of the British Eastern Fleet at Colombo and Tricomalee. With British reconnaissance forces decimated after the East Indies campaign, the British had no choice but to commit the MLD planes.

As the Japanese savaged allied merchant shipping in the Indian Ocean and along the coast of India and Burma, three Dutch Catalinas and their British counterparts flew a number of reconnaissance missions over the Indian Ocean and Japanese force April 5–9. Although three British PBYs were shot down, their reports resulted in a number of attacks on the Japanese carriers by British bombers that also suffered heavy losses. During this period, and the preceding three weeks of March, the exhausted Dutch were lucky to put even three PBYs into the air.

Between May and June, the MLD planes on Ceylon were joined by the PBYs in Australia. Upon their arrival, the squadron was redesignated 321 Squadron (Dutch) on July 1, 1942, and transferred to China Bay on the north coast of Ceylon, where it operated as part of the RAF's 222 Group. The base at China Bay was primitive and required a great deal of work by squadron personnel to make it operational. As the British allocated very few supplies to the Dutch, many facilities had to be built from scratch, including air raid shelters, magazines and workshops.

From December 1942 to January 1943, 11 new PBY-5A amphibians arrived at China Bay, providing the MLD with its first reinforcements since early 1941. Designated Y-74 through Y-80 and Y-82 through Y-85, these planes allowed the MLD to begin rebuilding and make a contribution to the war effort. For its part, 321 Squadron (Dutch) spent the remainder of the war flying long-range reconnaissance and A/S patrols over the Indian Ocean and Bay of Bengal.

The planes in Australia operated under American operational command until May 1942, when the remaining PBYs were transferred to Ceylon. The remaining X-boats were sold to the RAAF, which used them for transport duties and covert operations into occupied Sumatra and Dutch New Guinea. X-24, the last remaining MLD Dornier, was used for covert, long-range supply missions into Japanese-occupied Dutch New Guinea until it too was transferred to the RAAF in October 1943. However, the planes were virtually impossible to maintain due to a lack of spares, and the last Dornier was broken up in late 1944.

The loss of aircraft represented only part of the nearly insurmountable task facing the MLD during its attempts to rebuild after the fall of the East Indies. Admiral Helfrich had hoped to evacuate a large percentage of his naval stores from Java. However, the speed of the Japanese advance across Java and the late start of the KM's prearranged evacuation plan from the island precluded this.

Although fortunate to get a handful of ground personnel out of Java by ship, the MLD lost all its equipment, including tools, aircraft spares, engines and machinery. So when the surviving aircraft and ground personnel arrived in Australia and Ceylon, the MLD found it difficult to continue flight operations. Compounding the problem was that many of the seaplanes had not been properly serviced or overhauled since the outbreak of the Pacific War.

On a different scale, the Dutch learned much about where they stood with their American and British allies. Highlighted by what the Dutch saw as a virtual desertion by the British Royal Navy and the American Army Air Force during the final days on Java, relations took a downturn.[12] Matters were not helped as the Americans and British (the Americans in particular) proceeded to dominate Pacific War strategy. Despite Dutch efforts to direct the war effort toward the East Indies, American leadership pointedly ignored them and pursued a course back to the Philippines.

And although the KM and MLD enjoyed a good working relationship with the USN throughout the East Indies campaign, these relations cooled as the war progressed.[13] This can be attributed to Dutch inability to influence war strategies, which led them to maintain close ties with fellow colonial power Great Britain and the Royal Navy. However, there was still a certain amount of goodwill generated by the USN's decision to stand by the Dutch during the final days on Java although the East Indies campaign was clearly lost. At a time when the Royal Navy essentially abandoned the Dutch, American naval leadership, much to its credit, honored its commitment to the KM though few others would have questioned a decision to pull out.

It does not appear that this goodwill necessarily went both ways. There was deep resentment in certain circles of the USN regarding combined Anglo-Dutch efforts that resulted in the removal of Admiral Thomas C. Hart from command of the United States Asiatic Fleet and ABDA-FLOAT in February 1942. As fleet commander, both the Dutch and British felt that he was not aggressive enough, while the USN felt that "the two colonial powers were risking and losing American ships in a campaign of which they heartily disapproved on both strategic and tactical grounds."[14]

On this note, there were also serious ideological differences among the Dutch, British and Americans. Although all three nations fought a common enemy, Dutch and British motivations were far different from that of the Americans. The Europeans fought to preserve colonies that had been under their control for hundreds of years and that they considered to be an integral part of their respective empires. Thus, they were willing to fight to the bitter end to defend these territories, a concept many of the American troops in the East Indies could not understand.[15]

The United States as a nation was not an inherent colonial power, given its war of independence from Britain. For all practical purposes the Philippines were a largely unplanned afterthought of the Spanish-American War. Although the spoils of empire came with this victory, it was a situation this nation never would have pursued otherwise. And since the Philippines were well down the road to being granted independence by the United States in December 1941, many American servicemen also could not see the point in fighting to preserve a European colonial system that was diametrically opposed to the fundamental concept of democracy.

While not a major issue that can be related to the failure of the East Indies campaign, inter-Allied relations at the lower ranks are still interesting to study. In many instances, Australian troops found their Dutch counterparts in the field to be aloof, although their respective governments had worked closely together before the outbreak of war. The British at all levels did not entirely trust their Dutch allies and made a habit of withholding sensitive military information from them.[16] This included access to British radar installations and their codebreaking efforts.

But while American and British officers in the upper and middle ranks considered the Dutch to be extremely cooperative, the same view was not always true in the field. Relations at the lower ranks were often strained as many American enlisted men considered their Dutch allies to be somewhat arrogant and ungrateful. Some of these hard feelings were undoubtedly caused by the Dutch military's inflexibility toward the American airmen's situation.

Like other European colonial armies, Dutch forces in the East Indies were a "spit and polish" organization. As such, they adhered to strict rules and regulations similar to those experienced by American personnel in the Philippines before the war. However, the evacuation of USN aircraft to Java brought a flood of poorly equipped flight crews with them. The Dutch insisted that these expatriates conform to strict uniform regulations. But with so many of them escaping the Philippines with little more than the clothes they wore, this created problems.

Clothing issues aside, a number of more serious misconceptions lingered below the surface. By January 1942, few MLD airmen were impressed with the fighting record of their USN counterparts, and many were not shy with their opinions. On the other side, the men of PatWing 10, who had just been run out of the Philippines after a brief but bitter fight, did not think the Dutch had a right to talk when they had yet to see any "real" action, although this was far from true. A number of brawls between American and Dutch personnel did not help.

These feelings were reinforced by the fact that in mid-December, the war was still being conducted far north of Java. Japanese air domination had yet to take hold as it did in the Philippines, and many Dutch personnel acted as though there were no war on. There were no blackout measures in effect, and no one seemed overly concerned. But had the Americans been at home at the same time, they probably would have seen little different outside of California and the West Coast, which were hastily being prepared to defend against a feared invasion.

In addition, the Dutch had been engaged in a "Cold War" with Japan since May 1940. They had lived with the threat of Japanese attack for some 18 months before the Pacific War started and were far more prepared for the conditions that accompanied the outbreak of war than the Americans realized. At the same time, war seemed such a long way off in December, and few doubted the ability of the Dutch military to stop the Japanese once reinforced by the Americans.

American servicemen have also commented on the disappointment expressed by the Dutch that America had failed to do more. While the Americans felt they were fighting uselessly to defend Dutch territory, many Dutchmen felt let down by the lack of American aid.[17] Few expected Britain to make a serious effort to defend the East Indies. But after tremendous verbal support from President Roosevelt and a stringent economic embargo against Japan beginning in mid-1940, many believed the United States was prepared to go the distance in defense of the East Indies.

Although language played a role in increasing friction between Dutch and American servicemen, it was not the only reason. Following the attack on Pearl Harbor, the American government suppressed the full extent of the damage for several months. As a result, very few Dutchmen knew that the core of the USN's Pacific Fleet lay wrecked. Without it, the United States was apprehensive about its ability to defend against an invasion of Hawaii and the West Coast.

In addition, the United States was poorly prepared to defend itself or the Philippines— much less the East Indies— against Japanese attack. So when the Dutch complained about the United States not doing enough, many did not understand the "big picture" and expected the Pacific Fleet to sail in with thousands of ships, men and planes that simply did not exist at that stage of the war. It should also be added that thousands of American troops holding out in the Philippines harbored the exact same thoughts and wondered why their government was not doing more.

Nonetheless, despite losing 95 percent of its operational front-line aircraft and 50 percent of its total manpower in the East Indies, the MLD successfully rebuilt, letting it contribute to the rest of the Pacific War effort in a useful though limited role. By the end of the Second World War, the Royal Netherlands Navy had a solid base to build a post-war naval air force on. By successfully weathering a crushing defeat in the East Indies, the MLD was able to preserve its identity and establish a powerful legacy for subsequent generations of its personnel to build upon.[18]

Appendix 1

MLD Squadrons in the Netherlands East Indies

M.L.D. Commander(s):

Captain K.W.F.M. Doorman	August 17, 1938–May 5, 1940
Captain G.G. Bozuwa	May 5, 1940–January 16, 1942
Captain P.J. Hendrikse	January 16, 1942–March 3, 1942
	(KIA at Broome, Australia March 3)

GVT.1   **X-15, X-35, X-36**

1st Lieutenant J.H.J. Nepveu	December 7, 1941–December 29, 1941
	(KIA aboard X-15 December 29)

Based Sambas, Borneo, with support points at Kuching and the Natoena Islands. Seaplane tender at Sambas was the Government's Marine ship Poolster. Squadron transferred to Morokrembangan December 29, 1941, and disbanded January 2, 1942, due to losses.

- X-15 lost December 29, 1941—not replaced.
- X-35 and X-36 overhauled and put into reserve.

GVT.2   **X-11, X-12, X-25**

1st Lieutenant W.J. Reijnierse	June 17, 1941–March 3, 1942

Based Sorong, New Guinea, with support points at Morotai and Ambon. Mothership at Sorong was Governments Marine ship Rigel.

- All destroyed December 26, 1941, at Kalkas seaplane base on Lake Tondano.
- Squadron reformed as GVT.2(NEW) at Soerabaja with PBY-5 Catalinas.

GVT.2(NEW)   **Y-62, Y-63, Y-64**

1st Lieutenant W.J. Reijnierse	June 17, 1941–March 3, 1942

Activated January 19 at Emmahaven harbor at Padang (west coast of Sumatra).

- Y-63 lost February 28, 1942—not replaced.
- Y-62 evacuated to Australia from Tjilatjap March 6, 1942.
- Y-64 evacuated to Ceylon from Tjilatjap March 6, 1942.

GVT.3   **X-19, X-20, X-22**

1st Lieutenant G.F. Slottje, KMR	December 1941–December 31, 1942
(Naval Air Reserve Officer who was	
not commissioned by the Royal Naval Institute)	

Replaced GVT.8 at NAS Sambo at Singapore from December 10 to fly reconnaissance missions over South China Sea, Anambas Islands and Natoena Islands.

- Transferred Morokrembangan and disbanded December 31; reformed with PBYs.
- All three X-boats put into the reserve pool.

GVT.3(NEW)   Y-46, Y-49, Y-61

1st Lieutenant G.F. Slottje   January 16, 1942–March 1, 1942

Activated at Morokrembangan January 16 and operated from that base until March 1.

- Y-46 lost at Morokrembangan March 1, 1942 — not replaced.
- Y-61 lost at Morokrembangan March 1, 1942 — not replaced.
- Y-49 evacuated to Australia with MLD flight training school February 19, 1942.

GVT.4   X-13, X-14, X-21

Lieutenant-Commander S.H. Rosier   December 6, 1941–January 27, 1942

Based at Sambas, Borneo, on December 6, 1941, for reconnaissance flights over South China Sea. Group transferred to Morokrembangan and disbanded January 27, 1942.

- X-14 lost January 23, 1942 — replaced by X-19 from reserve pool.
- X-19 lost January 25, 1942 — not replaced.

GVT.5   X-26, X-27, X-30

1st Lieutenant H.V.B. Burgerhout, KMR   December 8, 1941–March 5, 1942
(Naval Air Reserve Officer who was not
commissioned by the Royal Naval Institute)

Based at Ternate, Anambas Islands, on December 7, 1941, for reconnaissance flights over the South China Sea and area south of the Philippines.

- X-13 lost February 7, 1942 — not replaced.
- X-21 lost February 25, 1942 — not replaced.
- X-27 lost December 23, 1941— not replaced.
- X-26 lost December 26, 1941— not replaced.
- X-30 returned to Morokrembangan December 26, 1941, and put into reserve pool.

GVT.5(NEW)   Y-65, Y-66, Y-67

1st Lieutenant H.V.B. Burgerhout, KMR   December 8, 1941–March 5, 1942
(Naval Air Reserve Officer who was not
commissioned by the Royal Naval Institute)
Reformed at Morokrembangan   December 28, 1941–January 12, 1942

Group reforms and reorganizes at Morokrembangan and becomes operational at Tjilatjap as of January 12.

- Y-67 badly damaged February 7, 1942, in ground collision with Y-65 — replaced by Y-71 and flown to Morokrembangan for repairs.
- Y-65 irreparably damaged and written off February 27, 1942 — not replaced.
- Y-66 destroyed March 4, 1942 — not replaced.
- Y-71 evacuated to Australia from Tjilatjap March 5, 1942.

GVT.6   X-28, X-29, X-31

1st Lieutenant J.G. Stegeman   December 10, 1941–March 3, 1942

Activated at Morokrembangan December 10, 1941, for reconnaissance patrols over Java Sea and along the south and east coasts of Java.

- X-31 lost February 13 — replaced by X-3 and X-23.
- X-29 lost February 11, 1942 — replaced by X-21.
- X-21 lost February 25, 1942.
- X-3, X-23 and X-28 evacuated from Lengkong, Java, to Broome, Australia, March 3, 1942.

GVT.7   X-32, X-33, X-34

1st Lieutenant B. Sjerp, KMR (Naval   August 1941–March 3, 1942
Air Reserve Officer who was not commissioned
by the Royal Naval Institute)

Transferred to Tarakan on December 6, 1941, for reconnaissance flights over Celebes Sea and Makassar Strait.

- X-34 lost December 17, 1942 — replaced by X-35.
- X-33 damaged in landing accident February 7, 1942 — replaced by X-13 and flown to Morokrembangan for repairs.
- X-13, X-32 and X-35 lost at Roti Island February 7, 1942.

GVT.7(NEW)   *X-1, X-20, X-24, X-36*

All reserve planes formed from the remnants of disbanded squadrons.

1st Lieutenant B. Sjerp   August 1941–March 3, 1942

Reformed at Morokrembangan February 1942. Based on Grati Lake near Modjokerto, Java.

- X-1 lost March 3, 1942.
- X-20 lost March 3, 1942.
- X-36 lost March 5, 1942.
- X-24 evacuated to Australia March 1942 and given over to RAAF April 19, 1942.

GVT.8   *X-16, X-17, X-18*

Lieutenant-Commander W. van Prooijen, KMR   December 3, 1941–December 20, 1941
(Naval Air Reserve Officer who was not
commissioned by the Royal Naval Institute)
Lieutenant 1st Class W.O.P.R. Aernout   December 20, 1941–March 1, 1942
(Naval Air Reserve Officer who was not
commissioned by the Royal Naval Institute)

Based at NAS Seletar/Singapore December 3–10, 1941. Replaced by GVT.3 December 10, 1941, and sent to Morokrembangan for overhaul.

- X-17 lost February 24, 1942.
- X-18 lost February 24, 1942.
- X-16 lost March 1, 1942.

GVT.11   *T-15, T-16, T-17*

1st Lieutenant J. Craamer, KMR   December 7, 1941–March 2, 1942
(Naval Air Reserve Officer who was not
commissioned by the Royal Naval Institute)

Based Morokrembangan December 7, 1941–March 2, 1942. Modified to carry depth charges; carried out reconnaissance and A/S patrols over Java Sea and Soerabaja.

- T-15, T-16 and T-17 destroyed by MLD personnel at Lengkong, Java, March 2 to prevent capture.

GVT.12   *T-18, T-19, T-21*

1st Lieutenant B.J.W.M. van Voorthuisen, KMR
(Naval Air Reserve Officer who was not
commissioned by the Royal Naval Institute)
                            OR   December 7, 1941–March 2, 1942
Lieutenant 1st Class W. Bierenbroodspot, KMR
(Naval Air Reserve Officer who was not
commissioned by the Royal Naval Institute)

Based Morokrembangan December 7, 1941–March 2, 1942. Modified to carry depth charges; carried out reconnaissance and A/S patrols over Java Sea and Soerabaja.

- T-20 lost February 3, 1942.
- T-22 lost February 3, 1942.
- T-18, T-19 and T-21 destroyed by MLD personnel at Lengkong, Java, March 2 to prevent capture.

GVT.13/GVT.14	4 × Fokker C.XI-W floatplanes attached to each squadron, including: W-1, W-4, W-8, W-10, W-11, W-12, W-13, W-14

Of these aircraft, five (possibly W-1, W-8, W-11, W-12, W-13) were based aboard the light cruisers Hr.Ms. *Tromp*, Hr.Ms. *Java* and Hr.Ms. *De Ruyter*, but the surviving seaplanes aboard the latter two ships were put ashore just prior to Battle of the Java Sea.

- W-4, W-10 and W-14 destroyed February 3, 1942.
- T-22 W-12 from *De Ruyter* shot down over Tjepoe, Java, February 18, 1942.
- T-22 Remaining aircraft flown to Lengkong, Java, March 2, 1942, and destroyed by MLD personnel to prevent capture.

GVT.16	Y-51, Y-56, Y-57
Lieutenant-Commander W. van Prooijen, KMR; Former commander of GVT.8. (Naval Air Reserve Officer who was not commissioned by the Royal Naval Institute)	December 20, 1941–March 2, 1942
1st Lieutenant A. van der Hoeden, KMR (Naval Air Reserve Officer who was not commissioned by the Royal Naval Institute)	January 19, 1942–January 21, 1942

Activated December 20, 1941. Based Tandjoeng Priok for patrols over Indian Ocean, Java Sea, Karimata Strait and Gaspar Straits.

Y-51 lost January 21 and replaced by Y-55. Group evacuated Admiral Helfrich and his staff from Java to Ceylon on March 2.

- Y-51 lost to Japanese fighters January 21, 1942 — replaced by Y-55.
- Y-55 evacuated from Toeloeng Agoeng to Colombo March 1, 1942.
- Y-56 evacuated from Bagendit Lake to Colombo March 1, 1942.
- Y-57 evacuated from Toeloeng Agoeng to Colombo March 1, 1942.

GVT.17	Y-58, Y-59, Y-60
1st Lieutenant F.J. Wissel, KMR (Naval Air Reserve Officer who was not commissioned by the Royal Naval Institute)	December 8, 1941–March 3, 1942

Based NAS Halong December 7, 1941, with seaplane tender Hr.Ms. Arend. Y-58 lost January 11 and replaced by Y-67.

- Y-58 lost January 11, 1942 — replaced by Y-67.
- Y-59 evacuated from Toeloeng Agoeng, Java to Broome, Australia, March 2, 1942. Destroyed March 3, 1942, at Broome.
- Y-60 evacuated from Toeloeng Agoeng, Java to Broome, Australia, March 2, 1942. Destroyed March 3, 1942, at Broome.
- Y-67 evacuated from Toeloeng Agoeng, Java to Broome, Australia, March 2, 1942. Destroyed March 3, 1942, at Broome.

GVT.18	Y-45, Y-47, Y-48
1st Lieutenant A.W. Witholt, KMR (Naval Air Reserve Officer who was not commissioned by the Royal Naval Institute)	January 16, 1942–March 8, 1942

Activated January 16, 1942, at Tandjoeng Priok to fly reconnaissance and A/S patrols over Sumatra, Borneo and Java Sea.

- Y-47 lost February 24, 1942.
- Y-48 destroyed March 3, 1942.
- Y-45 evacuated from Tjileuntja, Java, to Australia March 8, 1942. Was the last MLD aircraft to leave Java.

Appendix 2

MLD Dornier Do. 24K Flying Boats in the Netherlands East Indies

Aircraft	Status December 7, 1941	Remarks
X-1	Flight Training School December 7, 1941	Lost March 3, 1942, during the Japanese air raid on Broome.
X-2	Flight Training School April 1941	Destroyed April 24, 1941, during takeoff accident at Moro-krembangan while on training flight.
X-3	"	Lost March 3, 1942, during the Japanese air raid on Broome.
X-4	"	Lost November 13, 1941, in night landing accident at Morokrembangan while on training flight.
X-5	Flight Training School December 7, 1941	Evacuated to Rathmines NAS, Australia, February 19, 1942, with MLD flight training school. To RAAF April 29, 1942, and scrapped December 20, 1944.
X-6	"	Lost February 3, 1942, to strafing fighters in initial air raid on Morokrembangan.
X-7	"	Evacuated to Rathmines NAS, Australia, February 19, 1942, with MLD flight training school. To RAAF April 29, 1942, and scrapped December 20, 1944.
X-8	"	"
X-9	"	"
X-10	"	To RAAF April 29, 1942, and destroyed by fuel tank at Port Darwin March 11, 1944.
X-11	Operational with GVT.2 December 7, 1941	Burned on water at Kalkas Seaplane Base on Lake Tondano December 26, 1941.
X-12	"	"
X-13	Operational with GVT.4 December 7, 1941	Burned by Japanese aircraft February 7, 1942, at MLD support base on Rotti Island.
X-14	"	Lost in the early morning of January 23, 1942, while attempting to land on Songei River at Balikpapan during evacuation flight.
X-15	Operational with GVT.1 December 7, 1941	Shot down by Japanese bomber near Midai Island December 27, 1941.
X-16	Operational with GVT.8 December 7, 1941	Damaged March 1, 1942, during Japanese air raid on Tandjoeng Priok and possibly destroyed by MLD ground crews to prevent capture. Could also have been lost to mechanical failure over Indian Ocean during evacuation flight on March 1, 1942, after repairs by MLD ground crews.
X-17	"	Lost to Japanese fighters off Noordwachter Island following air raid on Muntok Harbor February 24, 1942.
X-18	"	"
X-19	Operational with GVT.3 December 7, 1941	Lost January 25, 1942, while attempting night landing at Soerabaja after a failed rescue flight to Greater Masalembo Island.
X-20	"	Lost March 3, 1942, during Japanese air raid on Broome.

157

Aircraft	Status December 7, 1941	Remarks
X-21	Operational with GVT.4 December 7, 1941	Lost February 25, 1942, to Japanese fighter while on night reconnaissance and minelaying flight over Bali and Lombok Straits.
X-22	Operational with GVT.3 December 7, 1941	Destroyed in Japanese air raid on Morokrembangan on February 5, 1942.
X-23	Reserve Status December 7, 1941	Lost March 3, 1942, during Japanese air raid on Broome.
X-24	Flight Training School December 7, 1941 October 1943	Evacuated to Australia March 2, 1942. Transferred to RAAF
X-25	Operational with GVT.2 December 7, 1941	Burned by Japanese fighters at Kalkas seaplane base on Lake Tondano December 26, 1941.
X-26	Operational with GVT.5 December 7, 1941	Burned by Japanese fighters at Kalkas seaplane base on Lake Tondano December 26, 1941.
X-27	"	Forced down at sea and lost December 23, 1941, as a result of damage suffered during MLD air raid on Davao, Philippines.
X-28	Operational with GVT.6 December 7, 1941	Lost March 3, 1942, during Japanese air raid on Broome.
X-29	"	Lost February 11, 1942, in night landing accident at Soerabaja following failed night evacuation flight to Bandjermasin.
X-30	Operational with GVT.5 December 7, 1941	Lost February 3, 1942, to strafing fighters in initial air raid on Morokrembangan.
X-31	Operational with GVT.6 December 7, 1941	"
X-32	Operational with GVT.7 December 7, 1941	Burned by Japanese aircraft February 7, 1942, at MLD support base on Rotti Island.
X-33	"	Destroyed in Japanese air raid on Morokrembangan on February 5, 1942.
X-34	"	Damaged by Japanese fighters December 17, 1941, during MLD air attacks on invasion convoy off Miri, British Borneo, and made forced landing.
X-35	Operational with GVT.1 December 7, 1941	Burned by Japanese aircraft February 7, 1942, at MLD support base on Rotti Island.
X-36	Operational with GVT.1 December 7, 1941	Evacuated to Australia March 3, 1942. Made forced landing on North Australia beach and burned by crew on March 5.
X-37	K-2 model that arrived Morokrembangan May 1940 with defective engines and was never operational with MLD	Destroyed February 3, 1942, in Japanese air attack on Morokrembangan.

Appendix 3

MLD PBY-5 Catalina Flying Boats in the Netherlands East Indies

PBY #	Left San Diego	Reached Manila	Reached Soerabaja	Remarks
Y-38	8/25/41	9/03/41	9/05/41	Never entered active service with MLD and attached to flight training school at Morokrembangan. Lost in collision with towboat February 9, 1942, after emergency landing.
Y-39	"	"	"	Never entered active service with MLD and attached to flight training school at Morokrembangan. Transferred to PatWing 10 January 19, 1942, and shot down by Japanese fighters over Makassar Strait February 5, 1942.
Y-40	8/31/41	9/11/41	9/13–14/41 (est.)	Never entered active service with MLD and attached to flight training school at Morokrembangan. Shot down over Madoera Strait while on training flight by Japanese fighters February 3, 1942.
Y-41	"	"	"	Never entered active service with MLD and attached to flight training school at Morokrembangan. Transferred to PatWing-10 January 19, 1942, and destroyed in Japanese attack on Darwin February 19, 1942.
Y-42	9/02/41	9/11/41	"	Never entered active service with MLD and attached to flight training school at Morokrembangan. Transferred to PatWing 10 January 19, 1942. Shot down by Japanese fighters near Makassar February 24, 1942.
Y-43	9/10/41	9/23/41	9/25-26/41 (est.),	Transferred to PatWing 10 January 19, 1942, and destroyed in Japanese raid on Morokrembangan February 5, 1942.
Y-44	9/13/41	"	"	Lost in landing accident at Tandjoeng Pinang, Banka Island, December 6, 1941.
Y-45	"	"	"	Evacuated to Australia March 8, 1942. Was the last Allied plane to leave Java before its surrender.
Y-46	9/18/41	10/07/41	10/9-10/41 (est.), '41	Heavily damaged during air raid on Morokrembangan March 1, 1942. Likely destroyed to prevent capture March 2, 1942.
Y-47	"	"	"	Lost in night landing accident at Tandjoeng Priok February 23, 1942.
Y-48	"	"	"	Damaged at Tandjoeng Priok and destroyed March 3, 1942.

	PBY #	*Left San Diego*	*Reached Manila*	*Reached Soerabaja*	*Remarks*
Y-49	9/30/41	10/12/41	10/14–15/41 (est.)		Evacuated to Australia with MLD flight training school February 19, 1942.
Y-50	"	?	1/16/42		Shot down by Japanese fighters over Soerabaja February 5, 1942. Possibly landed at Morokrembangan where written off March 1 and later destroyed by MLD personnel.
Y-51	"	10/10/41	10/12/41		Burned on Barito River (Borneo) by Japanese fighters January 21, 1942.
Y-52	?	10/12/41	10/15/41		Transferred to 205 Squadron and renumbered FV-Y December 12, 1941. Burned by JAAF fighters at Seletar January 17, 1942.
Y-53	?	"	"		Transferred to 205 Squadron and renumbered FV-U December 12, 1941. Irreparably damaged landing at Tandjoeng Priok February 18, 1942; blown up March 1, 1942, to prevent capture.
Y-54	?	"	"		Transferred to 205 Squadron and renumbered FV-W December 12, 1941. Destroyed at Broome March 3, 1942.
Y-55	10/18/41	11/03/41	11/5–6/41 (est.)		Evacuated from Java to Ceylon March 2, 1942.
Y-56	"	"	"		Evacuated Admiral Helfrich to Ceylon March 2, 1942.
Y-57	10/27/41	"	"		Evacuated Admiral Helfrich's staff to Ceylon March 2, 1942.
Y-58	"	"	"		Lost with entire crew over Kema January 11, 1942.
Y-59	11/02/41	11/09/41	11/11–12/41 (est.)		Lost at Broome March 3, 1942.
Y-60	10/27/41	11/03/41	"	"	
Y-61	11/02/41	11/09/41	"		Heavily damaged in initial Japanese raid on Morokrembangan February 3, 1942. Written off March 1 and later destroyed by MLD personnel.
Y-62	11/09/41	11/15/41	11/17–18/41 (est.)		Evacuated from Java to Australia March 6, 1942.
Y-63	11/08/41	"	"		Shot down by JAAF fighters off North Gebroeders Island February 27, 1942.
Y-64	"	"	"		Evacuated from Java to Australia March 2, 1942.
Y-65	11/17/41	11/02/41	11/4–5/41 (est.),		Irreparably damaged by IJN fighters over USS *Langley* March 4, 1942. Destroyed at Tjilatjap to prevent capture March 5, 1942.
Y-66	"	"	"		Destroyed in air raid on Tjilatjap March 4, 1942.
Y-67	11/19/41	"	"		Lost at Broome March 3, 1942.
Y-68	11/27/41	—	—		Destroyed at Pearl Harbor during Japanese attack December 7, 1941.
Y-69	"	—	—		Heavily damaged at Midway Island and returned to Consolidated plant at San Diego, California, for repairs. Joined MLD forces on Ceylon end of March 1942.
Y-70	"	?	12/41		At Wake Island December 7, 1942, en route to Java. Reached Java late December 1941 and later burned at Broome March 3, 1942.
Y-71	?	?	1/08/41		Reached Java via Atlantic route January 8,

	PBY #	Left San Diego	Reached Manila	Reached Soerabaja	Remarks
					1942. Evacuated from Java to Australia March 6, 1942.
Y-72	12/08/41	?	1/42		Reached Java via Atlantic route January 8, 1942. Unattached to a GVT when shot down by Japanese fighters over Waroe, Java, February 5, 1942. Transported back to Morokrembangan by truck; fuselage attached to wing and engine assembly of PatWing 10 PBY 22-P-12 and returned to active service as P-46. Evacuated to Australia March 1942.
Y-73	?	?	"		Irreparably damaged by Japanese fighters at Morokrembangan March 1, 1942.
Y-3	—	—	—		Damaged PatWing 10 PBY-4 (P-3) abandoned at Tjilatjap. Repaired by MLD personnel and flown to Australia. Transferred to RAAF March 1942.

Appendix 4

MLD Reserve Seaplanes in the Netherlands East Indies

Fokker T.IV (a)

Aircraft	Squadron December 7, 1941	Remarks
T-1	—	Damaged and written off October 16, 1937, following accident.
T-2	—	Written off and taken out of service 1939–40.
T-3	—	"
T-4	—	"
T-5	—	"
T-6	—	"
T-7	—	"
T-8	—	"
T-9	—	"
T-10	—	"
T-11	—	"
T-12	—	"
T-13	—	Damaged and written off October 12, 1937, following accident.
T-14	—	Damaged and written off May 26, 1941, following accident.
T-15	GVT.11	Destroyed by MLD personnel at Lengkong Lake to prevent capture March 2, 1941.
T-16	"	"
T-17	"	"
T-18	"	"
T-19	"	"
T-20	GVT.12	Destroyed at Morokrembangan by Japanese fighters February 3, 1942.
T-21	"	Destroyed by MLD personnel at Lengkong Lake to prevent capture March 2, 1941.
T-22	"	Destroyed at Morokrembangan by Japanese fighters February 3, 1942.
T-23	"	Destroyed by MLD personnel at Lengkong Lake to prevent capture March 2, 1941.
T-24	"	"

Fokker C.XI-W

Aircraft	December 7, 1941	Remarks
W-1	GVT.13 or GVT.14	Destroyed by MLD personnel at Lengkong Lake to prevent capture March 2, 1941.
W-2	—	Damaged and written off January 1939 following accident.
W-4	GVT.13 or GVT.14	Destroyed at Morokrembangan by Japanese fighters February 3, 1942.

Fokker C.XI-W

Aircraft	December 7, 1941	Remarks
W-5	—	Damaged and written off May 1939 following accident.
W-6	—	Damaged and written off August 7, 1940, following accident.
W-7	—	Damaged and written off September 26, 1939, following landing accident at Blinjoe, Banka; attached to Hr.Ms. *De Ruyter*.
W-8	GVT.13 or GVT.14	Destroyed by MLD personnel at Lengkong Lake to prevent capture March 2, 1941.
W-10	"	Destroyed at Morokrembangan by Japanese fighters February 3, 1942.
W-11	"	Destroyed by MLD personnel at Lengkong Lake to prevent capture March 2, 1941.
W-12	(Hr.Ms. *De Ruyter*)	Shot down by Japanese fighter near Tjepoe, Java, February 18, 1942.
W-13	"	Lost in accident June 17, 1941.
W-14	"	Destroyed at Morokrembangan by Japanese fighters February 3, 1942.
W-15	"	Destroyed by MLD personnel at Lengkong Lake to prevent capture March 2, 1941.

Fokker C.XIV-W

Aircraft	December 7, 1941	Remarks
F-1	MLD Flight Training School	Date of loss unknown, but likely destroyed in Japanese air attack on Morokrembangan February 1942. Or destroyed by MLD personnel March 1942 to prevent capture.
F-5	"	"
F-6	"	"
F-13	"	"
F-15	"	"
F-16	"	"
F-17	"	"
F-18	"	"
F-22	"	"
F-23	"	"

Appendix 5

Specifications for MLD Planes in the Netherlands East Indies

(Total Number Available, Approximately 130 Planes)

DORNIER DO. 24K-1/K-2 ("X" BOATS)

Type: Air\Sea Rescue\Reconnaissance Flying Boat
Crew: 6
Number: 37

*Performance:

Powerplant:	3 × 1,000 hp engines (Wright Cyclone GR1820 F-52)
Max Speed At 9,900 Feet:	211 mph
Cruising Speed:	137 mph
Maximum Range:	2,920 miles
Ceiling:	24,605 feet
	6 minutes to 6,650 feet

*Weight:	20,723 lbs empty
	35,715 lbs loaded

*Dimensions:

Wing Span:	88 feet, 7 inches
Length:	72 feet, 4 inches
Height:	18 feet, 10¼ inches
Wing Area:	1,162 square feet

Armament:	2 × 7.7mm Browning machine guns, 1 × 20mm Hispano-Suiza cannon, and maximum bomb load of 2,642 pounds.
Comments:	Design originally built to Dutch specifications for service in the East Indies. K-1 was the original model and was to be replaced by new Dutch-assembled K-2 versions. However, X-37 was the only K-2 version to arrive in the NEI before the invasion of Holland in May 1940.

*Do. 24K-1 Version

DORNIER DO. 15 "WHALE" ("D" BOATS)

Type: Reconnaissance Flying Boat
Crew: 4
Number: 10

Performance:

Powerplant:	2 × 750 hp Rolls Royce Eagle or Lorraine Dietrich engines; Do. Whale F models: 2 × 600 hp Lorraine Courlis engines
Maximum Speed:	143 mph

Cruising Speed:	124 mph
Range:	1,180 miles
	7 minutes to 9,842 feet
Weight:	10,362 lbs empty
	17,637 lbs loaded
Dimensions:	
Wing Span:	76 feet, 1½ inches
Length:	60 feet, ½ inch
Height:	17 Feet, 6½ inches
Wing Area:	1,033.34 square feet
Armament:	2 × 7.7mm machine guns, maximum bomb load of 2,200 pounds.
Comments:	In use with Netherlands East Indies Naval Air Force since the mid-1920s. Original order numbered 46 planes, but only 10 remained operational by the outbreak of the Pacific War.

CONSOLIDATED PBY-5 CATALINA ("Y" BOATS)

Type: Patrol Bomber Flying Boat
Crew: 7
Number: 36

Performance:	
Powerplant:	2 × 1,200 hp Pratt & Whitney R-1830-82 engines
Max Speed At 5,700 Feet:	200 mph
Cruising Speed:	115 mph
Range:	1,895 miles
Ceiling:	21,600 feet
Weight:	17,400 lbs empty
	33,389 lbs loaded
Dimensions:	
Wing Span:	104 feet
Length:	63 feet, 10 inches
Height:	18 feet, 11 inches
Wing Area:	1,400 square feet
Armament:	4 × .50 Browning machine guns, 4 × depth charges, 2 × torpedoes or 4 × 1,000 pound bombs.
Comments:	36 PBYs were completed for the Netherlands East Indies Naval Air Force at the Consolidated aircraft factory in San Diego, California between August and October 1941. Although the first PBY arrived at Soerabaja September 5 of that year, the last Catalinas did not arrive until January 1942, well after the outbreak of war with Japan. An additional 12 amphibious aircraft were still on order when Java fell and were delivered to the remnants of MLD at Ceylon from March 1942.

FOKKER T.IVA ("T" BOATS)

Type: Torpedo Bomber/Reconnaissance Floatplane
Crew: 4
Number: 11

Performance:
Powerplant: 2 × 768 hp Wright Cyclone SR-1820-F2
Max Speed At 2,624 Feet: 161 mph
Cruising Speed: 135 mph
Range: 970 miles
Ceiling: 19,360 feet
                                3 minutes, 6 seconds to 3,280 feet

Weight: 10,284 lbs empty
                                15,873 lbs loaded

Dimensions:
Wing Span: 85 feet, 11½ inches
Length: 57 feet, 9 inches
Height: 19 feet, 8¼ inches
Wing Area: 1,052 square feet

Armament: 3 × 7.7mm FN-Browning machine guns, maximum (internal) bomb
                                load of 1,764 pounds or 1 × torpedo under fuselage.

Comments: Designed for service in the East Indies and first flown in 1927. All 24
                                planes constructed were sent to the Far East. Eleven were left in Decem-
                                ber 1941, and served in auxiliary roles.

FOKKER C.XIV-W ("F" CLASS)

Type: Trainer/Reconnaissance Floatplane
Crew: 2
Number: 10

Performance:
Powerplant: 1 × 450 hp Wright R-975E-3 engine
Maximum Speed: 143 mph
Cruising Speed: 120 mph
Range: 590 miles
Ceiling: 17,720 feet
                                3 minutes, 48 seconds to 3,280 feet

Weight: 2,930 lbs empty
                                4,300 lbs loaded

Dimensions:
Wing Span: 39 feet, 5 inches
Length: 31 feet, 2 inches
Height: 13 feet, 11 inches
Wing Area: 342.22 square feet

Armament: 2 × 7.9mm FN-Browning or 7.7mm Browning machine guns. For air-
                                craft operating in Europe, 7.9mm was the standard caliber, while 7.7mm
                                was the standard for aircraft in the NEI. As these aircraft were originally
                                built and delivered to units in Holland, they would have been armed
                                with 7.9mm weapons; however, it is unknown whether they were
                                rearmed after their arrival in the NEI in mid-1940.

Comments: These aircraft were 11 survivors from the German invasion of Holland
                                in May 1940. They were initially evacuated to England and eventually
                                sent on to the East Indies later that year.

FOKKER C.XI-W ("W" CLASS)

Type: Cruiser Reconnaissance Floatplane
Crew: 2
Number: 8

Performance:	
Powerplant:	1 × 750 hp Wright Cyclone SR-1820
Max Speed At 5,750 Feet:	174 mph
Cruising Speed:	146 mph
Range:	453 miles
Ceiling	20,990 feet
	2 minutes, 24 seconds to 3,280 feet
Weight:	3,792 lbs empty
	5,622 lbs loaded
Dimensions:	
Wing Span:	42 feet, 8 inches
Length:	31 feet, 1 inches
Height:	14 feet, 9 inches
Wing Area:	430.4 square feet
Armament:	2 × 7.7mm FN-Browning machine guns
Comments:	Dual-purpose floatplane intended for shipboard and land-based operations. Entered service in 1938 and most sent to the Far East. Eight were aboard the cruisers Hr.Ms. *De Ruyter* and Hr.Ms. *Java*, but were later off-loaded for land operations. Only five were operational. Also operated aboard the cruisers Hr.Ms. *Sumatra* and Hr.Ms. *Tromp*, although the latter's aircraft was destroyed in a landing accident before the outbreak of war and was not replaced.

FOKKER C.VII-W ("V" CLASS)

Type: Light Reconnaissance/Trainer
Crew: 2
Number: 12 (Original Number Sent To East Indies)

Performance:	
Powerplant:	1 × 225 hp Armstrong Siddely Lynx engine
Maximum Speed:	100 mph
Cruising Speed:	81 mph
Maximum Range:	625 miles
Ceiling:	7,870 feet
	27 minutes to 6,560 feet
Weight:	2,643 lbs empty
	3.776 lbs loaded
Dimensions:	
Wing Span:	42 feet, 4 inches
Length:	31 feet, 2 inches
Height:	13 feet, 2 inches
Wing Area:	389 square feet
Armament:	1 × fixed forward firing Browning 7.7mm machine gun and 1 × flexible 7.7mm Lewis gun in observer's cockpit; assorted small bombs under aft fuselage.
Comments:	First flown in 1926. Twelve eventually sent to Naval Squadron in Far East. Six left in auxiliary capacity when Japanese attacked, although these might have been retired from service in 1941.

Appendix 6

Specifications for Japanese Planes Operating in the Netherlands East Indies

Fighters: Army

NAKAJIMA KI-27 "NATE"

Crew: 1

Performance:
Powerplant:	1 × 710 hp Nakajima Ha-1b Army Type 97 engine
Max Speed At 11,480 Feet:	292 mph
Cruising Speed:	217 mph
Maximum Range:	1,060 miles
Ceiling:	40,190 feet
	5 minutes, 22 seconds to 16,400 feet

Weight:	2,447 lbs empty
	3,946 lbs loaded

Dimensions:
Wing Span:	37 feet, 1¼ inches
Length:	24 feet, 8½ inches
Height:	10 feet, 8 inches
Wing Area:	199.777 square feet

Armament:	2 × 7.7mm Type 89 machine guns, 220 pounds of bombs.
Comments:	Although obsolescent, "Nates" were highly maneuverable and formed the backbone of the JAAF during the early months of the Pacific War. At the outbreak of hostilities it was being phased out and replaced by Ki-43 "Oscars." Though it had fixed landing gear, the "Nate" remained competitive against Allied fighter opposition well into the latter years of the war.

NAKAJIMA KI-43 "OSCAR"

Crew: 1

Performance:
Powerplant:	1 × 980 hp Nakajima Ha-25, Army Type 99 engine
Max Speed At 13,120 Feet:	308 mph
Cruising Speed:	199 mph
Maximum Range:	745 miles
Ceiling:	38,500 feet
	5 minutes, 30 seconds to 16,400 feet

| Weight: | 3,483 lbs empty |
| | 5,695 lbs loaded |

Dimensions:	
Wing Span:	37 feet, 6¼ inches
Length:	28 feet, 11¾ inches
Height:	10 feet, 8¾ inches
Wing Area:	236.805 square feet

| Armament: | 2 × 7.7mm Type 89 machine guns with maximum bomb load of 66 pounds. |

| Comments: | Just as maneuverable as the A6M "Zero," "Oscar" was an extremely dangerous opponent for Allied fighters, although it suffered the same weaknesses as its naval counterpart, including a substantial lack of armor. It was just entering service and replacing the "Nate" during the initial drive into the Pacific. Among the "Oscar's" other primary shortfalls was an initially weak armament. |

Fighters: Navy

MITSUBISHI A5M4 "CLAUDE"

Crew: 1

Performance:	
Powerplant:	1 × 785 hp Nakajima Kotobuki 41 or 41 KAJ engine
Max Speed At 9,840 Feet:	270 mph
Maximum Range:	746 miles
Ceiling:	32,150 feet
	3 minutes, 35 seconds to 9,840 feet

| Weight: | 2,681 lbs empty |
| | 3,684 lbs loaded |

Dimensions:	
Wing Span:	36 feet, 1¼ inches
Length:	24 feet, 9¾ inches
Height:	10 feet, 8¾ inches
Wing Area:	191.597 square feet

| Armament: | 2 × 7.7mm Type 89 machine guns, maximum bomb load of 132lbs. |

| Comments: | Similar to the JAAF's "Nate" in performance and armament, "Claude" was the IJN's first monoplane fighter. Although almost entirely replaced by the A6M "Zero" in December 1941, the "Claude" still equipped squadrons aboard three light carriers. |

MITSUBISHI A6M2 "ZERO" ("ZEKE")

Crew: 1

Performance:	
Powerplant:	1 × 950 hp Nakajima NK1C Sakae 12 engine
Max Speed At 14,930 Feet:	332 mph
Cruising Speed:	207 mph
Maximum Range:	1,930 miles

Ceiling:	32,810 feet
	7 minutes, 27 seconds to 19,685 feet
Weight:	3,704 lbs empty
	6,164 lbs loaded
Dimensions:	
Wing Span:	39 feet, 4½ inches
Length:	29 feet, 8¾ inches
Height:	10 feet
Wing Area:	241.541 square feet
Armament:	2 × 20mm Type 99 cannon, 2 × 7.7mm Type 97 machine guns with provisions for a 264-pound bomb load.
Comments:	The "Zero" comprised over 60 percent of all IJN fighter units when Pacific War broke out and formed backbone of the IJN fighter corps for entire war. It was a primary reason for the overwhelming success of Japanese onslaught during early days of the Pacific War.

Bombers: Army

MITSUBISHI K-21 "SALLY"

Type: Heavy Bomber
Crew: 5-7

Performance:	
Powerplant:	2 × 1,500 hp Mitsubishi Ha-101, Army Type 1 engines
Max Speed At 15,485 Feet:	302 mph
Cruising Speed:	236 mph
Maximum Range:	1,680 miles
Ceiling:	32,810 feet
	13 minutes, 13 seconds to 19,685 feet
Weight:	13,382 lbs empty
	23,391 lbs loaded
Dimensions:	
Wing Span:	73 feet, 9¾ inches
Length:	52 feet, 6 inches
Height:	15 feet, 11 inches
Wing Area:	749.165 square feet
Armament:	5 × 7.7mm Type 89 machine guns, 1 × 12.7mm Type 1 machine gun, maximum bomb load of 2,205lbs.
Comments:	The primary JAAF bomber during the early months of the Pacific War. Although successful in the early months of the war due to weak Allied fighter forces, performance fell dramatically as superior fighter resistance unmasked limitations of the "Sally."

Bombers: Navy

Mitsubishi G4M1 Model 11 "Betty"
Type: Medium Bomber
Crew: 7

Performance:

Powerplant:	2 × 1,530 hp Mitsubishi MK4A Kasei 11 engines
Max Speed At 13,780 Feet:	266 mph
Cruising Speed:	196 mph
Maximum Range:	3,748 miles
Ceiling:	?
	18 minutes to 22,965 feet
Weight:	14,991 lbs empty
	20,944 lbs loaded

Dimensions:

Wing Span:	82 feet, ¼ inch
Length:	65 feet, 7½ inches
Height:	19 feet, 8¼ inches
Wing Area:	840.927 square feet
Armament:	4 × 7.7mm Type 92 machine guns, 1 × 20mm Type 99 Model 1 cannon and a maximum bomb load of 1,764 pounds or one torpedo.
Comments:	The "Betty" formed the backbone of the IJN's bomber force throughout the Pacific War and was the most frequently encountered bomber in the East Indies. There were 120 operational at the time of Pearl Harbor. As with the "Sally" the "Betty" provided excellent service in the early stages of the war; however, as Allied fighter resistance stiffened, performance dropped dramatically.

Mitsubishi G3M2 "Nell"

Type: Bomber
Crew: 7

Performance:

Powerplant:	2 × 1,075 hp Mitsubishi Kinsei 41, 42 or 45 engines
Max Speed At 13,715 Feet:	232 mph
Cruising Speed:	173 mph
Maximum Range:	2,722 miles
Ceiling:	29,950 feet
	8 minutes, 19 seconds to 9,840 feet
Weight:	10,936 lbs empty
	17,637 lbs loaded

Dimensions:

Wing Span:	82 feet, ¼ inch
Length:	53feet, 11½ inches
Height:	12 feet, 1 inch
Wing Area:	807.3 square feet
Armament:	4 × 7.7mm Type 92 machine guns, 1 × 20mm Type 99 Model 1 cannon, maximum bomb load of 1,764 pounds or 1 torpedo.
Comments:	First entered service 1937 and was obsolete by 1941. 200+ were operational and on front-line duty at outbreak of the Pacific War, but were in the process of being phased out and replaced by G4M1s.

Miscellaneous Navy

AICHI E13A1 "JAKE"

Type: Long-Range Reconnaissance Floatplane
Crew: 3

Performance:
Powerplant:	1 × 1,080 hp Mitsubishi Kinsei 43 engine
Max Speed At 7,155 Feet:	234 mph
Cruising Speed:	138 mph
Maximum Range:	1,298 miles
Ceiling:	28,640 feet
	6 minutes, 5 seconds to 9,840 feet

Weight:	5,825 lbs empty
	12,192 lbs loaded

Dimensions:
Wing Span:	47 feet, 7 inches
Length:	37 feet, 1 inch
Height:	15 feet, 5 inches
Wing Area:	387.5 square feet

Armament:	1 × 7.7mm Type 92 machine gun; maximum bomb load of 551 pounds.
Comments:	Entered service late 1941, serving aboard large warships and aircraft tenders. Was replacing the E8N2 "Dave."

NAKAJIMA E8N2 "DAVE"

Type: Short-Range Reconnaissance Floatplane
Crew: 2

Performance:
Powerplant:	1 × 630 hp Nakajima Kotobuki 2 KAI 2 engine
Max Speed At 9,840 Feet:	186 mph
Cruising Speed:	115 mph
Maximum Range:	559 miles
Ceiling:	23,850 feet
	6 minutes, 31 seconds to 9,840 feet

Weight:	2,901 lbs empty
	4,189 lbs loaded

Dimensions:
Wing Span:	36 feet, ¼ inch
Length:	28 feet, 10¾ inches
Height:	12 feet, 7¾ inches
Wing Area:	285.24 square feet

Armament:	2 × 7.7mm machine guns; maximum bomb load of 132 pounds.
Comments:	"Dave" was found aboard virtually all capital ships, heavy cruisers and seaplane tenders, together with the "Jake," which was in the process of replacing it.

KAWANISHI E7K "ALF" RECONNAISSANCE FLOATPLANE

Type: Short-Range Reconnaissance Floatplane
Crew: 3

Performance:
Powerplant:	1 × 870 hp Mitsubishi Zuisei 11 engine
Max Speed At 9,840 Feet:	171 mph
Cruising Speed:	115 mph
Maximum Range:	1,147 miles
Ceiling:	23,165 feet
	9 minutes, 6 seconds to 9,840 feet

Weight:	4,360 lbs empty
	7,275 lbs loaded

Dimensions:
Wing Span:	45 feet, 11¾ inches
Length:	34 feet, 5½ inches
Height:	15 feet, 10½ inches
Wing Area:	469.31 square feet

Armament:	3 × 7.7mm machine guns; maximum bomb load of 264 pounds.
Comments:	Despite being obsolete at the start of the Pacific War, "Alf" was both rugged and easy to fly, making it highly popular with aircrews that flew it. This versatile aircraft operated aboard older Japanese Navy cruisers, seaplane tenders and with shore-based units in a wide range of roles, including reconnaissance, A/S support and convoy escort until mid-1943 when replaced by the "Jake."

Appendix 7

Marine Seaplane Tenders

Hr.Ms. *Arend*

Displacement:	1,011 tons (standard)/1,251 tons (full load)
Dimensions:	231 × 30 × 15b
Speed:	17 knots/11 knots (cruising speed)
Armament:	2 × 75mm deck guns, 1 × 7.7mm machine gun
Complement:	65

Launched by Fijenoord Shipyard in Holland in 1929 and completed a year later, Arend operated in the East Indies as an *opium jager* (drug interdiction vessel). When militarized in September 1939, she was assigned to the MLD as a seaplane tender. In late February 1942, she was badly damaged during an air raid on Tandjoeng Priok and later allowed to sink on the night of March 1–2.

Arend was raised by Japan's 102nd Repair Section and towed to Soerabaja in April 1943. After extensive modifications, she was renamed Patrol Boat 108 and joined the 22nd Special Base Force on July 31, 1944. USN aircraft off Makassar sank her on May 10, 1945.

Hr.Ms. *Valk*

Displacement:	1,011 tons (standard)/1,251 tons (full load)
Dimensions:	231 × 30 × 15b
Speed:	18 knots/11 knots (cruising speed)
Armament:	2 × 75mm deck guns, 2 × 12.7mm AA
Complement:	68

Valk was launched by Fijenoord Shipyard on October 19, 1929, and completed a year later. She operated with the Governments Marine in the East Indies as an *opium jager* (drug interdiction vessel) until militarized in September 1939 and assigned to the MLD as a seaplane tender. In late February, she was severely damaged during an air raid on Tandjoeng Priok and allowed to sink on the night of March 1–2.

She was raised by Japan's 102nd Repair Section on April 21, 1943, and renamed Patrol Boat 104 on September 1, 1943. She joined the 22nd Special Base Force on January 31, 1944, and was heavily damaged six months later. Laid up and later mined August 1945.

Hr.Ms. *Fazant*

Displacement:	624 tons
Dimensions:	158 feet × 28 feet × 9½ feet
Speed:	12¼ knots
Armament:	1 × 75mm deck gun, 1 × 7.7mm machine gun
Complement:	43

Laid down in 1929 at Soerabaja as a patrol boat for the Governments Marine, Fazant was launched in 1931. When the Governments Marine was militarized in September 1939, she was attached to the MLD as a seaplane tender. Fazant operated in this role throughout the East Indies campaign until scuttled at Tandjoeng Priok on March 1, 1942.

On July 31, 1944, Japanese Navy's 102nd Repair Section raised Fazant. After extensive repairs, commissioned into Imperial Japanese Navy on as *Patrol Boat 109* October 15, 1944. Surrendered at Batavia in 1945 and eventually transferred to the Indonesian Navy and renamed Kartika in 1951.

HR.MS. *REIGER*

Displacement:	624 tons
Dimensions:	158 feet × 28 feet × 9½ feet
Speed:	12¼ knots
Armament:	1 × 75mm deck gun
Complement:	40

Laid down in 1929 at Soerabaja as a patrol boat for the Governments Marine, Reiger was launched in 1931. When the Governments Marine was militarized in September 1939, she was attached to the MLD as a seaplane tender. Reiger operated in this role until mid-February, when she was ordered to help patrol the Soenda Strait after the fall of Palembang. She was sunk in this role by Japanese warships on the night of February 28.

HR.MS. *MEREL*

Displacement:	592 tons
Dimensions:	158 feet × 28 feet × 9½ feet
Speed:	12¼ knots
Armament:	1 × 75mm deck gun
Complement:	40

Built at Soerabaja as a patrol boat for the Governments Marine, Merel was launched in 1928. When the Government's Marine was militarized in September 1939, she was attached to the MLD as a seaplane tender. Although ordered to Padang by the Dutch naval high command on March 2, she was unable break out of Tandjoeng Priok and was scuttled there later that night.

HR.MS. *POOLSTER*

Displacement:	1,565 tons (standard)/1,929 tons (fully loaded)
Dimensions:	246½ (overall) × 39½ × 16
Speed:	12.8 knots (max)/11½ knots (cruising)
Armament:	1 × 75mm deck gun, 2 × 12.7mm AA
Complement:	60

Built at the N.V. Drydock Company at Tandjoeng Priok, Poolster was launched in May 1938. She operated with the Governments Marine as a salvage vessel until militarized in September 1939. In addition to operating as a seaplane tender for MLD aircraft, Poolster filled a number of other roles until the end of the East Indies campaign. On March 1, her captain requested permission to evacuate his ship to Australia, which was denied. He instead received orders to scuttle the ship, release the Indonesian crew from service and report to Bandoeng with his officers for further orders.

The 102nd Repair Section raised Poolster on September 21, 1943. Commissioned in IJN as salvage vessel Horei Maru and operated until sunk by U.S. Navy aircraft near the Philippines in January 1945.

HR.MS. *BELLATRIX*

Displacement:	773 tons (standard)
Dimensions:	176¼ (overall) × 30 × 10¼

Speed: 12 knots (max)
Armament: 1 × 75mm deck gun
Complement: 45

Built at the Rijkswerf in Amsterdam, Bellatrix was launched in 1914. She operated with the Governments Marine as a patrol boat until militarized in September 1939. In addition to operating as a seaplane tender for MLD aircraft, Bellatrix filled a number of other roles, including supply boat and aircraft tanker until the end of the East Indies campaign. She was scuttled in Tanjoeng Priok's inner harbor on March 1, 1942, with the Indonesian crewmen being released from service, while her officers were to report to Bandoeng for further orders.

Appendix 8

MLD Bases in the Netherlands East Indies

Primary and Support Bases

MVK Morokrembangan: The name Morokrembangan translates literally to "Mouth of the Krembangan River." Situated west of Soerabaja on the far side of the Kali River, the naval air station lay on Tandjoeng Perak on the Madoera Strait.

MVK Halong: Situated on Halong Bay five miles northeast of Ambon City. The minelayer Hr.Ms. *Gouden Leeuw* laid a barrage of 70 mines between December 16, 1941, and mid-January 1942. In addition, a sturdy log boom effectively closed the harbor.

MVK Priok: Located near Tandjoeng Priok, the harbor of Batavia; the naval air station lay west of the harbor.

Lake Toba: The naval air station lay at Prapat, on the east side the lake.

Tarakan: A major support base established near Lingkas on the southwest coast of the island.

Balikpapan: A support base that lay on the east side of Balikpapan Bay.

Pontianak: A support base that lay on the Kapoeas River, outside the city of Pontianak.

Kalkas: Established in 1940–41, this isolated support base lay on the south shore of Lake Tondano in Northern Celebes.

Koepang: A support base in West Timor that was only partially operational when war broke out. In December 1941 it contained berths for MLD aircraft.

Makassar: An auxiliary base offering accommodations for large numbers of aircraft in the roadstead.

Dore Bay: Located near Manokwari, New Guinea, this auxiliary base on the Vogelkop offered excellent water conditions and could be used easily and frequently. Manokwari also offered excellent conditions with berths for 6 to 12 aircraft.

Menado: Located in Menado harbor, this auxiliary base was not suitable for sustained flight operations. MLD pilots who encountered flash thunderstorms and other violent weather conditions detrimental to aircraft safety used it only as an emergency landing station.

Sabang: This auxiliary base was located at Poelau Weh in north Sumatra.

Sambas: Located on the Sambas River in Northwest Borneo, this auxiliary seaplane base had space to handle very large numbers of seaplanes.

Poelau Sambo: This auxiliary base was situated in Riouw Archipelago in the Singapore Straits. In December 1941 it could be made operational with a little technical support.

Sorong: Auxiliary base established on Dom Island in the Sele Strait on the northwest coast of the Vogelkop in western New Guinea.

Ternate: This auxiliary base on Molukka Island featured excellent water conditions that let it be frequently used. In addition, it offered ample space for large numbers of flying boats. In December 1941 GVT.5 was stationed here with orders to carry out reconnaissance flights between Ternate and Ambon. The Governments Marine ship Hr.Ms. *Bellatrix* served as mothership for the squadron.

Scatter Bases

BENOORD BAY: Located on Roti Island in the Lesser Soenda Islands.

BRANTAS RIVER: The river featured three scatter bases in East Java:
- Lengkong — The river offered enough space and open water for aircraft that required long takeoffs and landings. It was the only scatter base where MLD planes could takeoff and land at night.
- Modjokerto— Useable only by aircraft that could land and takeoff in short distances. Night operations were not possible.
- Djombang — A stretch of river nine miles from the city could handle aircraft with short landing and takeoff capabilities. As with Modjokerto, night operations were not possible.

RANOE KLINDOENGAN: This scatter base was located near Passoeroean in East Java. Nearby Klakeh functioned as a staging point for this base.

TJILEUNTJE LAKE: Located six miles west of Bagendit near Pengalangan on West Java.

KALABAHI: A little-used scatter base for MLD aircraft that was established south of Timor on Roti Island in the Lesser Soenda Islands.

ROTI ISLAND: This base was never more than marginally operational and had been built to serve as a scatter base only when the base at Koepang became untenable.

Chart 1

*Breakdown of MLD Losses by Month**

As seen in Chart 1, MLD losses were relatively small in the early months of the war. Although nearly 20 percent of all Do. 24 and PBY losses came in December, this figure is deceptively high. Of the eight flying boats lost in December, one was a landing accident, while another was lost at Pearl Harbor and four more in a single day at Lake Tondano. Subtract these losses from the month's total and one sees that the MLD lost only two boats in its daily air operations.

This trend remained consistent throughout January. However, as the Japanese advance moved south, it quickly became a tidal wave that denied the MLD use of its forward airbases. Whereas air combat with Japanese fighters remained comparatively scarce in the first two months of the war, their aggressive, fast-moving advance soon increased the number and frequency of these encounters.

By February and March there was virtually no spot in the NEI that remained free of Japanese air attack. With their fighters striking the naval air stations at Morokrembangan and Tandjoeng Priok almost at will, the MLD suffered more than half of its front-line aircraft losses in these two months alone. It was at this point that the Dutch and their American and British allies very quickly realized that there was literally no place for them to hide or safely operate.

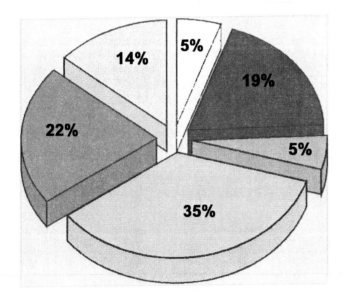

- ☐ Prewar
- ■ December
- ☐ January
- ☐ February
- ▨ March
- ☐ Evacuated

* *Do. 24 and PBY figures only*

Chart 2

*Breakdown of Do. 24 and PBY Losses by Month**

Chart 2 shows the breakdown of Do. 24 and PBY losses suffered by month during the NEI campaign. In December one can clearly see that the Dorniers by far suffered a disproportionate number of the MLD's front-line losses. This was because although large numbers of new PBYs had reached the East Indies from the United States, they had yet to begin phasing out the older German-built aircraft. So although two squadrons had reequipped with PBYs, Do. 24s were still the workhorses of the MLD's operational strength at the time of Pearl Harbor.

Although January saw a comparatively small number of MLD aircraft lost, the ratio between PBYs and Dorniers was almost even. This trend would remain consistent throughout February, although the number of Dorniers lost remained higher because of their established position in the front-line squadrons. But as attrition among the German-built flying boats mounted, squadrons were rotated back to Morokrembangan, where they were reequipped and retrained on Catalinas.

As the number of PBYs operating with front-line units began to grow, so did their losses. Although a good number of Dorniers remained in service, by the surrender of the NEI in March 1942, the PBY was well on its way to becoming the reconnaissance aircraft of choice for the MLD. Because of their relatively late arrival in combat, fewer of these aircraft were lost during the campaign, thus ensuring that a slightly higher number would survive to be evacuated.

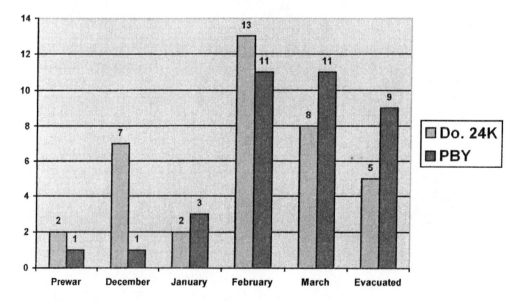

*Includes eight PBYs lost or destroyed after being transferred to the RAF and USN

Chart 3

*MLD Losses by Cause**

Chart 3 is a breakdown showing the cause of individual front-line MLD aircraft losses during the NEI campaign. Air combat consists of air-to-air action with Japanese aircraft, including fighters, bombers and seaplanes. AA fire includes ground and shipboard return fire against the Dutch planes, while accidents include aircraft lost to non-combat causes during takeoff or landing. Destroyed is used to describe aircraft blown up or otherwise permanently disabled on the ground to prevent their capture by the Japanese. These were typically aircraft that had been previously damaged, although they might or might not have been repairable.

Clearly the most vivid figure shown by this chart is the extraordinary (just under half) number of all front-line MLD aircraft lost on the ground. This number would be well over 50 percent if one figured in the substantial number of second-line, training and auxiliary aircraft lost by the MLD during the sledgehammer air strikes on Morokrembangan throughout February and March. These losses can be directly attributed to overpowering Japanese air superiority combined with weak fighter cover, poor AA defenses and a near complete lack of radar on the part of ABDA.

In comparison, only 16 percent of all front-line MLD aircraft lost came in the form of air-to-air combat. In all but a few cases, these losses amounted to single aircraft that had the misfortune to encounter a flight of Japanese fighters alone and unescorted while on a long-range reconnaissance patrol. It should also be noted that these numbers are very comparable to those losses suffered by PatWing 10, which also faced a complete lack of fighter cover and weak AA defenses.

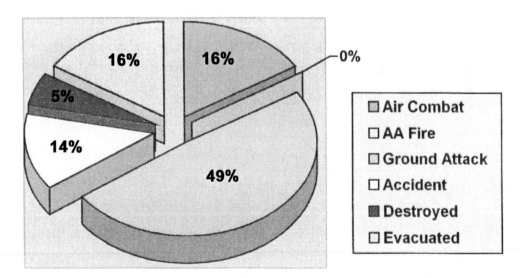

* *Do. 24 and PBY figures only*

Notes

Chapter 1

1. The Gouvernementsmarine was a civilian paramilitary police force similar in organization and function to the United States Coast Guard. Prior to the outbreak of the Second World War, its primary duties included drug interdiction, fishery regulation, search and rescue and the monitoring of Japanese spy vessels in the Netherlands East Indies. Following the outbreak of war in Europe, its ships were militarized in November 1939 and put under the command of the Royal Netherlands Navy.

2. The largest and best equipped of these forces were the Marechaussee, a paramilitary state police force charged with keeping order in both Holland and Dutch colonial territories throughout the East and West Indies. Like the Gouvernementsmarine, it was militarized in November 1939 following the outbreak of war in Europe.

3. Japan had long coveted a sustained presence in the Netherlands East Indies since before the First World War. As its government came more under the influence of nationalist military officers of the Imperial Japanese Army and Imperial Japanese Navy, the Dutch felt more threatened. Following the German occupation of Holland in May 1940, the Japanese went so far as to issue a formal list of "requests" regarding trade relations between the NEI and Japan, immigration laws and treatment of Japanese nationals. Had the NEI government accepted these stipulations, the archipelago would have effectively become a Japanese protectorate the same way French Indochina did in 1940–41 when it accepted similar Japanese demands following the fall of France.

Although all of these demands were firmly but politely rebuffed by the Dutch, the Japanese took steps to ensure that the East Indies would not come under the control of any other nation. In June 1940 the IJN went so far as to station a naval task force at the Pacific Island of Palau to ensure that Britain, Australia and the United States would not attempt to take the Dutch territory, willingly or unwillingly, into protective custody in the same way the United States did with the Danish territory of Greenland following that country's occupation by Germany in 1940. The formation was also intended to keep pressure on the Dutch East Indies government as the Japa-

nese presented greater demands and hinted at the possibility of war if they were not met.

4. Even so, there existed deep divisions between the Dutch government-in-exile, which had escaped to London in May 1940, and its colonial regime in the East Indies. Prior to the outbreak of the Pacific War, a sizeable nationalist movement existed that pushed for the liberation of the NEI in a wide variety of forms, ranging from those who wanted an autonomous territory with lax ties to Queen Wilhelmina to those calling for complete independence from the Netherlands. At the same time, many East Indies government officials had been born in the colonies and were subsequently viewed with some degree of suspicion as to exactly where their loyalties lay.

This is not to question their loyalty in the fight against Japan, but rather in regard to the fate of the NEI following the eventual defeat of Japan and the archipelago's subsequent reoccupation. Prior to the fall of Java in March 1942, H.J. van Mook, lieutenant governor of the NEI, had raised eyebrows among many in the Europe government when he openly called for Holland to loosen its colonial hold on the territory by allowing the NEI greater political representation, increased self determination regarding trade imbalances with the Dutch companies in Europe and by relaxing certain social imbalances for the Indonesian people.

These comments raised concern amongst the Queen's government, which was weakened by the fact that it itself was already in exile and had very little strength. Although nominally backed by the London government, the East Indies government was largely on its own and had experienced a great deal of political and foreign policy independence following the occupation of Holland. Combined with van Mook's comments, there was fear in London that certain Dutch colonial officials evacuated from Java in March 1942 might seek to create a separate Netherlands East Indies government-in-exile in Australia that would compete with London's goal of restoring the East Indies to full colony status following the war. To head off this very possibility, the London government replaced van Mook as lieutenant governor on March 25, 1942, and recalled him to London, where they could better control his actions. Ford, *Allies in a Bind*, pp. 37–38.

5. Prior to 1940, Germany was a major arms supplier of the Netherlands, providing its military forces with everything from seaplanes and shipboard catapults to anti-aircraft guns, precision optical equipment and small arms. But as Nazi German became more antagonistic toward the rest of Europe these ties were cut and the orders for new weapons and equipment lapsed.

6. Also listed as 1st Lieutenant W. Bierenbroodspot, KMR

7. In 1999-2000, a Dutch aviation group attempted to locate and salvage a number of these aircraft, whose remains reportedly still existed on the bottom of Java's Lengkong River. However, after a series of delays both attempts ended in failure and it appears that as this text is written that the aircraft will not be recovered anytime in the near future.

8. *De Ruyter, Java* and *Sumatra* shipped two aircraft each; records vary, so remains unclear if *Tromp* could operate one or two aircraft, although she appears to have only carried one aircraft immediately prior to the attack on Pearl Harbor. The Dutch destroyers and several of the larger GM patrol vessels were also capable of shipping a Fokker seaplane, although they rarely did as it eliminated the use of one of the after mounts on the destroyers. Aboard ship, their primary role was to conduct short-range reconnaissance and provide shell spotting during surface engagements.

Of the cruisers, only *De Ruyter* was equipped with a catapult that allowed her to launch floatplanes while underway. The others were forced to stop and lower their aircraft overboard; to recover the planes, all KM ships utilized the Hein Mat system, where the ship would tow a large mesh matt alongside the ship while simultaneously dumping oil on the water to break up the wave action. Upon landing, the aircraft would taxi onto the matt and be hoisted aboard. While effective in peacetime, stopping to launch and recover aircraft was not a preferred tactic in a war zone where the danger of lurking submarines was always present.

9. It is interesting to note that despite the MLD's successful operation of the Do. 24 for nearly four years beforehand, this was its first operational use with the Kriegsmarine.

10. These aircraft were primarily used to replace GVT aircraft that rotated in and out of Morokrembangan for repairs and routine overhaul. The latter was carried out at 200- to 400-hour intervals. However, the nature of their operations often meant that the flying boats were frequently subjected to operational periods that well exceeded these specifications.

11. All Dutch Catalinas were delivered without armament or weapons mounts, which were then installed by MLD personnel at Morokrembangan. This was presumably done as the Dutch had their own stocks of weapons and their bombs were of indigenous design and would not work with American bomb racks. Otherwise, the primary differences between the MLD Model 28 and USN Catalina were that all of the instrument panels had metric numbers and that related flight instructions and signage throughout the aircraft were posted in Dutch.

At the time of their order by the MLD, these boats were the newest version of the PBY Catalina then in production. But while the USN flew earlier PBY-4, PBY-3 and even obsolescent PBY-2 versions, which did not have self-sealing fuel tanks, the Dutch aircraft did, sometimes leading USN personnel to complain about a foreign power receiving the most modern equipment available while they had to make due with older aircraft.

12. With the pending threat of war and subsequent attack on Pearl Harbor, the MLD sought to have delivery of their remaining PBYs moved up.

13. The Dutch PBYs were built at the Consolidated Aircraft factory in San Diego, California. From there, chartered civilian flight crews ferried them across the Pacific via Pearl Harbor, Midway, Wake, Guam and Manila. At Manila, skeleton Dutch flight crews took control of the aircraft and ferried them south to Java via Tarakan or Balikpapan. Upon arrival in the NEI, they were outfitted with Dutch weapons and equipment and made ready for operational service.

14. Whereas the PBY-5 was a true flying boat that could be removed from the water only with great difficulty, the PBY-5A, and subsequent versions, was a true amphibian that could operate equally well from both water and land bases.

15. Information and other exchanges related to the British Royal Air Force taking over Dutch PBYs have been culled from the following ciphers:

August 11, 1941, PRO Air 8/461, Message for First Sea Lord from Admiralty

August 28, 1941, PRO Air 8/461, Message from Air Marshall A. T. Harris in USA to V. C. A. S. Whitehall

October 10, 1941, PRO Air 8/461, Message from Air Ministry Whitehall to Commander in Chief Far East

October 17, 1941, PRO Air 8/461, Message from Air Ministry Whitehall to Commander in Chief Far East

October 17, 1941, PRO Air 8/461, Message from Commander in Chief Far East to Air Ministry

November 14, 1941, PRO 8/461, Message from EASFAR to Air Minister Whitehall

November 20, 1941, PRO 8/461, Message from Air Ministry to EASFAR for Commander in Chief Far East

November 27, 1941, PRO 8/461, Message from EASFAR to Air Ministry Kingsway

December 1, 1941, PRO 8/461, Message from Air Ministry Kingsway to RAF Delegate Washington

December 9, 1941, PRO 8/461, Message from RAFDEL to AIRWHIT

December 16, 1941, PRO 8/461, Message from Air Ministry to EASFAR

16. This is a pattern that developed prior to Pearl Harbor and continued throughout the Singapore and East Indies campaigns. It appears that the British High Command regarded Dutch forces in the Far East as little more than a resource to be milked for their own needs, rather than a true ally. Time and

again, the British asked the Dutch to contribute valuable military resources, of which they had precious little to spare, for British national interests. Yet, Britain showed a great reluctance to make similar sacrifices in order to help rebuild Dutch military strength in the Far East.

17. Had all of these aircraft arrived, the MLD would have had a total of some 72 front-line aircraft. But as it was, the squadron never had more than 60 or so operational flying boats at any given time. This total includes both front-line and reserve aircraft, so the number in service with the active MLD squadrons was much lower.

18. There remains some confusion as to the actual number of STM-S2 models delivered. Although 24 floatplane versions were ordered, most sources believe that no more than 24 were actually delivered before the fall of Java.

19. The DB-7B was an attack version featuring a solid nose cone that housed four 20mm cannon, while the DB-7C was a torpedo bomber and could house a bombardier in a glass nose.

20. That the MLD ordered these aircraft to serve as transports is really no surprise, considering that they were already in service with KNILM, the Dutch civilian airline in the East Indies. Adoption of this extremely versatile and highly popular seaplane would certainly have simplified maintenance and training for the MLD, which would eventually draw heavily on KNILM flight crews and ground personnel to fill out its ranks once the Pacific War broke out.

21. The VS-310 was an export version of the Vought OS2U Kingfisher then just entering service with the USN. As with the Model 28-5MNE Catalina, the primary differences between it and its American brethren were Dutch-language control panels, metric instruments and instructions throughout the interior and exterior of the aircraft.

22. *Report of Mission Appointed to Enquire into and Verify the Requirements of the Netherlands East Indies Government for Munitions for Defense*, Headquarters Philippine Department, August 23, 1941.

23. *MS Tabian* on January 18 carrying seven aircraft; *MS Mapia* on January 20 carrying ten aircraft and *MS Weltevreden* on February 19 carrying seven aircraft. Information provided through correspondence with Bill Devins, January 30, 2002.

24. Personal correspondence with Jim Maas, Bill Devins, Bert Kossen, January and April 2002.

25. It was intended that MLD flight trainees would transition to these aircraft from the Ryan primary trainers; from there, they would again transition to front-line aircraft such as the Fokker T.IV and Dornier Do. 24. In the end however, virtually all of the MLD trainees went directly from the Ryan trainers to training operation on the front-line Fokkers and Dorniers.

26. KLM and KNILM airlines started the Pacific War with a combined total of 30 land-based aircraft and seaplanes. The land planes were used by the ML, and the seaplanes by the MLD, as supply and transport aircraft, although some continued to fly a limited number of passenger flights. These aircraft included
- 3 × Douglas DC-2
- 7 × Douglas DC-3
- 4 × Douglas DC-5
- 5 × Fokker F.VII and F.XII
- 4 × Grumman G.21a
- 4 × Lockheed L-14
- 1 × Sikorsky S-42B
- 2 × Sikorsky S-43

Of these 30 original aircraft, 11 escaped to Australia, where one DC-2 crashed almost immediately when it ran out of fuel during its evacuation flight from Java. In the East Indies campaign proper, KM and KNILM suffered no fewer than 19 losses, including
- 1 × DC-2
- 5 × DC-3
- 2 × DC-5 (one captured on Java)
- 5 × Fokker (all)
- 3 × Grumman G.21a
- 1 × Sikorsky S-42B
- 2 × Sikorsky S-43

Witter, *Het Vergeten Squadron*.

27. As with all aircraft from the "Grumman Iron Works," this highly versatile amphibian was both rugged and reliable, making it a popular choice for operations throughout the East Indies. In addition to KNILM, it was flown by a number of private and commercial owners, including oil companies and religious groups.

28. It appears that KNILM also operated a twin-engine de Havilland Dragon Rapide passenger plane that had likely been taken over from a commercial entity known as Servicos Aereas da Colonia Portuguesa da Timor, which had been formed by Spanish colonial authorities in 1940. This airline had been formed following prolonged Australian and Japanese efforts to set up airline passenger service between Timor, Australia and Palau. It provided weekly passenger service between the cities of Koepang in Dutch Timor and Dili in Portuguese Timor.

Although the Portuguese government owned and operated the airline, the Dragon Rapide was leased from KNILM. In addition, the plane's pilot and mechanic were also Dutch and whose salaries were paid by KNILM, which was to be reimbursed by Servicos Aereas da Colonia Portuguesa da Timor officials. However, the Koepang-Dili leg proved unprofitable and the airline almost immediately fell some six months behind on the aircraft's lease payments and crew salaries.

Nonetheless, the weekly flights continued when the Netherlands East Indies government stepped in and began to reimburse KNILM for its losses. Due to Timor's close proximity to Dutch territory, Japan wanted to establish a presence in neutral Portuguese territory for espionage purposes and was severely pressuring Portugal to make concessions. Because of these ongoing efforts, the Dutch believed that the intelligence on Portuguese-Japanese relations and Japanese operations in Portuguese Timor provided by the plane's crew during their flights into Dili justified the cost.

Archer, *Report on Portuguese Territory*. 1941.

29. As a result of the growing tidal wave of Japanese air supremacy over the NEI, by mid-February 1942 KNILM had lost one Grumman G-21a, one Sikorsky S-42B, one Sikorsky S-43 and two DC-3's. Casius and Postma, 40 jaar luchtvaart in Indie.

30. Helfrich, *Memoires*, Volume I, p. 274.

31. Although Admiral Hart updated Admiral Helfrich on a daily basis as a matter of courtesy regarding naval affairs, the Dutch admiral's only steady source of information of ABDA's strategic planning came from a naval staff officer whom he attached to the organization.

32. "It was not until 7 February that ABDA-AIR took over command of RAF and RAAF units in the Wesgroup area. Though on several occasions during the war the RAF obstinately and willfully chose to go its own way in spite of orders, the manner in which a British supreme commander and a British air commander tolerated a freewheeling organization within Wesgroup smacks of tacit collusion in the pursuit of a national interest at the expense of a wider inter-alliance commitment." Wilmott, *Empires in the Balance*, p. 275–76.

33. Haslach, *Nishi, No Kaze, Hare*, p. 112

34. As the threat of war in the Pacific loomed, Dutch intelligence agencies clamped down on Japanese espionage activities by outlawing the transmission of any information from the NEI in any language other than Dutch or English; this applied specifically to wireless messages and international phone calls. In the end, diplomatic pouches were one of the few secure methods of communications left between the Japanese consulate in Batavia and its handlers in Tokyo.

35. Information and related exchanges between Japanese counselor personnel and Tokyo has been culled from the following declassified United States intelligence documents:

Purple Intercept Code #895, From Batavia to Tokyo, August 28, 1941

Purple Intercept Code Circular #1947, September 6, 1941

Purple Intercept Code #659, October 22, 1941

Purple Intercept Code #1150, October 25, 1941

36. For this reason, the Dutch were always concerned to see concessions made by European nations to nationalist groups in other territories. Britain's formation of the state of Saudi Arabia in 1932 was viewed with particular alarm, as Indonesian Muslims promptly intensified their calls for a state of their own as well. Haslach, *Nishi, No Kaze, Hare*, p. 93.

CHAPTER 2

1. Neither the MLD nor the KM as a whole ever built an independent fighter arm prior to the Second World War. The primary reason was that shortly after the fighters were ordered for Perak, the KM voluntarily surrendered the air defenses of its naval and air bases to the KNIL (presumably for budgetary reasons), which then assumed responsibility for their protection in both Europe and the Netherlands East Indies. However, during the war MLD units based in England did operate a number of fighter aircraft from converted merchant carriers. And following the end of the war, the KM immediately established a carrier-based fighter and strike force using ships purchased from the Royal Navy.

Bosscher, *De Koninklijke Marine in de Tweede Wereldoorlog*, Volume 2, p. 437.

2. Much like the RAF, MLD pilots could be full officers or noncommissioned officers, the latter typically having the rank of Sergeant-Pilot.

3. Hooftman, *Van Farman tot Neptune: De Vliegtuigen van de Marine*, Volume 1, p. 41.

4. Just like the volunteer pilots who slipped into China to join the American Volunteer Group, it appears that these instructors were either ex-military or military reservists from the U.S. Marine Corps or USN. This would be a logical conclusion as the Dutch needed instructors with operational experience on military aircraft, and it is logical to assume that they would come from the military ranks.

Nine instructors returned to the United States shortly after the outbreak of war. However, three of them — Captain Willard Reed, USMC, Lieutenant Thomas Hardy (service unknown) and Lieutenant John A. Robertson, USN — remained on Java and flew combat missions with the 17th Pursuit Squadron (USAAF) and Patrol Wing 10 (USN). Although Hardy safely returned to the United States, Reed was killed when his P-40 crashed, and Robertson went missing aboard the PatWing 10 PBY P-42 (former Y-42) while on a reconnaissance mission over the Makassar Strait.

Edmonds, *They Fought with What They Had*, p. 288.

5. Hooftman, *Van Farman tot Neptune: De Vliegtuigen van de Marine*, Volume 1, p. 42.

6. According to Hooftman in *Van Farman tot Neptune: De Vliegtuigen van de Marine*, Volume 1, p. 41, a number of twin-engine Lockheed bombers were also ordered to facilitate the transfer of trainees from the primary trainers to Dornier and Fokker seaplanes. However, the author has seen no other mention of this order in either Dutch- or English-language sources.

7. Shores, *Bloody Shambles*, Volume 1, p. 64

8. Shores, *Bloody Shambles*, Volume 1, p. 42

9. Unlike the Commonwealth and American militaries, there was no strict color barrier in the KNIL, ML, KM or MLD for Eurasians of mixed Dutch-Indonesian ethnicity during the 1930s and 1940s. Eurasians were regarded as Dutch citizens and were afforded all of the same rights. This meant they could hold high-level government and military leadership positions, and many did, including General R.

Bakker, who served as chief of the general staff for the KNIL throughout the East Indies campaign.

10. A large number of these trainees were apparently later transported back to England, where they helped make up the RAF's 320 Squadron (Dutch).

11. In May 1941 48 of these aircraft were ordered from Australia. Of this number, 33 went to the ML-KNIL and 15 to the MLD, with 11 of the aircraft being made available to the VVC and its related flying clubs. Shores, *Bloody Shambles*, Volume 1, p. 40.

12. Six of these light training aircraft had been ordered from Germany prior to May 1940, but by December 1941, only three were still operational, the rest being lost in flight-training accidents.

13. Two aircraft available; it appears that these aircraft might have been former civilian aircraft.

14. An extensive list of MLD naval air stations and support bases can be found in Appendix 8 of this text.

15. Wijngarden and Staal, *Dornier Do. 24*, p. 38–40.

16. *Ibid.*

17. Messimer, *In the Hands of Fate*, pp. 202–03.

18. Military History Section of the KNIL, *Nederlands-Indie Contra Japan*, Part 1, p. 225–26.

19. *Ibid.*

20. *Ibid.*

21. *Ibid.*

22. *Ibid.*

23. *Ibid.*

24. *Ibid.*

25. *Report of U.S. Army Mission to Netherlands East Indies*, Exhibit B-I, Sheets 3–5, August 8–20, 1941.

26. Bosscher, *De Koninklijke Marine in de Tweede Wereldoorlog*, Volume 2, p. 394–95.

27. It should be noted that the operational composition of each MLD squadron varied greatly as aircraft were rotated in and out for repairs and routine maintenance. As a result, their composition in September 1939 was far different in most cases than on December 7, 1941.

28. Article 17 of Convention XIII of the Second Hague Conference clearly states that a belligerent warship entering a neutral port is typically guaranteed only 24 hours for the purpose of refueling, repairs or resupply, but cannot use this time to conduct activities, such as repairs, that could restore or strengthen its fighting capabilities. However, if additional time is required for repairs related to seaworthiness, the neutral power can grant an extension of up to 72 hours. At that point, the warship must leave or face internment by the neutral power.

It is unclear how this rule applies to merchant vessels, as neutral and belligerent powers have maintained normal trade relations for as long as there has been sea traffic. However, one can assume that the German merchant ships in East Indies ports either outstayed their allowed time and were formally prevented from leaving Dutch waters, or that they simply declined to leave port on their accord to avoid

capture by Royal Navy warships that continued to loiter nearby.

29. Throughout the Second World War, the Royal Navy rarely hesitated to violate the territorial waters of neutral nations in pursuit of their operational needs or national strategic goals:

In December 1939, following an engagement with the German battleship *Graf Spee* off the coast of South America, the Royal Navy cruiser HMNZS *Achilles* followed her adversary into Uruguayan territorial waters and initiated a brief fight, which was halted only when the Uruguayan cruiser *Uruguay* arrived on the scene to escort the German ship into Montevideo. Although the Royal Navy denies culpability in this instance and maintains that *Graf Spee* fired first while in neutral waters, the charts of *Achilles* showing her position and movements during this engagement were conveniently misplaced shortly afterward, so British claims could not be confirmed.

On February 16, 1940, the Royal Navy destroyers *Cossack*, *Intrepid* and *Ivanhoe* ignored protests from two neutral Norwegian warships and entered that nation's territorial waters. Still in neutral waters, *Cossack* forced the German merchant vessel *Altmark* aground and boarded her, killing eight German seamen in the process. They then proceeded to free 303 Allied merchant seaman being transported to Germany after being captured when *Graf Spee* seized their ships. Unchallenged by the Norwegian torpedo boats *Kjell* and *Skarv*, the British destroyers then retired from Norwegian waters.

Two months later, in direct violation of international law, the Royal Navy carried out a series of mine-laying operations inside Norwegian territorial waters between April 5–8, 1940. The reason given was that Britain remained unconvinced of Norwegian assurances to prevent German merchant ships from using Norwegian waters to transports raw materials to Germany. Although the Nazi invasion of Norway was already well under way before this operation took place, Germany later defended its invasion by stating that it was acting to protect Norwegian neutrality from British aggression.

30. Gill, *Royal Australian Navy 1939–42*, p. 250.

31. In reality, the Japanese likely could have invaded the NEI with little interference from either the United States or Britain. Although President Franklin D. Roosevelt stated that he would not tolerate additional Japanese aggression in the Far East, he clearly would have had immense trouble gaining the political and popular support needed for a declaration of war. At the time, Congress was divided between isolationist "Doves" and militaristic "Hawks" who pushed for a large US military build-up in order to confront Nazi Germany and Japan. The American people were themselves equally divided, and it is unlikely they would have supported military action against an Asian nation halfway around the world in order to help preserve a colonial territory for a European nation.

Likewise, England was enveloped by its war in Europe and Africa, and it is highly unlikely that Winston Churchill would have attempted to block the Japanese without a firm guarantee of support from the United States. So even though most Dutch oil from the East Indies went to Great Britain, it is just as likely that the British would have deemed themselves capable of surviving without it. However, it is also entirely possible that the British would have viewed an attack against the Dutch as being too great a threat against their naval base at Singapore and acted in defense of the Dutch anyway.

32. German naval intelligence.

33. Gill, *Royal Australian Navy 1939–42*, p. 250.

34. *Ibid.*

35. Netherlands Information Bureau, *Ten Years of Burrowing in the Netherlands East Indies*, p. 36.

36. Womack, *Sword of the Rising Sun, World War II* magazine, p. 36.

37. Although not overtly stated in Dutch records, this build-up by the Dutch was clearly a reaction to the earlier reports they had received in April 1940 concerning Japanese plans for surprise landings at key areas of the East Indies.

38. Netherlands Information Bureau, *Ten Years of Japanese Burrowing in the Netherlands East Indies*, p. 38.

39. This was clearly an attempt to coerce Japanese military officials into acting on their threat to prevent another power from taking the East Indies into protective custody. See Chapter 1, endnote #3.

40. Netherlands Information Bureau, *Ten Years of Burrowing in the Netherlands East Indies*, p. 38.

41. *Ibid.*

42. Honselaar, *Vleugels van de Vloot*, p. 116.

CHAPTER 3

1. The Japanese began landing troops in Malaysia and neutral Siam 70 minutes before the attack on Pearl Harbor began. Secondary landings took place at Prachaub, Siam (one transport), Jumbhorn (two transports), Nakhorn (three transports) and Khota Bharoe (three transports), while 18 transports landed the main force at Singora and Patani.

At Khota Bharoe, rough seas hampered the landings, as did stiff resistance from Indian troops of the 8th Brigade, who were well-supported by artillery. Offshore, the light cruiser *Sendai*, screened by the 19th Destroyer Division (*Isonami, Uranami, Shikinami* and *Ayanami*) and the minesweepers *Sokaitei, W-2* and *W-3* with several submarine chasers provided cover.

The destroyer Sagiri (headquarters ship for all landing beaches) and 20th Destroyer Division (*Amagiri, Asagiri* and *Yugiri*) covered the landings at Singora. The first wave of troops moved ashore at 2400, meeting only weak resistance from Thai police and military units. As they moved inland, the transports withdrew north, and the destroyers moved to join the escort off Khota Bharoe.

Sixty-five miles to the south, at Patani and Tepoh, the 12th Destroyer Division's *Shirakumo, Shinonome* and *Murakumo* covered troops landing at Patani. At Patani, troops of the 42nd Infantry Regiment initially met heavy resistance on the beach from the Royal Thai Army. This was soon overcome, and the destroyers withdrew to Khota Bharoe once the landings were complete.

The patrol boat *Shimushu* covered the operation at Nakhorn, as did the light cruiser *Kashii* at Bandon. The transports at Prachaub and Jumbhorn landed their troops without escort as no resistance was expected. None encountered any resistance, and the transports withdrew north and the warships to Khota Bharoe upon completion of the landings.

2. Greenwich Mean Time + 7½ hours.

3. The source of this information remains unknown, although it possibly originated from decoded radio intercepts or MLD reconnaissance flights from the Minahassa Peninsula. A third source could also have been the work of Dutch operatives, although this possibility is considered extremely remote by the author given Japanese security measures and the veil of secrecy that had been drawn over the Japanese Mandate Islands since the early 1930s.

4. Shores, *Bloody Shambles*, Volume 1, pp. 52–53.

5. Ibid, p. 54.

6. For the most part, these Japanese tenders operated F1M "Pete" seaplane fighters, which were highly maneuverable and versatile aircraft that proved to be extremely tough opponents for the Allied seaplanes they encountered throughout the NEI campaign. Some tenders also operated a small number of E13A "Jake" seaplanes, which were slowly replacing the "Pete" in front-line service. However, the limited number of "Jakes" soon disappeared as the NEI campaign progressed, allowing the obsolescent "Pete" to remain in front-line service, where it feasted on Allied flying boats.

Although seaplane tenders played a vital role in providing air cover and A/S support for numerous Japanese invasion convoys throughout the Philippine and East Indies campaigns, all paid heavily in lost aircraft. A number of these losses can be attributed to air action, but many more were the direct result of non-combat operational accidents. To make good the losses of "Petes" and "Jakes" and to keep the squadrons operating at peak efficiency, second-line E8N1 "Dave" seaplanes were also used, although the Japanese tried to keep them out of front-line service.

For example, when the tender *Sanuki Maru* set up a temporary seaplane base at Batan Island on December 10, 1941, to cover the initial stages of the Philippine campaign, she lost no fewer than six of her eight "Petes" in six hours due to heavy seas. It was not uncommon for the Japanese tenders to lose 2 aircraft for every 25 sorties they flew, making it extremely difficult to maintain a full complement of aircraft for extended periods of time. Nor was it uncommon for surviving aircraft to experience popped rivets and split seams in their floats. Personal correspondence with Allan Alsleben, June 2002.

7. Ministrie van Oorlog, *Nederlands-Indie Contra Japan, Deel IV*, pp. 32–34.

8. Bosscher, *De Koninklijke Marine in de Tweede Wereld Oorlog*, Volume 2, p. 126.

9. The barrage laid by *Tatsumiya Maru* during the night of December 6–7 numbered 456 mines, approximately 60–70 yards apart in a single, continuous line. Despite the presence of a suspected Japanese minelayer near Tioman Island, the Allies had no evidence to support the presence of the minefield or its precise location. Nonetheless, they ordered major surface ships to avoid the area.

The spread was laid along the anticipated sea route allied warships would take to reach the Japanese landing sites. Although the Royal Navy's major surface vessels avoided them, the mines resulted in the loss of the auxiliary patrol boat (also listed as an auxiliary minesweeper) HMS *Banka* on December 10. Likewise, the Dutch submarines *K-XVII* and *O-16* were lost to the barrage, the former with all hands on or about December 14, and the latter on December 12 with the loss of all but one crewman.

Royen van, *Hr.Ms. K-XVIII en Hr.Ms. O-16*, 1997. p. 40.

10. *Ibid.*

11. The identity of this ship is unclear; it could have been a Japanese transport making preparations to land troops on Malaya. However, in his book *Hr.Ms. K XVII en Hr.Ms. O 16: De ondergang of twee Nederlandse onderzeeboten in de Zuid-Chinese Zee (1941)*, Dr. P.C. van Royen e.a. states that it could have been a second minelayer. According to British and Australian naval sources, the auxiliary minelayer *Chose Maru* had also been ordered to accompany *Tatsumiya Maru* on her minelaying mission. However, *Chose Maru* turned back upon being sighted by British (Dutch?) aircraft and did not complete her mission.

12. Shores, *Bloody Shambles*, Volume 1, pp. 74–76.

13. Royen van, *Hr.Ms. K-XVIII en Hr.Ms. O-16*, p. 48.

14. Although the attack on Pearl Harbor officially took place on December 7, 1941, in the Far East, it fell on December 8 in the NEI because of the International Date Line.

15. "Citizens of the Netherlands East Indies! In its unexpected attack on American and British territories, while diplomatic negotiations were still in progress, the Japanese Empire has consciously adopted a course of aggression. These attacks, which have thrown the United States and the British Empire into active war on the side of already fighting China, have as their objective the establishment of Japanese supremacy in the whole of East and Southeast Asia. The aggression also gravely threatens the Netherlands Indies. The Netherlands government accepts the challenge and takes up arms against the Japanese Empire."

Mook, van, *The Netherlands Indies and Japan*, p. 130.

16. Since these aircraft belonged to a foreign nation (they were also *legally* considered civilian planes since they were not U.S. military aircraft), American neutrality laws prevented them from being armed while in U.S. territory. Nor could Dutch military personnel operate or fly aboard them while on the U.S. mainland.

As a result, the Dutch had two choices when it came to shipping the aircraft to the NEI: 1) transport them via ship at $20,000 per aircraft, or 2) fly them directly to Java at considerable cost savings of approximately $10,000 per aircraft, which included all operating expenses, such as fuel, flight crew wages and bonuses. The MLD chose the latter, and Consairways crews would ferry the aircraft across the Pacific to Manila, where Dutch crews took over. The flight across the Pacific typically took five to six days, followed by a two-week trip back to San Diego via commercial steamer. The flight from Manila to Morokrembangan usually took a couple of days and staged through either Tarakan or Balikpapan.

17. It appears that General van Oyen flew to Hawaii via Pan Am clipper because of American neutrality laws, which at the time prevented foreign military personnel from traveling aboard any aircraft other than civilian passenger planes while within the continental United States.

18. These ships belonged to the IJN's 7th Destroyer Division. A third destroyer in their group, the *Akebono*, had originally been detailed to take part in the Midway mission as well. However, she suffered damage to one of her propeller shafts prior to the departure date and was forced to remain in Japan for repairs. This chain of events has caused confusion in some sources over the years, many of which list *Akebono* in place of *Sazanami*.

Boeichio Kenshujo Senshishitsu (*Senshi Sosho*, Volume 5), *Hawaii Sakusen* (*Hawaiian Operation*); information and translations provided courtesy of Allan Alsleben.

19. *Naval Air Station Midway Island War Diary*, December 18, 1941, p. 6.

20. *Patrol Wing Two War Diary*, U.S. Naval Air Station Pearl Harbor, Territory of Hawaii, December 18, 1941.

21. Upon her arrival in Australia, Y-69 appears to have been attached to the MLD Flight Training School, which was evacuated from Java to Australia on February 19, 1942. She could also have been used to train flight crews who had formerly flown Dornier Do. 24s as the MLD continued its conversion to the PBY following the fall of the East Indies.

22. The arrival of Y-70 at Morokrembangan is also listed as December 16, 1941. Hooftman, *Van Farman tot Neptune*, Volume 1, p. 19.

23. It is unknown who flew Y-70 on this flight, as both Consairways flight crews (a total of eight men) at Midway had been left behind on the island when

Y-69 and Y-70 were returned to Pearl Harbor. However, the likely candidates would seem to be the displaced crew of Y-68, which had been destroyed on December 7. The Consairways flight personnel at Midway were not evacuated to Pearl Harbor until the morning of December 26 aboard the seaplane tender USS *Wright*.

Naval Air Station Midway Island War Diary, December 26, 1941, p. 8.

24. These forces consisted of the 4th Submarine Squadron (8 boats), 5th Submarine Squadron (6 boats) and the 6th Submarine Squadron (4 boats).

25. Y-52, Y-53 and Y-54, which were renumbered FV-Y, FV-U and FV-W, respectively, in RAF service.

26. Following the loss of Admiral Sir Tom Phillips with the battleship *Prince of Wales* and battlecruiser *Repulse* to Japanese bombers on December 10, the RN had no immediate plans to undertake any offensive action against the Japanese. *Prince of Wales* and *Repulse* had been the heart of the Far Eastern Fleet, and their loss was a crushing blow. The most powerful remaining Allied ships in the Malay Barrier were now the heavy cruisers *HMS Exeter* and *USS Houston*. But although supported by a host of light cruisers and destroyers, they were no match for the powerful Japanese units facing them.

The situation worsened on December 12 when the British Admiralty all but ruled out any future offensive action. The remaining RN ships would be used primarily for convoy duties between Singapore and the Indian Ocean. Since 1939, the RN had suffered grievous losses (particularly among its small ships) and now chose to concentrate its remaining heavy units at Ceylon to hold the Indian Ocean. As of 1941, RN losses included no fewer than 3 battleships, 3 aircraft carriers, 9 cruisers, 56 destroyers, 31 submarines, 23 small warships and 14 auxiliaries. The total was even higher when one counted the hundreds of small auxiliaries that had also been lost.

Following the loss of *Prince of Wales* and *Repulse*, the primary surviving ships at Singapore included the light cruisers *Dragon*, *Durban* and *Danae* with the destroyers *Encounter*, *Electra*, *Express*, *Jupiter*, *Stronghold*, *Tenedos*, *Vampire*, *Scout* and *Thanet*. Virtually all of these ships dated from the First World War and definitely could not be counted as frontline units. The RAN corvettes *Burnie*, *Goulburn*, *Bendigo* and *Maryborough* and armed merchant cruiser *Manoora* were also in harbor, as was the armed merchant cruiser *Kanimbla*. The destroyer *Isis*, from the Mediterranean Fleet, was refitting alongside the Australian sloop *Vendetta*.

On December 23, the RN announced its permanent plans following the loss of Force Z. The battleships *Revenge* and *Royal Sovereign*, together with *Dragon*, *Durban*, *Danae*, *Jupiter*, *Encounter*, *Electra*, *Express* and *Vampire* would form part of the Eastern Fleet surface forces at Singapore. Ironically, two elderly World War I–era cruisers (*Dragon* and *Danae*), which Admiral Phillips had refused to take to sea because of their advanced age, would now replace *Prince of Wales* and *Repulse*. But despite their attachment, *Revenge* and *Royal Sovereign* never moved to Singapore and remained with the main fleet at Ceylon.

27. Mostly likely these were either F1M "Pete" or E8N1 "Dave" floatplanes from the seaplane tender *Kamikawa Maru*.

28. Honselaar, *Vleugels van de Vloot*, pp. 140–41.

29. Netherlands East Indies Campaign Update, *New York Times*, December 19, 1941, Section L-6.

30. Bureau Maritieme Historie, *De strijd in Nederlands Oost-Indie: Verrichtingen van de MLD in Nederlands Oost-Indie Gedurende de Japanse Opmars*, p. 107. Provided courtesy of Jan Visser.

31. Visser, *Who Sank the Shinonome?*, p. 2.

32. According to *De luchtstrijd om Borneo* by P.C. Boer and *Verkennen en bewaken* by N. Geldhof, X-34 suffered mechanical failure, which forced her to make an emergency landing while en route to Miri. However, Japanese records clearly state that an engagement with an Allied flying boat took place over Borneo on this date. As there were no other engagements between Japanese aircraft and Allied flying boats that day, this could only have been X-34 and *Kamikawa Maru's* seaplane.

33. National Historical Society, *The Fall of the Philippines*, p. 113.

34. *Ibid.*

35. So poorly equipped were these troops that many of them, although armed, had weapons that were either broken, defective or otherwise did not work. In any event, none of them had more than a small handful of ammunition, which made the outcome of a fight for Jolo a foregone conclusion.

CHAPTER 4

1. Patrol Wing 10 consisted of two USN patrol squadrons, VP-21 (redesignated VP-101 in late 1940) and VP-26 (renumbered VP-102). VP-21 arrived in the Philippines from Pearl Harbor in September 1939 and was followed out a year later by VP-26 in December 1940; PatWing 10 was officially formed upon its arrival. Between the two squadrons, the reconnaissance wing operated a total of 28 PBY-4s, an earlier version of the MLD's Catalina flying boats, which were severely hampered by weak armament, and more important, a lack of self-sealing fuel tanks.

Badly weakened by Japanese aircraft in the early days of the Philippine campaign, PatWing 10 was reinforced by VP-22 in January 1942. This squadron had been present at Pearl Harbor on December 7 and had lost several aircraft during the attack. However, these aircraft were either repaired or replaced by the time VP-22 departed for Java on January 1, 1942. Unlike VP-21 and VP-26, the new arrivals operated a total of 12 newer PBY-5 Catalinas.

2. Messimer, *In the Hands of Fate*, p. 13

3. Four seaplane tenders supported the aircraft of PatWing 10. USS *Langley* had originally entered service with the USN in 1922 as its first aircraft car-

rier. She was converted into a seaplane tender in late 1936 as newer, larger ships rendered her obsolete in the carrier role. *Langley* was transferred to the Philippines in mid-1940 to support VP-21. There, she joined USS *Heron*, a converted "Bird"-Class minesweeper, which had served in the Philippines since the 1920s. Throughout the East Indies campaign *Heron* served as tender for PatWing 10's utility aircraft, which consisted of one SOC "Seagull," four J2F "Duck" and five OS2U "Kingfisher" seaplanes.

The USS *Childs* and USS *William B. Preston* were both former World War I "four stacker" destroyers of the "Clemson" Class that had been converted into seaplane tenders in 1938 and 1939, respectively. They were transferred to the Philippines in late 1940 to support the aircraft of VP-21 and VP-26. As converted destroyers, both possessed extremely good speed and above-average armament compared with other seaplane tenders.

4. At this stage of the campaign, this was most likely a long-range Kawanishi H6K "Mavis" from the Toko Air Wing then based at Palau, some 700 miles to the northeast. With a range of nearly 4,000 miles, the flying boat was operating well within its range.

5. The American crewmen obviously believed this was a Sikorsky S-42, clearly demonstrating that they had been briefed on the various types of aircraft operated by the Dutch.

6. Unknown to the American flight crews at the time, formation flights over Soerabaja were forbidden without first alerting the appropriate Dutch authorities, who were extremely concerned with the possibility of Japanese air raids on the city.

7. See reference on, Chapter 2, p. 18.

8. Throughout the NEI campaign, the tenders of PatWing 10 operated from a number of temporary seaplane bases throughout the Lesser Soenda Islands in the southeastern region of the East Indies. These included Morokrembangan (PatWing 10 HQ) and the islands of Soembawa (*Childs*), Timor (*Preston*) and Tanimbar (*Heron*). For the most part, *Langley* operated from either the port of Tjilatjap on Java's southern coast, or the Australian port of Darwin.

9. Shores, *Bloody Shambles*, Volume 1, p. 202.

10. *New York Times*, December 21, 1941, p. L-2.

11. The speed and efficiency in which MLD ground crews at Morokrembangan were able to repair routine battle damage often allowed the aircraft to be returned to operational status in record time. Although routine maintenance, such as 200- to 400-hour aircraft overhauls, and certain types of heavy battle damage could keep an aircraft out of service for several weeks, most were repaired and put back into action within a matter of days. However, this efficiency would be severely impaired once the Japanese began bombing and strafing Morokrembangan in early February 1942.

12. Honselaar, *Vleugels van de Vloot*, p. 146.

13. This is an interesting, perhaps fatally flawed, operational strategy on the part of Lieutenant Burg-

erhout. As American and British bomber raids over Germany and Japan would subsequently show, aircraft had a much higher chance of survival if they remained in formation during fighter attacks, as it offered a greater concentration of firepower. Likewise, fighters tended to single out individual aircraft that were crippled or otherwise isolated from the main formation.

14. This claim is not confirmed in Japanese records, as no Toko Air Wing flying boats were lost at Davao that day.

15. Honselaar, *Vleugels van de Vloot*, p. 147.

16. In Dutch, the word for fighter is "Jager," thus the gunner transmitting the letter "J" instead of "F" to notify his crewmates.

17. Japanese Defense Agency, *Boeichio Kenshujo Senshishitsu (Senshi sosho)*, Volume 23.

18. Although the specific damage to *Tonan Maru* is unclear, she was the only Japanese vessel hit that day.

19. The Beaufort (Wind Speed) Scale lists Force 6 conditions as a strong breeze with speeds ranging from 25 to 31 miles per hour (22 to 27 knots) with large waves in the area of 10 feet high, typically accompanied by some sea spray. On land, large tree branches move, wires whistle and umbrellas are difficult to control. Copyrighted information courtesy of Russ Rowlett, University of North Carolina-Chapel Hill.

20. In addition to commanding all naval forces, Hekking was also senior commanding officer in charge of all MLD flight and reconnaissance operations in the eastern half of the East Indies archipelago. However, given the dearth of naval forces at Ambon, the MLD aircraft stationed at MVK Halong were his only operational forces.

21. Shores, *Bloody Shambles*, Volume 1, p. 204.

22. GMT + 9 hours.

23. At the time of the attack, the Sikorsky had just recently arrived at Lake Tondano. Its pilot, Carl Rüpplin van Keftikon, was standing on the dock reviewing his cargo manifest with a KPM official from Menado. He reported hearing the sound of aircraft and then gunfire. So fast was the initial Japanese attack that by the time he turned to look, his plane was already in flames and three passengers still aboard were killed.

Witter, *Het Vergeten Squadron*.

24. It is interesting to note that the Japanese pilots, all of whom were universally liberal when it came to victory claims, actually understated their success at Lake Tondano on December 26. Although they had effectively annihilated two complete MLD squadrons, they claimed to have destroyed only three tri-engine flying boats and a large four-engine seaplane. Shores, *Bloody Shambles*, Volume 1, p. 204.

25. In addition, one of the wounded men died shortly after the New Year, thus bringing the total KIA for the raid to 18.

26. Another reason adding to the Dutch sense of security was the location of the seaplane base itself.

Kalkas was located directly at the foot of an 825-foot mountain; because this would make it difficult for fighters to pull up, the MLD believed this would help guard against sustained air attack from strafing fighters.

27. These were "Mavis" flying boats from the Toko Air Wing, which was still operating at Davao.

28. Lieutenant Burgerhout, commander of GVT.5, had sent a lengthy message to Captain Hekking at Area Combined Headquarters on Ambon immediately upon his return from the Davao raid. In it, he expressed his concern about trying to launch any more attacks from Lake Tondano. Burgerhout thought Kalkas was too exposed and that MLD aircraft on Lake Tondano should be withdrawn immediately to avoid a likely Japanese counterstrike.

Furthermore, Burgerhout believed that GVT.2 and GVT.5 had gotten lucky in their first attack and that the raid on Davao had achieved such good success only because the Japanese had been taken by surprise. He correctly anticipated that the Japanese would very quickly strengthen their air defenses, resulting in much heavier losses in future attacks. He stressed that it would be useless to try to attack a heavily defended target with flying boats in the face of heavy enemy defenses. Bosscher, *De Koninklijke Marine in de Tweede Wereld Oorlog*, Volume 2, pp. 517-18.

29. Following the attack on Lake Tondano, a meeting between Lieutenant Burgerhout and Captain Hekking took place on Ambon later on December 26. Although Burgerhout once again stressed his opposition to attacking heavily defended targets with flying boats, a simple fact remained — had not all but one flying boat of GVT.2 and GVT.5 been destroyed at Kalkas, the two squadrons would have been back over Davao the following morning. Despite strong warnings from senior MLD personnel, which were in line with the concerns expressed by Lieutenant Burgerhout, Admiral Helfrich personally ordered that another attack take place on December 27. *Ibid.*

30. Following the evacuation of Java, Lieutenant Burgerhout later wrote a highly critical report that raised serious concerns regarding a "lack of insight in the use of aircraft" by Captain Hekking and his subordinate, Lieutenant-Commander J. Luske, KMR, who together were responsible for the command of all naval and air operations in the Eastern East Indies from ACH on Ambon. The primary issue revolved around the fact that neither Hekking nor Luske had any aviation experience, yet they were responsible for controlling air operations in their sphere of command.

In response, Commander J.A.C. Broesder, commander of MLD units in Australia, wrote that MLD HQ had not been consulted when Admiral Helfrich and his staff had set up this command structure before the start of war. When word of this command structure did reach Captain Bozuwa at Morokrembangan, the war was already in progress, and he did not feel comfortable asking for such a radical change

at that point. So despite extensive talks among Broesder, Bozuwa and the commanders of GVT.2 and GVT.5 following their return to Java, there were no changes in the process of how KM officers were chosen to oversee MLD operations until the squadron had been evacuated to Australia and Ceylon. *Ibid.*

31. These aircraft were P-1, P-6, P-9 and P-11.

32. Honselaar, *Vleugels van de Vloot*, p. 158.

33. Shores, *Bloody Shambles*, Volume 1, p. 210.

34. Bosscher, *De Koninklijke Marine in de Tweede Wereld Oorlog*, Volume 2, p. 175.

X-34 from GVT.7 on December 17; X-27 from GVT.5 on December 23; X-11, X-12 and X-23 from GVT.2 on December 26; X-26 from GVT.5 on December 26 and X-15 from GVT.1 on December 29.

35. Helfrich, *Memoires*, Volume I, p. 242.

CHAPTER 5

1. The exact date of this transfer remains unclear, although it apparently took place sometime in the second or third week of January. The only correlating document is a Dutch naval report dated January 19, 1942, that confirms the transfer of Y-39, Y-41 and Y-42 from service with the MLD flight-training school to PatWing 10 in January 1942.

Author's correspondence (Reference numbers: 00/2163/71/AvdP and 00/2253/71/AvdP) with Dr. A.P. van Vliet, Dr. A.J. van der Peet and Dr. N. Geldhof of the Institute for Maritime History, The Hague, Netherlands, July 2000.

2. Although there is no written documentation to confirm this transfer, the author believes this is the most likely scenario. It is based on the fact that the original 40 PBYs of VP-21 and VP-26 were sequentially numbered P-1 through P-40, while those of VP-22 were numbered 22-P-1 through 22-P-12. As VP-22 was at full strength when it arrived on Java about the time the transfer took place in January 1942, the two original PatWing 10 squadrons absorbed all five of the transferred Dutch PBYs. In USN service they were also sequentially numbered P-41 through P-45.

It is known that Y-41 and Y-42 retained their original hull numbers and were put into USN service as P-41 and P-42, respectively. If Y-43 was the fourth transferred PBY, it would make sense that it would have retained its original hull number as well, entering service as P-43. The author's assumption is further based on the fact that there is no mention in any Dutch sources of Y-43 entering service with an operational GVT before or after the transfer took place in January 1942. Nor is there any mention of this Catalina being destroyed by the Japanese in combat or on the ground by Dutch personnel to prevent its capture when Java fell in March 1942.

On February 5, 1942, the USN PBY P-43 was destroyed during a Japanese air raid on Morokrembangan. From her serial number, it is known that this Catalina was a former MLD aircraft. Combined with the numbering sequence of Y-41 and Y-42, and given the total lack of any reference being made to Y-43 in Dutch service, the author believes this makes a strong, albeit circumstantial, case for Y-43 to be listed as the fourth PBY.

3. Although Y-50 had originally departed the Consolidated aircraft plant at San Diego, California prior to the attack on Pearl Harbor, she did not reach Morokrembangan until January 16, 1942. This was because while en route to Manila, she suffered heavy damage after running aground on a reef at Midway and had to be returned to San Diego for extensive repairs. Her late arrival at Morokrembangan, combined with the fact that it was a brand-new aircraft that had never seen combat, surely made it an attractive piece of equipment for the USN.

A second, although less likely, candidate for the fifth transferred PBY was Y-73, which also did not reach Morokrembangan until January 1942. The last of the Dutch PBYs to depart San Diego, it was rerouted and delivered to the NEI via a new, much longer route via the Atlantic Ocean, Africa and the Indian Ocean. She did not depart Dinnerkey, Miami, until January 6, 1942, and it is uncertain she could have made such a long flight and arrived on Java in time to be absorbed by PatWing 10. It is possible she was transferred to the USN prior to or immediately upon her arrival.

4. Edmonds, *They Fought with What They Had*, p. 262.

5. Dull, *A Battle History of the Imperial Japanese Navy*, pp. 52–53.

6. *Ibid.*

7. Hara, *Japanese Destroyer Captain*, p. 61.

8. *Langkoeas* was the former German merchant ship *Stassfurt*, which had been seized at Tjilatjap on May 10, 1940. When word came of German forces moving into Holland, the Dutch immediately enacted previously formulated plans to seize a total of 19 German merchant ships at various ports throughout the East Indies. All had previously been interned after entering then neutral Dutch territorial waters to avoid capture or destruction by Royal Navy warships.

9. It is likely these were Fokker T.IVs of GVT.11 and GVT.12, as they were the primary A/S aircraft operating from these ports at the time.

10. Bakker, *De K.P.M. in Oorlogstijd*, pp. 45–47.

11. *Ibid.*

12. *Djirak (TAN 8)* was one of 10 civilian tankers belonging to the Netherlands Colonial Steam Boat Company that were either chartered or militarized by the KM in 1939. All were used throughout the NEI campaign to transport fuel oil from outlaying refineries to Java to keep the East Indies naval squadron operating. Although all of the requisitioned tankers kept their civilian names, eight of them also received the designation TAN 1–8. The KM also utilized four KPM coastal freighters as benzine transports, which were designated BEN 1–4 in addition to their civilian names. Because these boats carried their highly flammable cargo in drums on deck, they quickly earned the nickname "Fire Boats."

13. Again, the muddied puzzle of PBYs transferred to PatWing 10 comes up. As previously discussed, Y-41 was nominally attached to the MLD flight-training school at Morokrembangan prior to being transferred to Patrol Wing 10. However, according to a Dutch source (Honselaar, *Vleugels van de Vloot*, p. 169), this was the PBY that sighted the wreck of *Djirak* on January 11. It is possible that Y-41 was still attached to the flight training school and was on a training flight, which is entirely plausible as the Kangean Islands are less than 100 miles north of Soerabaja. It is also possible that the flight-training school had already been shut down and Y-41 was flying reconnaissance missions prior to being transferred to PatWing 10 despite being unattached to a GVT at the time.

14. With the exception of Y-73, the identity, sequence and dates of arrival of these PBYs via the Atlantic is unknown. The only MLD PBYs that had not yet reached Java at this point in the campaign were Y-69 (damaged at Midway and returned to San Diego for repairs), Y-71, Y-72 and Y-73. But since Y-73 did not depart Miami until January 6, it can be safely ruled out.

15. These were 12 PBY-5A amphibians with the serial numbers Y-74 through Y-85, which were delivered to the MLD in September 1942.

16. It would appear that there was at least some friction between Admiral Helfrich and General ter Poorten, although the exact level and the extent are unknown. This primarily stemmed from the fact that Helfrich felt slighted by the ABDA command in more ways than one. Not only was Helfrich left out of the ABDA command structure, but according to the Dutch constitution, his position in the "Royal" Netherlands Navy afforded him greater military status than General ter Poorten, who, although an experienced general in his own right, was a member of the "Colonial" armed forces. However, by virtue of his seat on the ABDA command, ter Poorten now technically outranked Helfrich.

17. While Churchill and President Franklin D. Roosevelt got along famously on a personal level, it is less well known that the president considered the concept of colonial rule distasteful at best. For this reason, he consistently blocked any strategies during the Pacific War that might have helped strengthen British and Dutch efforts to restore their postwar colonial empires.

18. This ship was the former Japanese fishing vessel *Borneo Maru*, which had been seized and put into Dutch service at the outbreak of war. In some sources, the name of this ship is also listed as being *van Mastdijn*.

19. Bataafsche Petroleum Company, which owned the drilling rights on Tarakan.

20. Along with GVT.16 and GVT.17, GVT.18 was the only MLD squadron able to convert over to PBYs prior to the outbreak of war. All three were new

squadrons likely formed with new trainees and reservists. The first two units were already in service on December 7, but GVT.18 became operational only in mid-January 1942 and this was its first assignment.

21. The MLD base at Emmahaven was demolished during a Japanese air raid on January 27. This raid also sank the SPM steamer *Poelo Tello* and *Buyskes* (KPM), while damaging the KPM merchant ships *Mijer* and *Elout*. They also burned harbor warehouses and much material.

Emmahaven was hit again the next day, and *Elout* was lost, as was the KPM motorship *Boelongan*. The KPM ship *Van der Capellen* received shrapnel damage. Although Padang remained open, it proved increasingly difficult to operate from. It was critical that Padang remain open, as Java's railroads depended almost entirely on Sumatran coal transported via interisland steamer.

CHAPTER 6

1. Lieutenant-Colonel van den Hoogenband commanded the KNIL's 6th Infantry Battalion, which, like Lieutenant-Colonel S. de Waal's 7th Battalion on Tarakan, was to defend the port only long enough for the oil facilities to be destroyed. With that mission accomplished, he was to withdraw into the interior of Borneo to join other KNIL forces, or to begin guerrilla warfare if this were impossible.

2. Colijn might also have been chosen for the diplomatic task because his father had also successfully served as prime minister of the Netherlands in the 1930s.

3. Also listed as Parsipal in some Dutch sources.

4. Nortier, *De Japanse Aanval Op Nederlands-Indië*, p. 139.

5. One reason Colijn and Reinderhoff opposed destruction of the launch and its occupants was that they feared for the safety of the military prisoners and a number of female detainees the Japanese still held on Tarakan.

6. It appears that these men were evacuated aboard the aircraft of GVT.4, which were ordered back to Morokrembangan around the same time demolition of Balikpapan's facilities began.

7. Killed: 2nd Lieutenant R.H.J. de Vries, Sergeant-Pilot J. Steen, Telegraphist Mate A. Hensing and Aircraft Machinist Mate C.P. de Wit.

8. Due to the unexpected loss of the two Dorniers during the evacuation operation, a substantial number of demolitions personnel had to be left behind and could not be evacuated. Of this group, eight later reached Java aboard small native boats, while 10 more eventually marched overland and reached the Dutch airbase at Samarinda II in the interior of Borneo, from which they were flown to Java. KNIL HQ on Java lost radio contact with the remainder at the end of February.

9. Sakai, *Samurai*, pp. 57–58.

10. The minesweepers *W-13* and *W-14* had been sunk by Dutch shore batteries on Tarakan shortly after the garrison agreed to surrender. However, a well-defended coastal position did not receive word of the surrender, as its communications with the rest of the island had been cut on the first day of the invasion. So when the 11th and 30th Minesweeper Divisions moved to begin sweeping Tarakan's main harbor, the battery opened fire immediately, sinking the two Japanese ships. A short time later the battery surrendered and 85 men of its crew were promptly massacred.

11. Piloted by Lieutenant J.E. Dougherty, this plane was damaged and ran low on fuel, forcing it to set down on the beach at Greater Masalembo Island. There, the crew waited with the wrecked bomber for nine days until spotted by a low-flying B-17, which reported their presence. This report prompted MLD HQ to send out X-19; upon her loss, a PatWing 10 flying boat was given the job, which it completed successfully after a somewhat wild pickup of the bomber crew.

12. 2nd Lieutenant D.J. Bakker and Sergeant-Pilot W.J. Jansen.

13. Messimer, *In the Hands of Fate*, pp. 212–16.

14. Ministerie van Oorlog, *Nederlands-Indie Contra Japan*, Deel V, pp. 84–93

15. When interviewed by Dwight Messimer for his excellent text *In the Hands of Fate*, a number of former PatWing 10 personnel expressed hard feelings toward the Dutch. While some regarded the Dutch as ungrateful, others questioned the value of fighting for Dutch territory, perhaps unknowingly underscoring their own lack of commitment to the NEI campaign.

"The American-Australian joint effort was very successful, and relations between the two units were very friendly. Unfortunately, the same relationship did not exist in regard to American-Dutch relations. Generally speaking, men who were assigned to staff positions thought the Dutch were pretty good fellows. But most of the men who flew the patrol missions considered the Dutch as little more than 'haughty-taughty Krauts.'

"The Dutch are sore at us if we help them, and they have to feed us. And they gripe if we don't help them. To hell with the stingy louses!"

Don Chay, PatWing 10 crewman

"I hope no Dutchman hears this record, because all the Dutchmen that I ever came into contact with had the attitude that everything you did for them was just doing yourself a favor to do it for them. They had the attitude that it was just your duty to do these things for them, and you were honored to do it.'"

Nick Keller, PatWing 10 crewman

Messimer, *In the Hands of Fate*, pp. 133–34.

16. This attack originated from Davao and consisted of six H6K "Mavis" flying boats of the Toko Air Wing and 21 G4M "Bettys" from the Kanoya Air Wing. However, one of the flying boats crashed en route, and only three of the remainder reached Ambon, along with 14 of the "Bettys."

Shores, *Bloody Shambles*, Volume 1, p. 211.

17. Although three Buffalos were originally assigned to the defense of Ambon, one was lost during a landing accident, so that only two remained operational by the time of the first Japanese attack. Both of these fighters were shot down on January 15.

18. Despite the arrival of VP-22 and the transfer of the Dutch planes, most of PatWing 10's remaining aircraft were still older PBY-4 models without self-sealing fuel tanks. But even with these vital improvements, the newer aircraft of VP-22 were still easy prey for virtually any Japanese aircraft they encountered.

19. Although GVT.17 had pulled out, a small cadre of 20 officers and seamen under Commander J.J. Jager, KMR remained at Halong, where it continued to service a small number of PatWing 10 and MLD planes that periodically visited the base until it was captured.

20. At this point, Japanese AA defenses at Kuching consisted of at least eight 75mm guns and multiple light cannon and machine gun positions.

21. A Dutch intelligence agency that prior to the war had put most of its efforts into controlling Indonesian nationalist groups and Japanese espionage activities. After the fall of the East Indies, the Netherlands Interior Service also played a key role in continued Dutch operations throughout Dutch New Guinea.

22. Witter, *Het Vergeten Squadron*.

23. Shores, *Bloody Shambles*, Volume 1, p. 227.

24. *Ibid*.

25. Helfrich, *Memoires*, Volume I, pp. 304–05.

26. The identity and composition of this convoy is unknown. No invasion convoys are known to have been in the area of Boeton Island at this time, although it is possible that the ships observed belonged to a small supply convoy. At the same time, no Japanese ships were reported damaged or lost on the night of January 31.

CHAPTER 7

1. Shores, *Bloody Shambles*, Volume 2, p. 149.

2. Bosscher, *De Koninklijke Marine in de Tweede Wereldoorlog*, p. 581, note 418.

3. Ibid, pp. 252–53.

4. X-1 and X-24 joined the squadron after being overhauled following the closure of the MLD flight-training school in January. The remaining aircraft, X-20 and X-36, had started the war with GVT.3 and GVT.1, respectively. They had been overhauled and put into the reserve pool when GVT.1 was disbanded in early January and GVT.3 reequipped with PBYs in late December. It appears that these were the last available aircraft in the MLD reserve pool.

5. As previously detailed, Y-40 had previously served with the flight-training school and was never attached to an operational GVT. However, with the closure of the flight-training school in January due to a lack of new personnel, Y-40's operational status was unclear at the time of its loss.

6. Although it had been rebuilt into a command plane for Captain Bozuwa, X-37 still remained inoperable after having arrived on Java in May 1940 with a dead engine.

7. It is important to note that many second-line aircraft lost by the MLD during the Japanese air raids on Java cannot be confirmed or definitely attributed to a specific day. Many of the available Dutch sources conflict with one another regarding specific dates; nor can Japanese records be taken wholly at face value given their pilots' tendency to dramatically exaggerate and the fact that they also likely made repeat claims on wrecks of aircraft destroyed earlier. With these factors in mind, dates of loss for the single-engine Fokkers and Dornier "Wals" are approximate at best.

8. These were W-4, W-10 and W-14, which were likely still being used as advanced torpedo and weather-training aircraft for pilots who would fly the new Douglas DB-7 torpedo bombers then en route to Java.

9. *Bloody Shamble*, Volume 2, pp. 150–57. Chris Shores details the loss of 16 Allied fighters shot down or crash-landed and three flying boats and two B-17s shot down. In addition, he lists at least 10 — and possibly as many as 13 — flying boats and floatplanes being destroyed at anchor.

10. Bosscher, *De Koninklijke Marine in de Tweede Wereldoorlog*, Volume 2, p. 585, n. 62.

11. Messimer, *In the Hands of Fate*, p. 234.

12. As discussed earlier (see Chapter 5, endnotes 1-3), it is possible that Y-50 was not destroyed in this attack, as it might have been one of the five PBYs transferred to PatWing 10 in mid-January. Likewise, it is also possible that Y-50 received the serial number P-43 upon being transferred to PatWing 10 and was then destroyed on February 5. In the confusion, it is possible that records could have duplicated its loss in both USN and MLD records.

13. Shores, *Bloody Shambles*, Volume 2, p. 167.

14. *Ibid*.

15. JANAC, *Japanese Naval and Merchant Shipping Losses*, p. 30.

16. Shores, *Bloody Shambles*, Volume 2, p. 172.

17. Honselaar, *Vleugels van de Vloot*, pp. 186–87.

18. Killed outright in the initial crash were Sergeant-Pilot P.J. de Ru, the wireless operator Leading Seaman 1st Class J.J. Woltjes and Sergeant J. de Vries. The badly injured pilot who died the following day was 1st Lieutenant P.L.G. Adriani.

19. This action was consistent with the policies of both the KM and KNIL throughout the East Indies campaign. European evacuees were given top priority in the event of evacuation, while Indonesian civilians were typically left behind. However, it is unknown how many of the Indonesians would have left if given the opportunity, as their loved ones were attached to military units and they were quite often dependent on this arrangement for their livelihood.

20. Gill, *Royal Australian Navy, 1939–1942*, p. 563.

21. With no ABDA reconnaissance aircraft op-

erating over Japanese territory this far north, the information regarding those units in Indochina presumably came from Allied operatives operating within that territory. Given the deep divisions between Vichy French and Free French personnel at the time, it is reasonable to assume that the source of this information was a sympathetic French official who opposed the Japanese occupation of the colony.

22. Gill, *Royal Australian Navy, 1939–1942*, p. 565.

23. Japanese Defense Agency. *Boeichio Kenshujo Senshishitsu (Senshi sosho)*, Volume 23.

24. Shores, *Bloody Shambles*, Volume 2, pp. 75–76.

25. The weight of these air attacks was so great that the Japanese advance was temporarily halted as their landing barges took to cover along the tree covered banks of the Moesi River. However, as ABDA airpower waned in the face of Japanese counterstrikes, the barge convoy resumed its movement toward Palembang. Had ABDA-AIR been able to sustain its air offensive against the barges, the fight for Palembang might very well have had a much different ending.

26. Helfrich, *Memoires*, Volume I, pp. 332–33.

27. Bosscher, *De Koninklijke Marine in de Tweede Wereldoorlog*, Volume 2, p. 579, n. 383.

28. Although a figure of 143 officers and men is listed in Dutch sources, the precise complement of *Van Nes* is unclear. The normal prewar crew of a "*Van Galen*"–class destroyer was between 140 and 150 men. However, it is very likely that the crew of *Van Nes* was increased beyond her prewar complement to meet wartime needs.

29. A total of 96 magnetic mines were obtained from the Royal Navy, which wanted to deploy them around Singapore. But with the British surrender in Malaya, they were rerouted to Java, where the MLD successfully tested them for airdrop delivery using PBYs equipped with locally designed minelaying racks. However, only 24 of the mines were ever deployed, 8 in the Moesi River near Palembang and 16 in the Banka Strait following the fall of southern Sumatra. The remainder were never deployed due to inaction on the part of the KM high command.

Personal correspondence with Jan Visser, 2000–2001.

30. Bosscher, *De Koninklijke Marine in de Tweede Wereldoorlog*, Volume 2, pp. 253–54.

31. *Ibid.*

32. *Ibid.*

33. *Ibid.*

34. "En route to Malang we encountered a Dutch floatplane, and I broke formation long enough to send him crashing into the ocean." Sakai, *Samurai*, p. 68.

35. Ministerie van Oorlog, *Nederlands-Indie Contra Japan*, Deel IV, pp. 136–37.

36. Shores, *Bloody Shambles*, Volume 2, pp. 202–03.

37. Although the exact ownership of these Ryan trainers remains unclear, it appears that almost all of them were MLD aircraft and none were floatplanes.

38. Ward, Boer and Casius, *The Royal Netherlands Military Flying School 1942–1944*, p. 18.

39. *Ibid.*

40. *Ibid.*

CHAPTER 8

1. The simultaneous occupation of Bali and Timor would ensure that the Allied air route between Java and Australia was severed. Combined with the continued Japanese air strikes against Java, it was hoped that this would effectively deprive ABDA of air power it would desperately need to interdict the planned invasion of Java. At the same time, the loss of Bali would give the Japanese an advance air base from which to interdict sea movements reinforcing or evacuating the island.

2. The missing crewmen were the plane's commander, 1st Lieutenant S.A.M.J. Snep, Sergeant-Pilot P. v.d. Sloot, Petty Officer J.R. Kuikert, Wireless Operator A.W. v.d. Meer, Machinist Mate G.H. Hulsbergen, Machinist Mate Th. Schotten and Leading Seaman Djimoen, an Indonesian member of the crew.

3. *Patrol Wing 10 War Diary*, February 24, 1942.

4. *Ibid.*

5. *Ibid.*

6. The lost flight crew included the pilot, 2nd Lieutenant C. van den End, Sergeant-Pilot P. Mahu, Leading Seaman-Aircraft Mechanic W.J. Geurts, Aircraft Mechanic's Mate J.J. Pol, Aircraft Mechanic's Mate A.K. van der Pol and Seaman L.J. van Hasselt.

7. The identity of these attackers remains unknown, although they were most likely seaplane fighters from *Sanyo Maru* or *Sanuki Maru*, or possibly even Ki-27 "Nate" or Ki-43 "Oscar" fighters from Palembang. All were operating over the Soenda Strait and Eastern Java at this time. It is also possible that they were IJAAF bombers on an anti-shipping mission against ABDA convoys moving between Tandjoeng Priok and the Indian Ocean.

8. Bosscher, *De Koninklijke Marine in de Tweede Wereldoorlog*, Volume 2, p. 304.

9. Ibid, pp. 304–05.

10. This would be the second time that Sergeant-Pilot C. van Dijk narrowly escaped death at the hands of Japanese fighters. He was also one of the pilots of the KNILM Sikorsky S-42B flying boat lost during the air strike against the Kalkas seaplane base at Lake Tondano on December 26.

11. By this point in the East Indies campaign, the end was clearly in sight for Dutch rule on Java. Buoyed by these developments, the Indonesians abandoned their colonial masters in droves and openly welcomed the Japanese as liberators. As the Japanese advanced, rebellious Indonesians in virtually all parts of the archipelago frequently killed small groups of Europeans (particularly the Dutch) and informed the Japanese of the whereabouts of larger groups.

12. Messimer, *Pawns of War*, pp. 28–33.

13. *Ibid.*

14. Shores, *Bloody Shambles*, Volume 2, p. 241.

15. Messimer, *Pawns of War*, p. 60.

16. Gill, *The Royal Australian Navy 1939–1945*, p. 599.

17. *The Battle of the Java Sea*. Dir. Niek Koppen. Odusseia Documentaries, 1997.

18. Position reported as 6° 25' South, 117° 13' East.

19. Bosscher, *De Koninklijke Marine in de Tweede Wereld Oorlog*, Volume 2, p. 274.

20. Messimer, *In the Hands of Fate*, p. 267.

21. Bosscher, *De Koninklijke Marine in de Tweede Wereldoorlog*, Volume 2, p. 274.

22. *Ibid.*

23. Perhaps Admiral Doorman's greatest error during the Battle of the Java Sea was his decision to put the floatplanes of *Java* and *De Ruyter* ashore prior to leaving the ME. As a result, the CSF operated blindly throughout the battle, while the Japanese were able to track Doorman's movements step by step with the aid of floatplanes from their own cruisers.

In Doorman's defense, it can be said that in accordance with KM operational doctrine, his plans called for a night engagement with the Japanese. This philosophy, which had been developed long before the outbreak of the Pacific War, called for ML bombers to attack the Japanese far out at sea during daylight hours. The surface fleet would then initiate a night action in which destroyers would make a series of torpedo attacks designed to reduce the enemy's fighting strength. Doorman would then slowly withdraw with the Japanese in pursuit, dragging their warships across a line of submarines, which would further reduce their numbers. The bombers would strike the Japanese force again beginning at dawn. At some point, the CSF would engage the invasion convoy and turn it away from Java.

Another reason for Doorman's leaving his floatplane ashore was the fact that neither *De Ruyter* nor *Java* was equipped with hangars. This meant that they would have been left dangerously exposed on their catapults throughout the battle, providing a serious fire threat if hit by Japanese shells. Likewise, only *De Ruyter* was equipped with a catapult, and Doorman was not inclined to have *Java* stop in order to launch and recover her seaplanes while operating in a battle zone.

24. Bosscher, *De Koninklijke Marine in de Tweede Wereldoorlog*, Volume 2, p. 280.

25. *Ibid.*

26. *Ibid.*

27. Following the loss of Tarakan, Balikpapan and Palembang, the CSF was experiencing a severe shortage of fuel, and many ships were unable to fuel completely before and after the Battle of the Java Sea. ABDA aircraft, including the MLD, were also facing shortages, as the refineries at Palembang had been the sole source of high-grade aviation fuel in the East Indies. However, it appears that the shortages did not hamper the Dutch as much as the American and Com-

monwealth units, because the Dutch apparently reserved much of the available fuel for their own forces.

28. This signal came in response to a directive from Admiral Helfrich that read, "The Enemy Has Been Sighted West of Bawean [Island], You Must Attack."

Bosscher, *De Koninklijke Marine in de Tweede Wereldoorlog*, Volume 2, p. 282.

29. Shores, *Bloody Shambles*, Volume 2, p. 238.

30. Messimer, *In the Hands of Fate*, p. 268.

31. As a result of these torpedo hits, *Java* sank in approximately 15 minutes, while *De Ruyter* followed some two and a half hours later. Both cruisers went down with heavy loss of life.

32. Bosscher, *De Koninklijke Marine in de Tweede Wereldoorlog*, Volume 2, p. 610, n. 349.

33. In fairness to Doorman, it must be stated that this mine barrage was actually laid several miles from its reported position after a Japanese reconnaissance plane sighted the minelayer *Gouden Leeuw*. Fearful of air attack, her captain dumped his entire cargo well short of the minefield's stated position, although only a small handful of the mines were actually armed.

Chapter 9

1. The title of this chapter is drawn from the final conversation between Vice-Admiral Helfrich and Governor-General van Starkenborgh as the Admiral prepared to evacuate Java for Ceylon. Helfrich would later write of the conversation in his memoirs:

"It was a solemn farewell. Jonkheer Tjarda van Starkenborgh's last words were, 'This is the end of a courageous fight Admiral. This moment moves me. I remain and wish you luck.' There are moments that remain sharp in one's memory. This is without a doubt, one of them."

Helfrich, *Memoires*, Volume 1, p. 441.

2. Information regarding the subsequent flight operations of Y-72 with PatWing 10 in Australia provided courtesy of squadron veterans Larry Katz and Paul Stevens, whose original flight log books provided clear proof of its evacuation from Java.

3. Y-55, Y-56 and Y-57.

4. Although this version of X-16's destruction is recounted from Shores, *Bloody Shambles*, Volume 2, p. 249, it should be regarded as highly suspect. Virtually all Dutch language sources list X-16 as being destroyed on the ground in inoperable condition at Tandjoeng Priok on or about March 1, 1942. Several of these sources state that X-16 was crushed by falling debris when demolition crews, to prevent its capture, blew up the hangar it was in. Given the detailed descriptions from the participants, it is likely that this story was true, but with another seaplane in place of X-16.

5. Y-59, Y-60 and Y-67.

6. X-1 (from the flight training school), X-20, X-24 and X-36.

7. According to Hugo Hooftman on p. 21, Vol-

ume 1 of *Van Farman tot Neptune: de vliegtuigen van de Marine Luchtvaart Dienst*, Y-50 and Y-61 were written off by the MLD at Morokrembangan on March 1. They would then be destroyed by MLD ground personnel to prevent their capture several days later when the air station was abandoned.

8. Shores, *Bloody Shambles*, Volume 2, p. 311.

9. The single-engine floatplane might have been one of the older C.VII, C.VIII or C.XIV aircraft still in service with the MLD as auxiliary hacks.

10. The possibility of this aircraft being a four-engine S-42B should be treated with extreme skepticism. As far as the author knows, the KNILM operated only one of this type aircraft, which served as the flagship of the airline's seaplane fleet. And as noted earlier in Chapter 4, it was destroyed at Lake Tondano on December 26.

11. Y-62 was also slated for evacuation duties from Lake Bagendit but was left behind at the last minute when its material condition was considered to be too poor by Admiral Helfrich's party. It remained at Lake Bagendit until March 5 when ordered to join Y-45 at Lake Tjileuntja.

12. Helfrich, *Memoires*, Volume 1, p. 443.

13. Details for the evacuation of the KM and MLD from Java had been planned well before the outbreak of the Pacific War. It was recognized that if and when the Japanese landed on Java, the course of the war would be out of the Navy's hands and would depend solely on the abilities of the KNIL. With little role to play in the campaign at that point, Admiral Helfrich would evacuate as many of his remaining ships and men as possible to Australia and Ceylon.

14. In a show of solidarity to the Indonesian people, the East Indies government had not only ordered that all Dutch citizens be engaged in some type of war activity following Pearl Harbor, but it had also forbidden the evacuation of any Dutch civilians from the NEI prior to March 1942. Nor were they permitted to transfer their finances to more secure financial institutions in Australia, Ceylon or America. Ever the paternalistic colonial masters, the Dutch were naively determined to show the Indonesian people that theirs was a brotherly fight against the naked militaristic aggression of Japan. Unfortunately for the Dutch, little did they realize just how deep disaffection with their rule ran amongst the common Indonesian. So that when the Japanese appeared on the shores of Java, they were greeted as conquering liberators after 300 years of Dutch colonialism.

15. Bosscher, *De Koninklijke Marine in de Tweede Wereldoorlog*, Volume 2, p. 344.

16. Shores, *Bloody Shambles*, Volume 2, p. 337.

17. Technically Admiral Koenraad held the rank of captain, but he was temporarily promoted to flank rank in order to effectively oversee destruction of the ME and ensure the evacuation of its personnel to Tjilatjap and Wijnkoops Bay.

18. Bosscher, *De Koninklijke Marine in de Tweede Wereldoorlog*, Volume 2, p. 337.

19. Ibid, p. 345.

20. *Ibid.*

21. Honselaar, *Vleugels van de Vloot*, p. 221.

22. Given the propensity of Japanese pilots to strafe anything that moved during their air strikes, it remains unclear whether Shibata's orders were strictly humanitarian in nature, or rather that he wanted his pilots to be sure to have enough ammunition to destroy as many of the Allied flying boats as possible.

23. Bosscher, *De Koninklijke Marine in de Tweede Wereldoorlog*, Volume 2, p. 346. In *Vleugels van de Vloot*, p. 221, Honselaar lists the same number of dead and missing but gives a figure of 32 wounded. Again, he lists most of the dead and wounded as women and children. Hugo Hooftman on p. 24 of *Van Farman tot Neptune: de vliegtuigen van de Marine Luchtvaart Dienst*, Volume 1 lists 48 dead and 32 wounded, including 16 MLD personnel among the dead.

24. Hendrie, *The Catalina Aircraft in World War II*, pp. 96–97.

25. The bulk of this section is drawn from Mervin W. Prime's *Western Australia's Pearl Harbour: The Japanese Raid on Broome*, pp. 13–18.

26. On the Do. 24, the stummel is the short float on the lower hull that protrudes from either side of the aircraft in order to help stabilize it while operating on the water.

27. The premature burning of X-36 to prevent its capture, despite the relative safety Australia provided, clearly shows the mindset of the Dutch flight crews following their exhausting campaign in the NEI and the mental stress brought on by the evacuation of Java. At the direction of X-36's Russian pilot, the passengers and crew burned the flying boat by loading it with mattresses and other flammable materials that they then covered in engine oil and set aflame.

28. *Barentz* was in the final stages of being converted into a seagoing repair ship for the KM when hit during this attack.

29. This last-minute decision would later cost Bozuwa his life, as he was killed only days later aboard the transport *Poelau Bras* when Japanese bombers sank that ship off the coast of Sumatra.

30. Although there is absolutely no evidence to suggest this was the case, at this point in the campaign, one must certainly wonder whether the flight crew of Y-62 received the message yet chose to ignore it. After all, at this point the fight for Java was all but over, and the plane's crew certainly could not have been happy about turning back toward territory that was bound to be captured in the immediate future.

31. The aircraft in question is unclear, and it is also possible that Rijnders and his crew had orders to retrieve Y-48, which was also under repair at MVK Priok.

32. It is unclear whether Witholt actually had any orders, or whether he simply chose to evacuate the PBY from Java on his own initiative. In either event, there were virtually no senior MLD or KM officers

remaining on Java to approve or disapprove of his decision!

33. Witholt attempted to take off three times, but bad weather and unfavorable wind conditions prevented him from doing so, forcing the crew to endure a night of uncertainty on the lake.

Hooftman, *Van Farman tot Neptune*, Volume 1, p. 24.

34. 1st Lieutenant G. Mulder, KMR.

35. With this flight, Y-45 became the last MLD plane to leave Java just before the island was engulfed by the Japanese. In an ironic twist of fate, on September 5, 1945, despite being the oldest aircraft in the squadron's inventory, Y-45 was also the first MLD aircraft to fly over Java following the Japanese surrender in the NEI. It carried emergency relief supplies, which were dropped into civilian internment camps on Java and Celebes.

36. Bosscher, *De Koninklijke Marine in de Tweede Wereldoorlog*, Volume 2, pp. 339–40.

37. Bezemer, *Geschiedenis van de Nederlandse Koopvaardij in de Tweede Wereldoorlog*, Volume 1, p. 746.

38. Keffikon was the same pilot who had lost his S-42 seaplane at Lake Tondano while standing on the dock talking to a KPM agent.

CHAPTER 10

1. As stated earlier, the British Army operated the only land-based radar units in the East Indies and apparently did not consult with the Dutch on its operational use beyond its initial placement.

2. Helfrich, *Memoires*, Volume 1, p. 442.

3. Although no individual numbers exist for MLD losses, in *De Koninklijke Marine in de Tweede Wereldoorlog*, Volume 3, p. 359, n. 2, Bosscher lists the KM as a whole to have suffered 1,653 dead during the NEI campaign. In addition, another 3,847 men were captured, many of whom would also die in captivity through brutal, substandard treatment by their Japanese captors. Of those killed, more than half (938 or 57 percent) were lost during the Battle of the Java Sea aboard the cruisers *De Ruyter* (367), *Java* (512) and the destroyer *Kortenaer* (59).

4. As a result, the Dutch had virtually no bargaining power and thus absolutely no say in how the war in the Pacific was orchestrated or executed. At the same time, it should be pointed out that even the British with their sizeable Far Eastern Fleet and large number of land forces in India also soon found themselves to be unwanted players in the Pacific campaign. With the land war dominated by the United States Army under General Douglas McArthur, and the naval war likewise dominated by the United States Navy under the command of Admiral Chester Nimitz, the NEI quickly became a backwater in American plans to retake the Philippines and isolate Japanese forces in the Pacific. Likewise, the Dutch and British also both soon realized that President Roosevelt's plans for a postwar Asia

provided little support for the reestablishment of European colonial empires once hostilities ended.

5. These numbers do not appear to include personnel of the GM, which was demilitarized immediately prior to the surrender of Java in early March. Although a number of these ships, including the MLD's seaplane tenders, had the range to reach Australia, it was feared that their largely Indonesian crews could not be coerced to leave their families behind if given the order to evacuate the NEI. As a result, virtually all of the ships were scuttled with their lower deck hands being released from service with final pay and three days of food. The European personnel and officers, however, were ordered to report to Soerabaja or Batavia for further duty.

6. Groen and Touwen-Bouwsma, *Nederlands Indië 1942 — Illusie en ontgoocheling*, p. 139.

7. *Ibid.*

8. *Ibid.*

9. *Ibid.*

10. With all flight training transferred to the United States, the Dutch sold their remaining Ryan trainers to the Australian government, which transferred them to the RAAF. Many survived the war and long beyond. As late as 1990, photos show one of the ex-Dutch planes to still be flying in the hands of a private owner in Australia. Restored to mint condition, the Ryan is painted in the markings of the RAAF and travels the air show circuit throughout Australia.

11. Of these, approximately 100 were Dutch or Indonesian flight personnel.

Hooftman, *Van Farman tot Neptune*, Volume 1, p. 25.

12. Although the circumstances that led to the withdrawal of the USAAF from Java can easily be justified, the evacuation itself was chaotic and unorganized for the most part. Also, no one had bothered to inform the Dutch of the evacuation, who were, to say the least, shocked by the sudden pullout of American forces. This led Major-General Ludolph van Oyen, commander of the ML, to bitterly denounce the USAAF withdrawal as little more than desertion in the face of the enemy.

So amplified were van Oyen's comments that General George C. Marshall, commander-in-chief of the US Army, immediately ordered an official enquiry. Although his enquiry subsequently disproved the Dutch claims, it did pointedly reveal a complete lack of liaison communications between USAAF leadership on Java and their Dutch allies. In the end, van Oyen accepted Marshall's verdict and later wrote a warm letter thanking the USAAF for its efforts to defend Java.

Edmonds, *They Fought with What They Had*, p. 403.

13. Teitler, *Sea Power on the Decline*, pp. 72–73.

14. *Ibid.*

15. For many Dutch in the Far East, the NEI were the only home they had ever known, having been born and raised there. Although they were staunchly

loyal to Holland and Queen Wilhelmina, they were unwilling to sacrifice the East Indies in order to buy time for a stronger defense to be mounted elsewhere, as was the strategy employed by the United States in the Philippines. Unlike the Philippines, the Dutch were literally fighting for their homes and not just an expendable colonial territory. So when the British and Americans sought to convince the KM to withdraw its few remaining ships from the NEI after the Battle of the Java Sea, their pleas fell on deaf ears for this very reason. Likewise, most Americans failed to appreciate the significance the East Indies held for these people.

16. The author has no clear rationale to support this assertion, although perhaps the English regarded the Dutch, on a subconscious level, as being a bit too similar to their German enemies in language and culture.

17. Messimer, *In the Hands of Fate*, p. 134.

18. So valued was the contribution and sacrifices of the MLD during the East Indies campaign that the Netherlands government ordered that the entire service be awarded the Militaire Willemsorde der 4e klasse, the highest Dutch military award for bravery. Normally this award is reserved for individuals, but it was felt that the MLD merited the award as a whole. Queen Wilhelmina approved the request, and the MLD was so honored on April 9, 1942. Her award speech read:

"In the fight against Japan from the declaration of war on December 7, 1941, [the MLD] without exception, provided excellent service and performed outstanding deeds, including reconnaissance, air attack, anti-submarine duties, minelaying and convoy escort, against an overwhelming enemy, giving their utmost effort and lives in uninterrupted air battles to inflict great losses on the enemy."

Bibliography

Air Ministry. *There's Freedom in the Air: The Official Story of the Allied Air Forces from the Occupied Countries.* London: HMSO, 1944.

Angelucci, Enzo. *The Rand McNally Encyclopedia of Military Aircraft 1914–80.* Chicago: Rand McNally, 1981.

Archer, C.H. *Report on Portuguese Timor, May 3, 1941,* AA Series A816 No. 19/301/822, Relations with Portuguese Timor. Appointment of Commonwealth Representative, Occupation of Portuguese Timor, 1940–1941.

Bakker, Ir. H. Th. *De K.P.M. in Oorlogstijd: Een Overzicht van de Verrichtingen van de Koninklijke Paketvaart-Maatschappij en Haar Personeel Gedurende De Wereldoorlog 1939–1945.* Amsterdam: J.H. de Bussy. 1950.

Bezemer, K.W.L. *Geschiedenis van de Nederlandse Koopvaardij in de Tweede Wereldoorlog,* Volume 1. Amsterdam: Elsevier, 1987.

Bosch, J.W.T. *De militaire luchtvaart van het Koninklijke Nederlands Indisch Leger in oorlog, 8 dec. 1941–9 maart 1942.* Manuscript Ypenburg: n.p., 1973.

Bosscher, Dr. Ph.M. *De Koninklijke Marine in de Tweede Wereldoorlog,* Deel 1. Franeker: Wever, 1988.

_____. *De Koninklijke Marine in de Tweede Wereldoorlog,* Deel 2. Franeker: Wever, 1988.

_____. *De Koninklijke Marine in de Tweede Wereldoorlog,* Deel 3. Franeker: Wever, 1988.

Bryan, E.H., Jr. *Pacific War Atlas.* Honolulu: Tongg, 1945.

Dull, Paul S. *A Battle History of the Imperial Japanese Navy 1941–45.* Annapolis: Naval Institute Press, 1978.

Dulm van, J.F., and F.C. van Oosten. *50 Jaar Marineluchtvaartdienst 1917–1967.* Den Haag: Bureau Maritieme Historie, 1967.

_____. *De Marineluchtvaartdienst, 1917–1967.* Marineblad 77: 459–599. 1967.

Edmonds, Walter D. *They Fought with What They Had: The Story of the Army Air Force in the Southwest Pacific, 1941–42.* Washington, D.C.: Zenger, 1982.

Francillon, Rene J. *Japanese Aircraft of the Pacific War.* Annapolis: Naval Institute Press, 1988.

Geneste, Willem. *75 Jaar Vliegende Marine: "Never a Dull Moment."* In Woord en Beeld. Den Haag: Marinevoorlichting, Ministerie van Defensie, 1992.

Gill, G. Hermon. *Royal Australian Navy 1939–1942.* Canberra: Collins (Australian War Memorial), 1985.

Gillison, Douglas. *Royal Australian Air Force 1939–1942: Australia in the War of 1939–1945, Series III (Air),* Volume 1. Canberra: Australian War Memorial, 1962.

Groen, Petra and Elly Touwen-Bouwsma. *Nederlands Indië 1942 — Illusie en Ontgoocheling.* The Hague: Sdu Uitgeverij Koninginnegracht, 1992.

Haaff, P.S. Van 't, and M.J.C. Klaassen. *Gedenkboek: Honderd Jarig Bestaan Der Adelborsten-Opleiding Te Willemsoord 1854-1954.* Bussum: Van Dishoek, 1954.

Haslach, Robert D. *Nishi No Kaze, Hare: Nederlands-Indische inlichtingendienst contra aggressor Japan.* Weesp: Van Kampen, 1985.

Headquarters, U.S.A.F.F.E. And Eighth U.S. Army (Rear). *Monograph No. 66: The Invasion of the Netherlands East Indies (16th Army).*

_____. *Monograph 69: Java-Sumatra Air Operations Record, Dec. 1941–Mar. 1942.* Tokyo. 1946.

_____. *Monograph 101: Naval Operations in the Invasion of Netherlands East Indies.* Tokyo. 1945.

Helfrich, C.E.L. *Memoires van C.E.L. Helfrich,* Deel I. Amsterdam: Elsevier, 1950.

_____. *Memoires van C.E.L. Helfrich,* Deel II. Amsterdam: Elsevier, 1950.

Hendrie, Andrew. *Flying Cats: The Catalina Aircraft in World War II.* Shrewesbury: Airlive, 1988.

Honselaar, L. *Vleugels van de Vloot: De Geschiedenis van de Marine Luchtvaart Dienst.* Rotterdam: Wyt, 1950.

Hooftman, Hugo. *Van Farman tot Neptune: De vliegtuigen van de Marine Luchtvaart Dienst*, Volume 1. n.p.: Zwolle. 1964–65.

_____. *Van Farman tot Neptune: De vliegtuigen van de Marine Luchtvaart Dienst*, Volume 2. n.p.: Zwolle. 1964–65.

_____. *Van Glenn Martins en Mustangs. Alle vliegtuigen die hebben en vlogen bij het KNIL, de Indische Militaire Luchtvaart.* n.p.: Zwolle. 1967.

Japanese Defense Agency. *Senshi Sosho, Volume 10: Hawai Sakusen (Hawaiian Operation).* Boeichio Kenshujo Senshishitsu, ed. Tokyo: Asagumo Shimbun, 1967.

_____. *Senshi sosho, Volume 24: Hito Mare homen kaigun shinko sakusen (Philippines/Malaya).* Boeichio Kenshujo Senshishitsu, ed. Tokyo: Asagumo Shimbun, 1969.

_____. *Senshi sosho, Volume 23: Ran'in Bengaru wan homen kaigun shinko sakusen (Dutch East Indies).* Boeichio Kenshujo Senshishitsu, ed. Tokyo: Asagumo Shimbun, 1967.

Joint Army-Navy Assessment Committee, The. *Japanese Naval and Merchant Shipping Losses During World War II by All Causes.* Washington: U.S. Government Printing Office, 1947.

Jordan, Roger. *The World's Merchant Fleets, 1939.* Annapolis: Naval Institute Press, 1999.

Le Nobel, Anton. "Marineluchtdienst is 60." *Air Britain Digest* 29(5): 107–110. 1977.

Messimer, Dwight R. *Pawns of War: The Loss of the U.S.S. Langley and the U.S.S. Pecos.* Annapolis: Naval Institute Press. 1983.

_____. *In the Hands of Fate: The Story of Patrol Wing Ten, 8 December 1941— 11 May 1942.* Annapolis: Naval Institute Press, 1985.

Mikesh, Robert C. *Japanese Aircraft Code Names & Designations.* Atglen: Schiffer Publishing, 1993.

Ministrie Van Oorlog, Hoofdkwartier Van De Chef Van De General Staf, Krijgsgeschiedkundige Afdeling. *Nederlands Indie Contra Japan, Deel III: Overzicht Van De Na Het Uitbreken Van De Oorlog Met Japan In De Z.W. Pacific Gevoerde Strijd.* Gravenhage, 1954.

_____. *Nederlands-Indie Contra Japan, Deel IV: De Verrichtingen Van De Militaire Luchtvaart Bij De Strijd Tegen De Japanners In En Om De Bondgenootschappelike Luchtstrijdkrachten.* Gravenhage, 1956.

_____. *Nederlands-Indie Contra Japan, Deel V: De Strijd Op Borneo En Op Celebes.* Gravenhage, 1957.

Mollo, Andrew. *The Armed Forces of World War II: Uniforms, Insignia and Organization.* New York: Crown, 1981.

Mook, Hubertus J. van. *The Netherlands East Indies and Japan: Battle on Paper 1940–1941.* New York: W.W. Norton, 1944.

Morison, Samuel Eliot. *History of the United States Naval Operations in World War II, Volume III: The Rising Sun in the Pacific 1941— April 1942.* Boston: Little, Brown & Company, 1982.

Münching von, L.L. n.d. *De materieelverliezen der Koninklijke Marine in de Tweede Wereldoorlog 1939–1945.* n.p.: Den Haag, 1968.

Netherlands Information Bureau. *Ten Years of Japanese Burrowing in the Netherlands East Indies: Official Report of the Netherlands East Indies Government on Japanese Subversive Activities in the Archipelago During the Last Decade.* New York: Netherlands Information Bureau, n.d.

Nortier, J.J. *De Japanse Aanval Op Nederlands Indië. Deel 2: Borneo.* Rotterdam: Ad. Donker, 1992.

Oosten, F.C. van. *The Battle of the Java Sea.* Annapolis: Naval Institute Press, 1976.

Orita, Zenji, with Joseph D. Harrington. *I-Boat Captain.* Canoga Parks, CA: Major, 1976. Press Conferences. *New York Times* December 1941–March 1942, Section A.

Prime, Mervin W. *Western Australia's Pearl Harbour: The Japanese Raid on Broome.* Bullcreek: Royal Australian Air Force Association, n.d.

Richards, D., and H. Saunders. *The Royal Air Force 1939–1945*, Volumes 1–3. London: HMSO, 1974.

Rohwer, Jürgen. *Axis Submarine Successes of World War Two: German, Italian and Japanese Submarine Successes, 1939–1945.* Annapolis: Naval Institute Press, 1999.

Rohwer, J., and G. Hummelchen. *Chronology of the War at Sea 1939–45: The Naval History of World War Two.* Annapolis: Naval Institute Press, 1992.

Royen, Dr. P.C. van. *Hr.Ms. K-XVIII en Hr.Ms. O-16: De ondergang van twee Nederlandse onderzeeboten in de Zuid-Chinese Zee (1941).* Amsterdam: Van Soeren, 1997.

Sakai, Saburo, with Martin Caidin and Fred Saito. *Samurai!* New York: Bantam, 1978.

Sectie, Overzeesche Gebiedsdeelen. *Het Koninklijk Nederlands Indische Leger in den Strijd Tegen Japan.* Maastricht: Leiter-Nypels, 1945.

Shores, Christopher, and Brian Cull with Yasuho Izawa. *Bloody Shambles. The First Comprehensive Account of Air Operations over South-East Asia, December 1941–May 1942. Volume 1: The Drift to War to the Fall of Singapore.* London: Grub Street, 1992.

_____. Christopher and Brian Cull with Yasuho Izawa. *Bloody Shambles. The First Comprehensive Account of Air Operations over South-East Asia, December 1941–May 1942. Volume 2: The Defense of Sumatra to the Fall of Burma.* London: Grub Street, 1993.

Teitler, Gerke. *Sea Power on the Decline: Anti-Americanism and the Royal Netherlands Navy, 1942–1952. European Contributions to American Studies.* Amsterdam: Free University Press, 1986.

Thomas, David A. *The Battle of the Java Sea.* New York: Stein & Day, 1968.

Visser, Jan. *Who Sank the Shinonome?* Unpublished white paper. Oldemarkt, The Netherlands, 2002.

Wagner, Ray. *American Combat Planes.* Garden City: Doubleday, 1968.

Ward, O.G., P.C. Boer, and G.J. Casius. *The Royal Netherlands Military Flying School 1942–1944.* Den Haag: Afdeling Maritieme Historie van de Marinestaf, 1982.

Weal, Elke C. *Combat Aircraft of World War Two.* London: Bracken, 1985.

Wijngaarden, Pieter van, and Prudent Staal. *Dornier Do. 24: Herinneringen aan een legendarische vliegboot.* Bergen n.h.: Bonneville, 1992.

Wilmott, H.P. *Empires in the Balance: Japanese and Allied Pacific Strategies to April 1942.* Annapolis: Naval Institute Press, 1982.

Winslow, W.G. *The Fleet the Gods Forgot: The U.S. Asiatic Fleet in World War II.* Annapolis: Naval Institute Press, 1982.

Witter, Renee. *Het Vergeten Squadron: Het verhaal van de Nederlandse vliegers die tegen Japan hun vergeten strijd vochten.* Bussum: Holkema & Warendorf, 1976.

Womack, Tom. *Island Fortress: The Invasion of Tarakan.* Unpublished manuscript. Dallas, Texas, 2002.

_____. *For God, Queen and Country: The Allied Defense of the Malay Barrier, December 1941– March 1942.* Unpublished manuscript. Dallas, Texas, 2002.

Young, Donald J. *First 24 Hours of War in the Pacific.* Shippensburg: Burd Street Press, 1998.

PERSONAL CORRESPONDENCE

Horan, Mark E. Windsor Locks, CT. August 2000.

Jones, Mark. Ridgefield, CT. 2000–2004.

Katz, Larry. Blytheville, AR. 2002.

Kossen, Bert. Huizen, The Netherlands. 1999 — 2005.

Stevens, Paul F. Nashville, TN. May 2002.

Visser, Jan. Oldemarkt, The Netherlands. 1999 — 2005.

Vliet, Dr. A.P. van, Dr. A.J. van der Peet and Dr. N. Geldhof. *Institute for Maritime History.* The Hague, The Netherlands. July 2000.

Index